BISON
BOOKS

Jackson, Mississippi
An American Chronicle
of Struggle
and Schism

JOHN R. SALTER JR.

With a new introduction by the author

UNIVERSITY OF NEBRASKA PRESS
LINCOLN AND LONDON

Library of Congress Cataloging-in-Publication Data
Salter, John R.
Jackson, Mississippi: an American chronicle of struggle and schism / John R. Salter Jr.;
with a new introduction by the author.
p.   cm.
Originally published: Hicksville, N.Y.: Exposition Press, c1979
ISBN 978-0-8032-3808-4 (pbk.: alk. paper)
1. African Americans—Civil rights—Mississippi—Jackson. 2. Civil rights workers—
Mississippi—Jackson—Biography. 3. African American civil rights workers—Mississippi—Jackson—Biography. 4. Jackson (Miss.)—Race relations. 5. Evers, Medgar Wiley,
1925–1963. 6. Salter, John R. I. Title.
F349.J13S25 2011
976.2'51—dc23   2011024646

INTRODUCTION

As an older teen, I shot my huge Coming of Age Bear deep in the vast Sycamore Canyon wilderness area in northern Arizona. At that point, I became a man. The fiery spirit of the Bear and his abundantly fine qualities—intelligence, courage, stamina, instinct—are with me always and have served me very well and faithfully on my swift and rocky River of No Return.

It is now almost half a century since the rise and climax of the massive, non-violent Jackson Civil Rights Movement of 1962–63—the greatest grassroots up-heaval in the history of the Magnolia State and one of the truly major movements of the 1960s. It also featured some of the bloodiest resistance by every repressive resource—"lawmen" and hoodlums and vigilantes—that Mississippi could muster; the movement's examples of martyrdom are many, including the assassination of our good friend and colleague NAACP field secretary Medgar W. Evers. In those days, I was the adult advisor of the North Jackson NAACP Youth Council, and that of the student group at private, almost completely African American Tougaloo Southern Christian College. It was that committed and courageous assembly of young people who sparked the sweeping economic boycott of Jackson, which we broadened into the full-scale Jackson Movement. I was the chair of the Strategy Committee of that nonviolent revolution.

This book of mine, *Jackson, Mississippi*, tells the story of that great struggle. It's the most fully detailed account of any major, local civil rights movement. I wrote this book—my basic work on the movement in Jackson—with the greatest care, from my own very clear recollections drawn from consistent and pervasive personal involvement at every step of the way. (And those recollections remain precisely and indelibly engraved in my mind to this moment.) I utilized a host of primary documents, some of which are in my collected papers (housed at the Wisconsin Historical Society, Madison, and at the Mississippi Department of Archives and History, Jackson) and some of which remain with me personally. I did a great deal of careful cross-checking on certain points with other people who were, in various ways, involved in our effort (attorney William M. Kunstler, for example). I included nothing in the book that could not be backed up by documents or the confirmation of other knowledgeable persons. And the book, very well reviewed, has never been challenged in any factual or thematic sense.

A few years ago, I received a most welcome message sent by Dr. Colia Liddell Lafayette Clark, a native of Jackson who in the fall of '61 asked me to become advisor to the then small NAACP Youth Council. She, a very notable activist in her own good right, wrote this to her colleagues:

I received a note from Hunter Gray Bear (John [R.] Salter [Jr.]). Hunter Bear was my professor at Tougaloo College and one of the sharpest organizers in both the southern civil rights movement and labor movement in the USA. He agreed to serve as advisor to the newly organized Jackson, Ms NAACP North Jackson Youth Council in 1961. This was no small decision. Under his tutelage and guidance and with the oversight of Medgar Wylie Evers, the North Jackson NAACP Youth Council would produce a mass movement and the most successful boycott of a downtown district in the deep south. Only Ida B. Wells's boycott of Memphis in the 19th century can compare. Jackson, Ms' downtown folded and has never reopened with its string of shops and department stores. This was no easy work and like Medgar and so many others Hunter Bear was targeted for death. He was seriously wounded in a freak car wreck (point of death), beaten a number of times in demonstrations but refused to yield even from pressure within the struggle. Those years are detailed in a book by Hunter Bear (John R. Salter [Jr.]) entitled: *Jackson, Mississippi: An American Chronicle of Struggle and Schism*. The book is out of print, but should be in most college libraries. Today, Hunter Bear has returned to his native land in the West and to his Native roots to continue organizing and building grass roots struggle and a new generation of youthful organizers.

Hear him for he is worthy to be heard.

Colia L. Clark

I'm an organizer—a working social justice agitator. I've been one since the mid-1950s, and I'll always be one. I have always lived and worked in the borderlands—the often isolated and therefore overlooked and lonely settings where calls and cries for justice are frequently ignored until activist grassroots organization is sparked and moving.

In many respects, being an organizer is one of the toughest trails anyone could ever blaze. An effective organizer seeks to get grassroots people together—and does; develops ongoing and democratic local leadership; deals effectively with grievances and individual and family concerns; works with the people to achieve basic organizational goals and develop new ones; and builds a sense of the "New World to Come Over the Mountains Yonder"—and how all of that relates to the shorter-term steps. An effective organizer has to be a person of integrity, courage, commitment, and a person of solidarity and sacrifice. The satisfactions are enormous.

This is an organizer's book—centered primarily on the development and life of the Jackson Movement but encompassing other campaigns of mine. This introduction provides autobiographical material on the factors that have led to my embracing the Romany trail of an activist organizer. It also updates the flow of events since my book initially appeared thirty-one years ago, when I was on the Navajo Nation, to the present, and my current location in the mountains of eastern Idaho. (The reader is advised that this, necessarily limited by space, covers only what I feel to be the major mountains and canyons on the trail.)

I was born from the Four Directions as John Randall Salter Jr. I grew up in wild and rugged mountains and canyons at and around Flagstaff, (Coconino County) Arizona. It was a quasi-frontier atmosphere where you learned early on how to fight—and fight effectively. You also learned and appreciated the sensible use of firearms. From my childhood on, I was an avid hunter—usually a loner—and, as I grew into adolescence, an explorer of vast wilderness areas in our setting.

My father was an essentially full-blooded American Indian of the far-flung Wabanaki Confederacy, originally from the Northeast: Mi'kmaq and St. Francis Abenaki (in his family's case, increasingly involved and mixed with the akin Penobscots). There are also, in our makeup, strains of St. Regis Mohawk. Dad was born Frank Gray, but as a child, he was adopted and partially raised by William Mackintire Salter and Mary Gibbens Salter, very prominent New England liberals who changed his name to John Randall Salter. My mother, an Anglo, was from an old western "frontier" family. Dad was a noted artist, a professor at Arizona State College/Northern Arizona University, and was always deeply involved on behalf of the regional Indian Nations—primarily Navajo and Laguna. Our very close ties to those Nations continue to this day. My mother taught for years in the Flagstaff education system, where she forged its earliest multicultural programs in her classes.

I've organized all over this country—the Southwest, Pacific Northwest, New England, Chicago, the Midwest, up-state New York, the northern plains, the Rockies. Trained as a sociologist, I've taught at a number of colleges—again, all over this land. Sometimes it's been full-time organizing and part-time teaching; or full-time teaching and full-time organizing; or simply organizing (which can be double-duty work in its own right!). I've worked with grassroots people from all sorts of ethnic backgrounds in militant and democratic organizations and movements. My focus has consistently been Native rights, civil rights and liberties, union labor.

I started doing fully adult work as I entered my teens—many tough jobs across northern Arizona as those earlier years moved on, including much forest fire fighting and fire lookout work and other challenging endeavors. Since I was a big kid, I had no problem at all representing myself as being a good deal older than I really was.

Entering the U.S. Army, I served a full hitch—very honorably by the army's standards—and was out at the beginning of 1955, just as I was becoming twenty-one. At that point, I faced a major life directional crossroads. So I then made an extremely significant Vision Journey: I went down the length of the very vast and deep Sycamore Canyon when the upper snow melted in the late spring of '55. That extremely rugged wilderness region has always been my most special setting—bar none. My parents hoped (and Mother pushed) for a "respectable" career, to which I was resistant. And so that magnificent trip through Sycamore—coming home to my very special land—was in largest part to organize my own thinking. It took several days, and I had a full backpack and a Winchester 30/30. I know of no other person in those days—and maybe even to this day—who ever made that trip.

In the course of that Great Trek, I explored some vast side canyons coming down off the western rim. I saw ancient Indian ruins in cliff settings—the location of which I would never reveal. The entire journey featured all sorts of wild game—much of it not afraid of me at all—and I saw hundreds of elk antlers, seasonally shed in winter grazing areas. At one point, I saw huge bear tracks—very fresh—under sycamore trees that had been clawed eight feet up or so. This was grizzly sign—even though no grizzlies were supposed to exist anywhere in Arizona by that time. At another point, while resting on a knoll above Sycamore Creek, I heard a noisy crashing sound coming toward me through the brush. I waited. Suddenly, a huge, jet-black long-horn bull emerged, limping from an old wound on one back thigh evidenced by lion or bear claw scars. He drank from the creek. When he had finished, I asked him quietly, "How are you doing today?" He jerked his head up—he had never, I'm sure, seen a human before—and looked directly at me. Then he turned and plunged back into the brush. He was a direct descendant of many generations of purely wild cattle, stemming from Spanish gold-mining operations in the latter 1700s. Eventually, when the geology had shifted into the Great Verde Fault, I found rose quartz—gold-bearing quartz—but I would never reveal the location of that, ever.

When I finally "came out" in the comparatively "civilized" Verde Valley, I was very much together. Not long thereafter, I went with my family to Mexico, where Dad painted and lectured. I spent the month studying that fascinating nation's radicalism and Native and union movements, and then I moved on to sociology at the University of Arizona and eventually to Arizona State University—fine enough. But almost immediately I fortunately connected with radical and democratic—and consistently embattled—industrial unionism. My life-long vocation—calling—began and feathered out from that point.

I and my good spouse, Eldri (with a Scandinavian/Finnish/Saami background), entered the Closed Society of Mississippi in the ominous summer of 1961. And that for sure, as my *Jackson, Mississippi* discusses at great length, was a River of No Return.

In 1978 we arrived at Navajo Community College (now Dine' College) on the Navajo Nation (*Dine'* means "The People"). It was the very first of the now thirty-six tribally controlled Indian colleges in the United States. Navajo Community College (NCC) was launched at the end of the '60s, primarily by my father's art protégé and very close family friend Ned A. Hatathli. I can well remember Ned—at our Flagstaff home countless times—talking about his dream as early as the late '40s: a free and democratic bicultural Navajo college controlled by the grassroots. He, far more than anyone else, brought that to fruition.

The lands of the Navajo Nation are vast and beautiful and sometimes mysterious—larger than the state of West Virginia. The Nation's membership population is almost three hundred thousand (as of 2010). The primary campus of the college is located at remote Tsaile (Say-Lee, "Place by the Lake"), elevation seven thousand feet, under the beautiful Lukachukai Mountains—and ninety-five road miles from Gallup, New Mexico. There is an important branch campus at Shiprock, New Mexico, and several smaller ones.

Ned died tragically in 1972. Six years later, we came to NCC for a stint of several years. I taught in educational and social sciences and did several other things with the college; Eldri wound up teaching in the almost all-Navajo Tsaile Elementary School.

The students at NCC, mostly Navajo but some from other tribes, were just fine. So were almost all faculty and staff and most administrators. And all of that remains the case to this moment. Whatever the setting, anywhere, it's a consistently fascinating challenge to teach the mysteries of sociology and its collateral dimensions. That always requires an approach that's sensitive, deft, intricate, and practical. When the context is bicultural, the challenge is broadened and deeply complex. But I had grown up very much indeed within the Navajo country, and a major dimension of my teaching forte is telling interesting and meaningful stories with a significant point. Things went very well in my classes. My students at Navajo (as has been the case everywhere) were quite interested in my personal experiences and observations in the Southern Civil Rights Movement and elsewhere.

I became chair of educational and social sciences and, for a time, chair of the Academic Standards Committee and that of the Curriculum Committee. I was also chair of the Grievance Committee, which fortunately, no matter how long our deliberations, always found unanimously for the worker (faculty and staff). I was also a consistent and very determined and effective advocate for students, staff, and faculty. I was among those who set up a student court system—very friendly to the students, of course—to keep tribal police off our campus. We were successful in that. And, at their request, I joined the NCC president and regents in Washington lobbying. Very significantly, I was also deeply involved in anti-uranium/anti-nuclear efforts, and I wrote widely for U.S. and global publications on this topic. I have studied and written on the horrific uranium tragedy—"the yellow rock that kills"—since 1957. There are now many bones under the turquoise sky.

Around that point, our fourth child, Josephine (Josie), arrived—born at Gallup, New Mexico, at the end of 1979. Our daughter Maria had been born at Jackson in 1962; John at Raleigh, North Carolina, in 1965; and Peter at Chicago in 1969.

My father had very recently died. Fortuitously for me, there had been, since we first arrived, the presence of the noted Navajo artist and Code Talker Carl Nelson Gorman, whose large office was shared by several traditional, highly trained medicine men. Carl and my father had been good friends, and each much respected the other's work. I spent a good deal of time with Carl Gorman and the resident medicine men, and I credit them all for helping me adjust to my father's passing.

At the conclusion of the 1981 spring term, after three years at NCC, we left for the American Indian studies department at the University of North Dakota (UND). The evening before our departure, there was a surprise party for us—attended by faculty, staff, students, and several administration people, including President Dean Jackson. He presented me with a fine silver and turquoise bolo tie, carrying the symbol of the college. It was only one of three of such made by a topflight Navajo silversmith (the other two had been presented to then senator Barry Goldwater and to the president of the Exxon Corporation). Another fine gift was the portrait *Navajo Woman*, done by the noted Navajo artist Harry Walters, who, with his wife, Anna, gave that great painting to us at the same honoring event. It always hangs proudly in our home for all to see.

Those gifts, to be treasured always, were part of a very significant complex given by the Dine' land and its people that we took with us when we left the Navajo country: vastly renewed wells and springs of strength and newly honed vision, broadened and extended.

There was a significant event in late 1979, to which my son John and I drove from Tsaile. During late October and early November of that year, a major and genuinely historic retrospective on the Mississippi Movement—"Mississippi's Freedom Summer Reviewed: A Fifteen Year Perspective on Progress in Race Relations, 1964–1979"— was held at Jackson under the joint auspices of Tougaloo and Millsaps Colleges. For the better part of a fascinating week, several dozen program participants gathered. Some were old Mississippi Movement activists, and others were liberals of good will and outside academicians. A welcome presence was the courageous and involved professor James W. Silver, formerly of Ole Miss and author of the notable work *Mississippi: The Closed Society (1964, 1966)*. There was considerable wrangling, pleasant and otherwise, over the meaning of it all before session audiences, which often numbered close to a thousand. The consensus was that much had happened in Mississippi and other hardcore southern areas that was good: the development of the very right to organize and dissent and vote, widespread desegregation, and a substantial reduction in terror.

But the dichotomies became very apparent on the question of to whom should the credit go—and what had gone wrong and why. Some of the blacks who had "made it" (not all of them by any means, however) and most of the liberals felt matters were well up on the mountain and gave a heavy measure of credit to the Kennedy and Johnson administrations and to the concept of federal involvement in general. Activists, whether currently engaged or not, vigorously disputed both of these contentions, gave primary credit for what victories had been won to the courage of the grassroots people, and pointed to the economic poverty and relative powerlessness that continue to grip the South and nation regardless of race.

My part in the affair was to discuss "Race Relations in Mississippi before 1964." My paper, which I had given at Ole Miss two days before to an enthusiastic gathering of the Black Students' Union, covered the background and development of the Jackson Movement and its ramifications. I concluded:

> If we could have gone on, really cracking Jackson, who knows what 1964 would have been in Mississippi? Only the Creator can tell us now.
>
> The black youth of Jackson were exhausted and discouraged. Many dropped away or eventually went into other civil rights groups. The middle class re-treated. Low-income poor people, who had just been into the primary thrust of the movement, never had an opportunity to really gain a confident footing. Thus the Jackson Movement passed into history and legend. Though other strains of activity came into the capital city in the years to come, there was never again a viable, ongoing upsurge from within Jackson itself. . . . Divisions between the national NAACP and other civil rights organizations deepened permanently.
>
> On the positive side, the Jackson Movement—particularly in the massive demonstrations following the murder of Medgar Evers—destroyed forever the self-serving segregationist myth of Mississippi black satisfaction. The boycott, nourished by the blood of May and June, lived on, eventually winning some victories and draining white Jackson merchants into grudging compliance with the 1964 Civil Rights Act. The passage of that legislation was certainly enhanced by the many forms of martyrdom characterizing the struggle in Jackson. And in other parts of the state, efforts continued and mounted, aided by the rapidly

growing national focus upon Mississippi, which, until the tragedies of Jackson especially, had seemed a lonely and isolated backwater.

So it went down. In the end, the Jackson Movement brought forth the most magnificent display of basic human grassroots courage that many of us have ever witnessed—courage that nonviolently and effectively confronted the raw brutality of a garrison police state. But it could not withstand the subversion by the corporate liberals of New York and the self-styled "pragmatism" of those splendid scoundrels residing in Camelot on the Potomac.

That drew a cheering, standing ovation from the very large audience. But more to the point: in the years since *Jackson, Mississippi* first appeared, there has been no attempt to refute my contentions regarding the conduct in Jackson of the national NAACP and the federal government.

We arrived at Grand Forks, North Dakota, late in the summer of 1981. Both Eldri and I had old "frontier" roots in the state. One branch of my mother's family, Scots from Ontario, had settled in Dakota Territory as early as 1870, developed a very large land base, and raised horses. My maternal grandfather, Thomas Hunter Heath, later a college-trained engineer, grew up on that ranch. My grandmother on that side, Marie Senn Heath, who was probably the first full-time female college professor (domestic science) in North Dakota, came from Kansas and Missouri territorial stock. Her father, my great grandfather, Michael Senn, was a Swiss immigrant, an abolitionist, one of the earliest settlers in Kansas Territory, a Union Army soldier, vigorously denounced atrocities against Indian people, was a founder of the Knights of Labor, and was a major leader of the Kansas Populist Party. My grandmother was a fighter for women's suffrage and many other good causes.

Although Eldri was born at Moose Lake, Minnesota, her father, the Reverend John Johanson, a mainline Lutheran clergyman, came from an old homesteading family in north central North Dakota. When we arrived in the state, he was chaplain at a large nursing home at Northwood, not far from Grand Forks. Her younger brother, Arnie, was chair of philosophy at nearby Moorhead State University, Minnesota. Eldri's parents and other family were delighted we were in the immediate region.

Initially, and for a few years, matters seemed to go well at UND. Its student body numbered around twelve thousand or so, with about three hundred Native students. The latter were mostly from the four reservations in the state—two of these Sioux (Spirit Lake Tribe, Standing Rock Tribe), one the Three Affiliated Tribes (Mandan/ Hidatsa/Arikara), and the Turtle Mountain Chippewa Band. Eldri has cousins in the Turtle Mountain Nation.

A smoldering problem within UND was that the strong academic commitment of its previous president—retired a few years before I arrived—was not enthusiastically shared by his successor, whose style of management favored several pet dimensions and was relatively indifferent to most others. This was manifested by significant inequities in his fiscal appropriations; arts and sciences, not close to the president's heart, was low on the totem pole. This uneasy equilibrium held together, more or less, until tax measures that would have been beneficial to higher education generally in the state were killed by a statewide referendum. This was in 1989. At that point, a myriad of increasing and ever-proliferating internal problems began.

Over a span of thirteen years, almost always involving summer teaching as well, my UND experience featured thousands of fine students—Native and non-Native. I liked virtually every one of them (as I have everywhere). I was, as I have always been, an extremely popular teacher with consistently large and sometimes huge class membership, even in my quite challenging Federal Indian Law. I was also deeply involved in the UND Honors Program, taught honors courses over the years, and served a term as chair of the program. And I was a member of the graduate faculty.

But, with the exception of my students and several good faculty friends outside my department, my later years at the university were not pleasant. I was the only Native American on the faculty who was tenured and a full professor. During my long sojourn at UND, I was also the only full-time Indian faculty person among the three full-time faculty in our Indian studies department. The ethos within our unit became, for me, increasingly uncomfortable. For four years I was departmental chair, but even that was, despite my best human-relations efforts, an often uneasy stint for me.

As always, I consistently organized hard-fought social justice campaigns. Among those in the North Dakota context:

The successful fight against entrenched and multifaceted police racism at Grand Forks. I served for many years as the primary organizer and "spark plug" of the mayor's Committee on Police Policy and as the advocate for victimized people.

The successful exoneration of—and major religious freedom victory for—the defendants in the viciously intensive federal attack on the Native American Church (the peyote faith) at and around the Devils Lake Sioux Reservation (now Spirit Lake Tribe or Spirit Lake Dakotah Nation). I coordinated all legal defense and all community, regional, and national support.

The successful fight against the UND administration's Faustian pact with Union Carbide to "test burn" dioxin-producing PCBs at UND, which would have endangered everyone in the whole Grand Forks region. We ended this whole scheme forever.

The successful fight against broad-based and deep Anglo racism at Devils Lake, North Dakota, bordering the Spirit Lake Tribe's reservation. A hard-fought and long-going campaign, we made many significant breakthroughs in this 1950s-type situation, utilizing a wide variety of creatively effective tactics: nonviolent confrontation, lawyers, regional and national publicity, an economic boycott.

I also chaired the Community Relations Board at Grand Forks.

In addition, I successfully handled several hundred individual and family advocate cases involving virtually every conceivable situation.

I and others, over the years, consistently pushed bona fide union organization for UND faculty and staff—working with the American Federation of State, County and Municipal Employees, the National Education Association, and the American Federation of Teachers. Along the way, I held several elected leadership positions, and we successfully processed many grievances indeed. (At one point, about 1989, I very publicly denounced UND as "a big plantation"—a characterization carried widely by news media.)

When you fight for social justice, you make enemies. I was, of course, subjected to a great deal of incessant and covert back-knifing at the university. My social justice activism was the primary source of my increasing difficulties in the UND setting. A key contributing factor was some marked faculty jealousy at my increasingly large classes regardless of specific subject area. Eventually, those two dimensions joined forces. Laced into this toxic mix, in some quarters, were murky threads of racism.

Native students and many non-Native students were consistently with me at every point. At one juncture in 1993, hundreds of students signed a petition on my behalf when surreal but eventually unsuccessful administrative efforts were made to block all student enrollment in my courses; supportive Native persons from around the country also telephoned and wrote to UND's president. So you also make a great many friends—and I had an enormous number in the Native community, among working people and in other grassroots settings, and among students. Many of them are still fine friends to this very moment.

In 1988 I was honored with the annual UND Outstanding Faculty Advisor Award—given by the student government. In 1989 North Dakota governor George A. Sinner and the State King Commission presented me with the Annual Martin Luther King, Jr. Award for my historical and ongoing social justice activities. Also in 1989, the North Dakota State Department of Public Instruction (Indian Education/Equity Programs) awarded me its Annual Civil Rights and Social Justice in Education Award. The commanding general and officers of Grand Forks Air Force Base presented me in 1989 with an excellent plaque and dinner in recognition of my historical and contemporary human rights work. Native students, Native student organizations, and Native prison inmates honored me with many fine gifts: blankets, star quilts, bead work, leather work, hand-carved crafts.

At the conclusion of the 1994 spring semester, I formally retired from UND. When it became known that I was retiring at the end of that academic year, all of my classes boomed even more. At the end of my UND experience, May 1994, I was making a salary of $36,500 per year. It may have been the lowest salary in that faculty rank of full professor in any state school in the United States. But Native students gave me an excellent dinner, replete with gifts that I shall always treasure.

During this era, two more great children entered our family via our oldest daughter, Maria: Thomas Gray Salter, now an MD, and Samantha Salter, presently in college. Thomas, very much our grandson/son, is one-half Mississippi Choctaw. They all lived with us for many years, and Maria still does. A few years ago, Thomas added a new dimension to our family when he married Mimie (Yirenga) Chilinda, a sharp young lady from Zambia and the United Kingdom who shares his professional commitment to medicine and health. Other grandchildren—all fine kids—have emerged via John (Nancy), Peter (Dawn), and Josie (Cameron).

Our family, powerfully cohesive, has become a small horde.

There were a number of Mississippi matters during that general North Dakota time period. In 1987 Krieger Publishing brought out *Jackson, Mississippi* in paperback.

And there was this: In late March 1988, I and my oldest son, John, in the Deep South for several speaking engagements, had dinner one evening at an excellent restaurant on the outskirts of Jackson. Our host, Erle Johnston, had grown up in Grenada in north Mississippi, was a veteran newspaperman, a much older person than I, and had been, in the old days, a shrewd, mortal, and deadly adversary. A leading figure in the Ross Barnett administration—public relations director of the State Sovereignty Commission ("Watchdog Agency") and then its head—he came to see more clearly than anyone else in that whole camp the bloody abyss into which the then dominant (White) Citizens Councils Movement ("States Rights/Racial Integrity") was taking Mississippi. As early as 1962, calling himself "a practical segregationist," he resigned from the Citizens Councils and began to criticize the council leadership as "extremist."

A bit later, in a truly extraordinary move given his surroundings, he proceeded in two significant steps to cut off a long-standing state government subsidy (interracial tax dollars) to the White Councils that had been regularly channeled through the Sovereignty Commission. The fiery national council leader, Bill Simmons of Jackson, immediately called on Governor Barnett to fire Johnston, but Barnett, loyal to an old friend, refused. Johnston caught heavy flak but hung on. He was then calling Simmons "The Rajah of Race."

Johnston, the very first moderate (of sorts) in the old Mississippi segregationist camp, continued his own strange journey onward into the surrealistic transitional administration of the new governor, former lieutenant governor Paul B. Johnson Jr. (1964–68). Erle served increasingly as a kind of race-relations mediator in the early on and sometimes chaotic rapidly desegregating racial situation.

He left state government in 1968, by then quietly convinced of the validity and necessity of racial integration, to return to his newspaper, the *Scott County Times*. Years later, he ran for mayor of his substantial town of Forest and won—with virtually all of the many black votes. As mayor, he once desperately called me in North Dakota for advice on how to deal with a heavy snowfall. I was, of course, experienced with that problem and was quite helpful to him. Basically I told him, "You've got sun and warmth. Just let it melt off. That's the Navajo way." He took my advice. Around this same time, he conveyed the concerns of Ross Barnett about our frigid plight "way up there in that awful North Dakota." We received the same message via letter from Mrs. Virginia Durr of Alabama, who with her late lawyer husband, Clifford, had been a pioneer fighter for civil liberties and civil rights as far back as the '30s. (Mrs. Durr was a sister-in-law of U.S. Supreme Court justice Hugo Black.)

Erle Johnston wrote a number of good books on Mississippi. As time went on, he sent me copies of them all. His initial one, *Roll With Ross*, is a study of Ross Barnett and that very turbulent administration. I reviewed it, favorably, for the quarterly *Journal of Southern History*. The issue came out in November '81, along with a review of my own book—and that's how Erle and I connected in post-war Mississippi.

A 1990 book of his, large and full and very honest, is *Mississippi's Defiant Years, 1953–1973: An Interpretive Documentary with Personal Experiences*. It carries an eloquent foreword by his old friend, also from Grenada, William F. "Bill" Winter. Bill Winter, as Mississippi state tax collector in the old days, was the one significant public official at any level who flatly refused to join the Citizens Councils. His own gubernatorial administration, 1980–84, was one of the very best Mississippi has ever had. In his foreword to *Defiant Years*, Winter wrote: "This is a book about a time and place that will forever be etched in the memory of those of us who lived in Mississippi in the 1950's and '60's."

Mississippi's Defiant Years (which opens with a tribute to longtime black civil rights activists Aaron Henry and Charles Evers) carries a number of testimonials from various persons of some prominence in the Mississippi milieu. The back book cover conspicuously features four of those: Gen. William D. McCain, president emeritus of the University of Southern Mississippi; Hodding Carter III, secretary of state for Jimmy Carter, among many things; myself (then John R. Salter Jr.); and the noted American historian from USM Neil R. McMillen.

Only in Mississippi.

As we ate on that late March 1988 evening, Erle and I and John were surrounded in the restaurant by a lively throng of high school students celebrating a friend's birthday. The honoree was black and the group very well mixed on a black/white basis. As this racially encouraging but now long-commonplace event proceeded, Erle, in response to a question from me, talked about the status and health of the once huge and powerful Citizens Councils—no friends of his to the bitter end! He told us they'd moved their "national headquarters" several times and were now in very modest quarters. He'd been over there to look at their extremely large library.

"They sit each day at a long table and talk about the old days. Got a lot of books in there, and sometimes they just sit and read."

"Is my book there?" I asked.

"You bet it is," he grinned. "At least three copies."

"Bill Simmons, is he there?"

Erle nodded. "Faithfully, from what I hear."

"And Dr. Evans?" (Medford Evans, arch-ideologue and former college English professor—and the father of the *Indianapolis Star*–based national conservative writer M. Stanton Evans.)

"He, too," said Erle. "Last I heard. And all the old guard."

Only a very few years after that, the Citizens Councils hung it up and went formally out of business.

From the far but living past: In 1994 there was the conviction in Mississippi of Byron de la Beckwith for the murder of Medgar Evers. Back in the mid-1960s, two all-white juries had deadlocked. Thirty years later, Beckwith was given a life sentence. Already an old man and always remaining an unreconstructed white supremacist, he died several years ago at the Mississippi State Penitentiary.

We remained at Grand Forks for three years after I left UND. I continued advocacy and general social justice activities. And I continued to see, and often assist, a good number of students.

I also did something else during this period. For many years, I had wanted to change my name—from the adoptive Salter handle visited upon my father back to our original name of Gray. I had held off doing this because of possible confusion to students. But I effected the shift in the district court at Grand Forks in 1995, becoming John Hunter Gray. Eldri now uses the Gray name as well.

Our initial home at Grand Forks was some distance from the Red River of the North—safe distance, we were assured by many. And we were not required to have flood insurance at any point. But I didn't trust the Red. In 1991 I moved our family well to the west of Grand Forks into a pleasant, somewhat newer home. In May 1997 Eldri and I stood and looked at the massive floodwaters of the Red River. Those, born of a dozen blizzards and having engulfed virtually all of Grand Forks (forcing the evacuation of over fifty thousand people), had stopped only three hundred yards from our 'way out home.

We decided then to move—back to the Mountain West. We picked Idaho, southeastern Idaho, specifically the Pocatello setting. I knew the town, a railroad center with phosphorous mining and refining, from my early wanderings and a few later ones. But it was the rough country around Pocatello that pulled me especially—yanked with the greatest poignancy.

A major figure and a direct ancestor in my own family (and, in a strong sense, our culture hero) was John Gray (Ignace Hatchiorauquasha), a St. Regis Mohawk who, with his sixteen-year-old Mohawk wife, Marienne Neketichon (Mary Ann Charles), had come into the Columbia and Snake River country in the early nineteenth century with the fur trade. He emerged as the leader of the Mohawk (with some St. Francis Abenaki) fur hunters and was an effectively fierce advocate in their dealings with the British and American fur companies. He was also a formidable knife fighter. The Grays had maintained their key southeastern Idaho winter camp in an upper valley always visited by sun during the days and surrounded by high, rough ridges. All of this was covered by junipers and sage and was very good indeed for lookout scouting. The location is not far to the west of the Portneuf River and a few miles west of Pocatello.

And so we came to Pocatello in the summer of '97: myself and Eldri; our youngest daughter, Josie; and my oldest daughter, Maria, and her two children—Thomas and Samantha. Rescued by me just before the Red River flood struck, Maria and her little group had lost everything. Our families now joined, we brought our cats, our rabbit, and a turtle on the long westward trek out of the western plains and into the Montana mountains and down into southeastern Idaho. I bought a home 'way far up on the western frontier of Pocatello, right on its very edge. It's less than an hour's up-hill hike to the high hills and small mountains and the special valley and protective ridges of my ancestors. Wild country is only a good stone's throw from our backyard. And that is exactly how and why we came here.

But no sooner had we arrived than it became clear that my reputation as a "known agitator" had preceded me. Police began almost immediate surveillance. We began having weird phone problems—sometimes with a crudeness reminiscent of our civil rights years in the Deep South. People skulked around our home in early morning hours. Heavy mail delays, including innumerable stalled and sometimes opened priority packages, became commonplace. (Three detailed complaints on my part to regional postal inspectors at Seattle went unanswered, unacknowledged.) Our

garbage was surreptitiously searched. Idaho State University—here at Pocatello—
was tellingly resistant, swiftly so, when I sounded it out about part-time teaching.
Several faculty members, initially friendly, began fleeing when they saw me. All of
this and much more, including harassing phone calls, continued for several years.
Some of these issues still remain, and I keep two loaded firearms in our home. But
with only an exception or two, our neighbors, people who've gotten to know us on
a personal basis, are always friendly and fine.

Late in 1998, we got our first computer, absorbing it into our family culture as
quickly and smoothly as Geronimo had embraced his Winchester Model 1876 lever-
action rifle. Our human contacts increased tremendously. And not much more than
a year later, we launched our rapidly growing Lair of Hunterbear website. Initially
it was to refute defamatory stuff and to publicize our harassment here in Idaho, but
it came to feature as well all sorts of interesting written pieces of mine: activist,
informative, and reflective.

Soon after getting here, I found myself being interviewed in friendly fashion
by the local newspaper—the first of several times—and I've given many enthusiastically well-received social justice talks to groups ranging from Bureau of Land
Management/Caribou National Forest personnel to a large annual gathering of
Democrats at Idaho Falls.

We were pleased when Roy Wortman, professor of history at Kenyon College,
put forth in 2000 an excellent essay, "'I Consider Myself a Real Red': The Social
Thought of American Civil Rights Organizer John R. (Salter) Hunter Gray." This
was published in the web magazine *The Journal of Indigenous Thought*, by Sas-
katchewan Indian Federated College (now First Nations University of Canada),
and otherwise widely circulated. This greatly broadened our horizons and contacts.

Before long, in addition to other activities, I began hiking in the rugged turf
above our home and far beyond, sometimes with Maria and always with our Sheltie.
Often I and the dog did it by ourselves, starting in the darkness well before dawn
and trekking several miles before the sun rose. Soon we were doing it daily—and
we did that for a long time. I drew creative insights and strength from these trips,
transposing my thoughts into computer-driven posts and substantial written pieces.

There were times, in the high country, when we encountered winds of sixty
miles per hour on high and dangerous ridges, but we kept going. Sometimes, in
late fall and early winter, I could stand 'way up with clouds below me and the hill
and mountain tops poking through like islands in a vast white sea. And there was
much wildlife: deer, sometimes moose, plenty of coyotes, some of whom began
to follow us with regularity. At least once a mountain lion paced us evenly, not far
below our trail, for several hundred yards. Owls, becoming used to us, sat quietly
in their respective perches as we passed through.

Once, after several inches of snow had fallen under a bright full moon, I came
home and wrote this about our 'way up, partially hidden valley: "In our Gray Hole,
the ghosts often dance in the junipers and sage, on the game trails, in the tributary
canyons with the thick red maples, and on the high windy ridges—and they dance
from within the very essence of our own inner being. They do this especially when
the bright night moon shines down on the clean white snow that covers the valley

and its surroundings. Then it is as bright as day—but in an always soft and mysterious and remembering way."

In the spring of 2003, Eldri and I—and our plain, bare-bones Jeep Cherokee—went to Chicago. There, I was the featured speaker at the annual Founder's Day of the Ethical Humanist Society of Greater Chicago (Ethical Culture). The topic was William Mackintire Salter, Dad's adoptive father. Salter had been a major leader of the Ethical Movement and had founded the Chicago group ages before. Trained in philosophy, he was a courageous and dedicated social activist on a number of critical and controversial fronts over many decades. But, old and brittle beyond his years, he was not suited for fatherhood.

Although the adoption of my father had been a rough trail, and our family's retrospective view of William M. Salter was, to put it delicately, "uneven" and frequently hostile, when I spoke at Chicago I made a kind of genuine peace with his ghost. I linked him, as a social justice influence on myself, with my Swiss immigrant activist great grandfather and with John Gray, fighting leader of the Mohawk and Abenaki fur hunters in the Far West.

As July 2003 began and moved on, I sensed a kind of strange tiredness. I brushed it off, but it became more acute. On my last trip in the darkness with our Sheltie, I was almost dead tired in the latter stages. I finally went to a clinic.

At that point, a nightmare began. Blood tests indicated an odd version of profound anemia. The initial physicians decided I had cancer. A colonoscopy was ordered, but in the context of severe anemia, I suffered two cardiac arrests. The colonoscopy produced nothing, but its botched nature brought my resistance close to zero. That was the first of what became three extremely close brushes with death, stemming from medical malfunctions, within a period of three months—even after this malady was accurately diagnosed as systemic lupus erythematosus (SLE), a relatively rare genetic autoimmune disease. SLE has a special, predatory preference for Native Americans, blacks, Chicanos, some Asian groups, and women in general. It has no cure and is frequently lethal. (In retrospect, it's clear that I had earlier, moderate brushes with this at various points in my life—but I'd ignored those, just kept going, and they faded.)

Some medics gave me up for early death. One asked Eldri—while I lay in a coma—how she felt about my just "slipping away." Of course Eldri said, with uncharacteristic vehemence, "Never!" Another strongly advised me to speedily divest myself of my possessions. I had Last Rites from the Roman Catholic Church. But I am inherently tough, and I refused to die. And I also had the positive forces generated by Things Unseen. The spirit of my Great Bear goes with me, always.

By this time, another physician—who had been my primary doctor early on—had entered the situation. He was a young Mormon and medically conservative. I was opposed to taking any chemo drugs, and he supported this. Gradually, matters began to improve. In late 2004 I was doing some limited hiking. By 2010 things were much, much better. And now, eight years after the onset of the full-scale systemic lupus assault, and as per nine detailed pages of laboratory blood test results, I have been told that I have "no active lupus" within me and that all organs are just fine. This obviously full remission is a quite rare event in cases of this disease.

Through all of this, my mind has remained very clear and unfettered. Physically inhibited but with computer technology, I began doing even more published writing and also some public speaking on a wide variety of social justice topics, including systemic lupus. With its preference for "minority people" and women, the disease strikes many of us as a very real civil rights issue, urgently crying out for adequate research monies. I was privileged to have a significant segment on an oft-repeated installment of NPR's *Infinite Mind* program in which I discussed lupus and Natives and the civil rights implications. But, by far and away, the major thrust of my writing encompasses the actual practice of bona fide organizing and such accompanying dimensions as issues, strategies, tactics, pragmatism, and vision—through explicitly focused material and many personal accounts of significant campaigns.

Friends and family are extremely important in crisis situations of this sort. Early in 2004, they put together a most impressive tribute to me, which has been placed on our Hunterbear website. It includes dozens of fine messages from old friends and new, plus an impressive communication signed by twenty-five former Tougaloo College students from the class of '64. They wrote:

> The Tougaloo Class of '64, meeting for our 40th Reunion, sends heartfelt greetings to Professor and Eldri Salter and their family. We remember their time with us (and we with them)—their encouragement, guidance and welcoming home. Above all, we remember their commitment to the Civil Rights Movement and their faith in us. For all of these gifts we say, "Thank you, thank you." We are saddened to learn of Professor Salter's infliction with lupus. We want him and his family to know that our hearts and prayers are with them as they face this life's challenge. His support and inspiration are living legacies for all who were fortunate to know him, especially the Class of 1964. For this we are ever grateful.

Dr. Willa Cofield (Willa Johnson) of Halifax County, in the northeastern North Carolina Black Belt, wrote the following letter. As the field organizer for the Southern Conference Educational Fund, I had spent almost two years successfully organizing, county by county, a very hard-fought campaign to bring that rigidly segregated, poverty-stricken, and Klan-infested region into the twentieth century.

> I'd like to share my own impression of John Salter, whom I first saw on a 1963 television newscast being mercilessly pummeled by a group of white men. The attack took place during a Black student demonstration in Jackson, Mississippi. A few months later, John appeared in my rural, eastern North Carolina community, where we Black people were staging our own demonstrations.
>
> Originally from Flagstaff, Arizona and part-Indian, he was young, intense, smart and completely committed to social justice.
>
> Salter's civil rights record, his obvious sincerity, as well as his willingness to take on the local racists, soon won over the most skeptical among us. For over a year, he worked in our community, facing daily death threats, abuse, and the virulent hatred of local white people.
>
> With John Salter's help, we initiated a countywide voter registration drive,

and when local officials set up obstacles, John convinced a battery of topnotch lawyers to challenge the county board of elections in court. Our side won. For the first time since the disenfranchisement of Blacks in the late nineteenth century, thousands of eastern North Carolina Blacks registered.

In the 1980s, those voters helped send two Black men to the North Carolina Legislature. In 1992, they sent Eva Clayton, a Black woman, to Congress where she served for many years.

John Salter was not present for the victory celebration or for the happy bus trip to Raleigh for the inauguration of Thomas C. Hardaway as Representative from our District, but many of the bus passengers recalled Salter's courageous work during the 1960s. He had helped break the fierce Southern wall of resistance, thereby setting the stage for the Voting Rights Act and the election of Black people to local, state, and federal legislative bodies.

John drove with us the morning six of our children, including my own six-year-old daughter, integrated the local white school. He found lawyers and financial support, and we successfully battled the school officials and politicians who tried to kill our movement by firing Black teachers.

In communities throughout the South, John Salter is remembered for his selfless leadership and courage and as a man deeply and passionately opposed to injustice.

Since the Civil Rights Movement of the 1960s, I have met many of his former Tougaloo College students. All remember him with the greatest respect and admiration.

John has never flinched from taking unpopular positions. Those of us who benefited from his determination to act upon what he believed right consider that very quality a key factor in making him one of the truly great leaders of our time.

Sincerely,
Willa M. Cofield, PhD,
Enfield, North Carolina and Plainfield, New Jersey

Also, through kind nomination by an old friend and former student, Alice Azure, Mi'kmaq, a gifted poet, I was greatly honored in 2005 with the Elder Achievement Award from the Wordcraft Circle of Native Writers and Storytellers.

The challenges, problems, and often outright horrors that are coming at long-suffering humanity from the very Four Directions are obviously as numerous as needles on a tall yellow pine. And they constitute an enduring and compelling clarion call of many echoes for sensibly altruistic commitment and tangible action by as many people as possible. A basic approach is grassroots social justice community organizing—which I have always seen as Genesis. This can be volunteer in nature or "professional" and paid. It can involve, in the statistical sense, large-scale endeavors but also much smaller ones—whenever or wherever any human beings are suffering, efforts to help are never "small."

Any kind of organizing work, volunteer or otherwise, engenders some headaches along with a great many satisfactions. If you should be interested in becoming involved as an organizer over the long trek, I have this advice: It's a migratory trail, and you certainly won't get rich. But Eldri and I, married fifty years, have four wonderful children (and many fine grandchildren). Recently, our oldest son, John, wrote this:

> Except for his refusal to be walked on by any boss, my father was never like Abner Snopes, but like that peculiar family in Faulkner's "Barn Burning," we were always loading up the wagon with our battered furniture and moving, moving, moving. We lived in North Carolina, we lived in Vermont; we lived in Chicago, Cedar Rapids, Iowa City, Seattle, and Rochester, New York. We lived on the Navajo Nation, we lived in Grand Forks, North Dakota. Our houses were never too grand, never too squalid. Not much survived the moves but our family, and, of course, the steady parade of visitors, people in rags and suits, people coming to see Hunter—people in need: in need of money, advice, food, sanctuary from the Feds, respite from self-destruction; people with plans, problems, with energy that could benefit from focus.

So if you are an aspiring social justice organizer—"bright eyed and bushy tailed"—recognize that you can't practice that always critically needed vocation and have the things about which Thorstein Veblen wrote so well and indictingly in his classic attack on conspicuous consumption, *The Theory of the Leisure Class.* You'll get your skull cracked, your hide cut, and you'll often get fired. But I'd rather have those memories than money.

"You're wired not to know fear," son John (a perceptive writer) remarked during a long phone conversation when I was in the deepest pits of the battle with systemic lupus. "You were born that way." And my youngest son, Peter (an astute journalist), commented: "This is coming out of nowhere, but I've decided you're the toughest S.O.B. I know. . . . I'm glad I've never had to stand on the other side of the negotiating table from you."

They're right. And I have heard essentially that from many people over many decades. Since I have never known fear, I cannot claim courage. But I can claim optimism. I see the basic nature of people and the world itself as good. And so, with my organizer's backpack, I continue to climb the mountains toward sun and life.

Almost half a century ago, an initially small group of young black people—high school and college students—and their quite young half blood Native advisor set out to build a movement that would fundamentally shake and crack the capital city of Jackson—the very heart of Mississippi, itself the nearest thing to a garrison police state that has ever existed in this country.

And that great saga now lies directly ahead on this trail.

John R. Salter Jr. (Hunter Gray)
In the mountains of eastern Idaho

To
TIM MCGOWAN AND CAROL SCHWARZ,
COMMUNITY ORGANIZERS

JACKSON, MISSISSIPPI
An American Chronicle of Struggle and Schism

1

It was a clear, pleasant morning in mid-October, 1961.

The class was American Government and, although a sociologist, I was teaching it. We had spent most of the hour talking about such matters as student involvement in that society which lay out and beyond the gates of the college—various things that a student could and should do, simply because he or she was a human being. It was a bit cooler than it had been, fall was just arriving; and on occasion we all looked out of the window, grateful that the intense heat of summer was beginning to wane.

Not all of the students contributed to the discussion of ways and means of improving the larger society. Not that all didn't feel that it needed improvement; indeed they felt it did. But most also felt, and indicated one way or the other, that it would be many decades before their society underwent substantial improvement. Even in our classroom, comparatively safe as it was, were the penetrating fingers of a fear deliberately manufactured and implemented in a wide variety of ways by the power structure of the state in which we lived: Mississippi.

Ours was a black college—Tougaloo Southern Christian College— a few miles north of the Mississippi capital of Jackson. It was certainly a unique institution in the state. Formerly an old plantation, it had almost a century before become a school for black people and was now operated under the auspices of two northern-based churches: Congregational and Disciples of Christ. It was free from state control. The Tougaloo faculty was, and had always been, interracial; and with the exception of two white girls, neither from Mississippi, who had come only a few weeks before, the student body was black. Unique indeed was Tougaloo; and we viewed it as the only comparatively "free" island in the whole, sovereign State of Mississippi.

The students who came to Tougaloo came from many parts of Mississippi—some from families which could afford the school's minimal tuition and board and room, and others with scholarship aid. Nearly all of them felt that, once out of college, they would go North to a future which, whatever limitations it might have, would offer them more than their home state did. In many respects, the Tougaloo students were just like students anywhere. But in other respects, they were not: for no matter from where they came—larger towns and cities such as Jackson, Biloxi, or Meridian, or small towns like Greenwood, Canton, and McComb, or

3

hamlets or isolated sharecropper cabins in the rural areas, whether their families were moderately well-to-do or poor—they were black, and they were black in the most repressively racist segregation complex in the United States. As such they bore, one way or another, the scars of their past and present and of the future that they felt they could never enjoy.

Many in that American Government class, although quite certain that their society required fundamental change, saw no way in which that change could be effected, and certainly saw no possibility of their playing a role in effecting it. We concluded that class by deciding that we would all have to do something—something more—and as everyone left, I picked up my books and notes and prepared to go. A girl waited for me by the door.

Her name was Colia Liddell; she lived in Jackson and was probably the only member of that class, and one of the few students at Tougaloo, who was trying to bring about a change. I knew that Colia was active in what there was of the National Association for the Advancement of Colored People, which, as she freely conceded, was not a strong group—either in Jackson or in Mississippi.

Colia Liddell was a little hesitant about what she had to ask me that day. She was president, she reminded me, of the Youth Council of the NAACP in Jackson. Now we had, she went on, two days or so before, discussed in class the effort of the Freedom Riders to desegregate the bus terminals in Jackson. As a consequence of those civil rights efforts, the Interstate Commerce Commission several weeks before had issued a formal ruling making it clear that interstate public conveyance terminals were not to be segregated—and this ruling was going into effect on November 1. So would it be possible, Colia asked, for me to be the speaker at a little community mass meeting they were having in Jackson on the night of October 30, in order to explain to the people just what the ICC ruling really meant?

I thought it over for a moment. Colia had told our class harrowing accounts of some of the difficulties she and other members of her group had had with the Jackson police. But after a class session like this, I thought, who was I to refuse to speak at an NAACP mass meeting—even if it was in Jackson, Mississippi?

I told her certainly, I'd be glad to be the speaker. She said that she would spread the word and try to ensure a good turnout.

A few hours later I mentioned her request to another faculty member. He told me that he was glad it was I, not he, whom they'd asked. "This is a tough state," he told me. "It's going to get worse before it gets any better."

I agreed, but told him I thought I'd speak at the meeting anyway.

I hadn't been in Mississippi long; I had come with my wife, Eldri, a few weeks before on September 1. We had come a long way to get to Mississippi. Although born in the East, I had grown up in the northern

Arizona mountain town of Flagstaff. She was from Minnesota and had spent most of her life in and around Minneapolis and St. Paul. Back in the spring we had been married at Superior, Wisconsin, where Eldri was a staff member of a Lutheran organization, working with students, and where I had just spent a year teaching sociology at a state college.

We were both in our mid-twenties. Eldri's father was a clergyman in the American Lutheran synod, and the views of both her parents on human rights were fully consistent with deepest traditions of Christian brotherhood. Eldri herself had worked as a social worker in South St. Paul. And even if Arizona, my state, was far indeed from being a bastion of liberalism, I had grown up in a family that stressed the traditions of equalitarian democracy. My father was a Wabanaki (Abenaki) Indian—one of the "People of the Dawn"—from the Penobscot bands of Maine and the Micmacs of Quebec and the Maritime Provinces. His mother had left a poverty-stricken home at the age of ten to work full time as a domestic for white people. The economic deprivation that always followed her greeted my father at birth.

Eventually he was adopted and partially raised by William Mackintire Salter, a prominent New England liberal who was a brother-in-law of the noted philosopher William James. Salter had been a founder of the Ethical Culture Society, was an active member of the almost completely white Indian Rights Association, and was one of the fifty or so men and women who, in 1909, had signed the call to organization of the NAACP. Yet, despite the intellectual liberalism of William Salter and his substantive commitment to human rights, he endeavored to turn my father into a white person. In this he did not succeed; my father remained very much a Wabanaki, and the relationships between William Salter and his dark foster son became strained and bitter. In his mid-teens, my father left the Salter home to make his own way, and eventually, following a series of unique experiences—including a sojourn in Mexico during the Zapata/Madero revolution, in which he was part of an altruistic gun-running operation serving the Indian peasants—Dad graduated from the Art Institute of Chicago and became a highly successful artist. Later he took an M.A. and an M.F.A. from the University of Iowa—but he always remained an Indian. Coming to Northern Arizona University at Flagstaff as chairman of its art department, he served there until his retirement.

Although my mother's family was a rather conservative white one with early frontier origins, it had encompassed Abolitionists and Union soldiers, Kansas Populist party leaders, Knights of Labor and Debs socialists, and several participants in utopian-colony endeavors. My maternal grandmother had been the first woman to receive a master's degree in the history of Kansas and had been an active campaigner for women's rights. My mother carried with her a primary commitment to social justice.

Flagstaff, Arizona, itself was certainly no "beloved community" of good fellowship. It had a large native American, Chicano, and black population—and prevalent white racism featuring, among all of its other manifestations, a number of restaurant signs indicating "No Indians or Dogs Allowed." Violence was a tool of almost ethical nature as far as a great many of the residents were concerned. But along with many others—Indian, white, black, Hispanic—my parents had "moved and shook" the town in positive directions. I was growing into my late teens, and all of this had played a powerful role in making me—a "half-breed"—whatever I was in my social philosophy.

Like many Americans, Eldri and I, long before we had met one another, had been stirred by such developments in the South as Little Rock, and the Montgomery bus boycott, and the wave of sit-ins that began in the upper South. In May, 1961, up in Wisconsin, we looked at the newspaper and read of the Freedom Rider crusades through the Deep South and, especially into Alabama and Mississippi, saw the pictures of the burning buses and those of beaten and bloody people. We decided to go South ourselves—down into Mississippi.

And so we came, I as a college teacher, she as my wife. Yet we knew even before we arrived that it was conceivable that we would become "involved" in matters beyond the scope of actual teaching. Once on the scene, however, it became clear that simply to be at Tougaloo was "involvement" in large measure, since the power structure of Mississippi was inclined quite negatively toward the college.

The first night on campus, staying temporarily at the home of Dr. A. D. Beittel, the president, who, although a white man originally from the North, had spent much of his life in the South, we saw an indication of how the college was viewed. Dr. Beittel went into Jackson that night to sit on a TV panel discussion where he was interviewed by a number of Mississippi newsmen, all of whom wished to discuss with him the college's policy of "allowing" civil rights activities on the part of students, and of doing such strange things as "allowing" the Freedom Riders to stay at the college when they had all returned to Mississippi for their arraignment in the local courts. Quietly and courteously he explained integration as he saw it—how it was desirable, how it was the law of the land, how students had the right to peacefully protest. But the men who asked him the questions, although courteous enough themselves, were rigid, hard, adamant; and the interview had closed with the mediator, a tough-looking old man, taking the position that if Tougaloo was going to keep on getting involved in civil rights, there would most likely "be more trouble."

Later that same night a woman named Hazel Brannon Smith and her husband came to Tougaloo to see Dr. Beittel. We talked with them, learned that they were among the extremely few outspoken white "moderates" in Mississippi. She was from a rural county to the north, Holmes County, and she was a newspaperwoman who, because of her stand favoring justice for all Mississippians, white and black alike, had been subjected to constant segregationist pressure—most of it spearheaded by the racist organization, the Citizens Council, and most of it designed to cut off her advertisers. Her husband, once director of a hospital in the county, had lost his job because of Citizens Council pressure. The Smiths had seen the TV interview, and they felt that Tougaloo would come under increasing pressure itself in the days ahead. This embattled couple congratulated Eldri and me for having come to the college, and we in turn were a little surprised that this was considered a "brave" thing to do—even to come to Tougaloo.

In the days ahead, however, we came to realize a little more what the Smiths meant. White people, traveling up and down the highway in front of the college, frequently "looked hostile" in the direction of the school. The local press in Jackson, and other news media as well, avowedly racist and completely uninhibited, leveled frequent attacks in the direction of Tougaloo. When the two white girls, Joan Trumpauer, who had been a Freedom Rider and who had served several weeks at the state penitentiary at Parchman, and Charlotte Phillips, a Swarthmore transfer, arrived to enroll, the segregationists became quite upset, and for a few days there was the possibility of police arrest of, say, Dr. Beittel. The line dividing Hinds and Madison counties cut right through the campus, and although Madison County was silent, the district attorney for Hinds County gave a public statement that he was "investigating the matter." The college, however, pointed out that its ninety-year-old charter, granted by the state during Reconstruction, said nothing about race. Finally, the controversy over the two girls died down, although for weeks much of a wildly critical nature was said about all this in the local news media. Then too, Tougaloo students, especially those who had college stickers on their cars, often had "trouble" in their hometowns. It was quite clear that the college was far from being in the good graces of Mississippi.

But aside from this attachment to the college in a teaching capacity, we had not become immediately involved in direct civil rights activities. For one thing, Eldri and I were learning about Jackson, and Mississippi in general—trying to get the lay of the land—and there was a great deal to learn. For another, there really wasn't, we were surprised to learn, much civil rights activity at all anywhere in the state.

The Supreme Court school desegregation ruling came in 1954; the Montgomery bus boycott developed soon after that; the sit-ins spread out from Greensboro, North Carolina, in 1960, over much of the South. But not much at all had happened, or was happening, in Mississippi. In April, 1960, a number of blacks had attempted to use a "white" beach down on the Gulf Coast, had been attacked by a mob, and had been arrested and jailed. Almost a year later nine Tougaloo students had sought to use the all-white library in Jackson; they had been arrested immediately for "breach of the peace" and thrown into jail. Later, after they had been released on bail bonds of $500 each and were in court for trial, Jackson police, using clubs and dogs, had dispersed a number of black sympathizers who were standing quietly outside the courthouse. As was always the case in civil rights matters, the Tougaloo students were found guilty in the local courts and had to begin the long process of appeal. When students at another black college, Jackson State, which was under the thumb of state authorities, attempted to stage a march protesting this whole situation, they too were dispersed with clubs and dogs.

Shortly after this, the Freedom Riders began to ride into Jackson, attempting to use the bus-terminal facilities on an integrated basis. They were met at the state line by Mississippi law-enforcement officers, escorted into Jackson, and, as soon as they sought to use the facilities, were arrested—in the end, almost 350 of them. Their trials were still going on, one and two at a time, although by late summer the Riders had all been bonded out of jail.

About the time that we came to Mississippi, the embryonic Student Nonviolent Coordinating Committee (SNCC) had sent a few workers, under the leadership of a former New York teacher who had just arrived in the South, Bob Moses, into the southwestern part of the state—to Amite, Pike, and Walthall counties. It was a pioneer effort based mostly around voter registration and included some attempts to desegregate a couple of McComb lunch counters. Police harassment and arrest of the SNCC workers, physical violence, reprisals against local blacks who participated in the efforts—including the expulsion from school of many black high-school students in McComb, and finally, the murder of a black farmer, Herbert Lee, who had been active in the SNCC campaign, by a white state legislator who was never indicted by a jury—broke the SNCC efforts in southwestern Mississippi within a few weeks.

A few days before Colia talked with me, half a dozen Tougaloo students had attempted to picket the black portion of the segregated Mississippi State Fair in Jackson. That had been ended immediately by police dogs and instant arrest, and the students had, a day or so before, been released on $500 bail bonds. That incident, however, did at least successfully spread the word to blacks to stay away from the fair.

But not much was really happening with respect to civil rights activity in Mississippi. One could always read of efforts in other southern states, even efforts which, in part at least, were successful. But nothing much was happening in Mississippi.

There was a good reason for this: Mississippi was functioning, in the purest and most cold-blooded sense of the word, as a garrison state that viewed itself not only as being prepared for war but as already fighting a war.

Of all the southern states, it had always had the highest number of blacks, proportionately, and the rationale of slavery—the "inherent biological inferiority" of blacks—had never been as deeply and universally accepted by any other society within the United States. More than most areas, Mississippi had been a land where a very small proportion of the population had exercised control of economic factors, largely agricultural, and because of that control had wielded the whip hand over the political structures. Running all through the history of Mississippi were the threads of violence, a trait derived from its frontier-like nature; indeed, as one authority put it, Mississippi was the "wild West" of the South.

The Civil War struck Mississippi especially hard economically, since its wealth concerned, in very large numbers, black slaves; and from that and other standpoints, it never recovered. Its period of Reconstruction had seen a substantial number of black officeholders, although never a majority, and they had functioned well. But after a few years, the North had terminated its partial alignment with southern black political leaders; the Hayes-Tilden Compromise in 1877 had given the South clear mandate to do whatever it wished with respect to its treatment of blacks; and soon white supremacy was again total. Mississippi itself, in 1890, emerged as the spearhead of the Jim Crow laws in the South—legislation designed to institutionalize segregation in every aspect of life. Then again, Mississippi took the lead in a massive and successful campaign designed to disfranchise southern blacks. Then, to root even deeper the climate of fear that had always prevailed, thousands of southern blacks were lynched—more in Mississippi than any other southern state.

By the early 1900s Mississippi was, from the day and place that a man was born to the day and place that he was buried, a total segregation complex. Still poverty-stricken, even its populist protests were perverted by racism, and Mississippi's populist leaders were among the most virulent anti-black demogogues the nation has ever known, even as they up to a point, lashed out against the plantation elite.

World War I brought little change to Mississippi. Nor did the 1930s, nor, so far as that goes, World War II; and even if the post-World War II era saw a bit of a wane in the almost total provincialism, it saw no change, really, in the racial status quo. Black and white Mississippians moved back into the same old patterns if and when they returned from war.

Through the years, then, Mississippi went essentially the way it wished: refusing to recognize its mounting social and economic problems, let alone doing anything about them; blaming its ills on the Federal government, the remainder of the country, "communist conspiracies," blacks. And Mississippi, wrapping itself up in the myths of the antebellum era—which, increasingly, came to be a period viewed as having been the ultimate in utopian living—launched periodic crusades, such as the Dixiecrat maneuver, to make that long-ago era a new reality. And it reacted to the increasing failure of those crusades by building ever higher its barricades of hatred and suspicion.

For a white man—if he was a planter, businessman, professional—Mississippi could be a comfortable place in which to live. For a poor white man Mississippi was rough, with little industry and low wages and the humiliating presence of the aristocratic snobbery that lingered from the old days. For a black, any black, Mississippi was hell: unequal facilities, if indeed any facilities; disfranchisement—and total exclusion from any participation in the decision-making process; always the most menial jobs and the rankest poverty; the status of an animal; terror.

It became worse.

Came Monday, May 17, 1954, and the Supreme Court decision that not only opened the door toward, someday, the integration of the school system, but that, reversing old precedents, even then could be seen as an initial step toward the ultimate destruction of all segregation barriers. Stunned, the South, Mississippi, reeled from this decision; but there were some who did not. And as they had so many times in the past, Mississippi segregationists took the initiative in mobilizing against desegregation.

In late May, 1954, a circuit judge from Brookhaven, Mississippi, Tom P. Brady—who had once taught sociology at the University of Mississippi—delivered a speech entitled "Black Monday" to the Greenwood, Mississippi, chapter of the Sons of the American Revolution. He outlined what he felt should be done with respect to the Supreme Court decision. Some weeks later, *Black Monday* emerged as a tract that was widely distributed, first in Mississippi, then throughout the South. All of the old paranoia was crystallized in the pages of Judge Brady's book:

> . . . Whenever and wherever the white man has drunk the cup of black hemlock, whenever and wherever his blood has been infused with the blood of the negro, the white man, his intellect and his culture have died.

The Fourteenth Amendment and the Federal government were bitterly castigated, and Brady warned that the "Supreme Court can play King Canute to its heart's content—but laws like bullets cannot kill a sacred custom."

Judge Brady felt that the southern and border states should take the initiative in organizing into a tight federation which, as he put it, would be open to "all other States which are vitally interested in stopping and destroying the Communist and Socialist movement in this country," and which could work through such means as widespread publicity—and political action, even to the point that it could, if warranted, develop a "third national party."

The Brookhaven jurist saw this proposed organization working zealously at the southern grassroots. "We must teach our children," said he, "the truth about communism, its infiltration of our country, and the facts of ethnology."

And pointing out that most blacks in the South were employed by whites, he called, if necessary, for large-scale economic reprisals—mass firings.

Within weeks after the publication and initial distribution of Judge Tom Brady's strident call to arms, a handful of men, very much inspired by the judge's position, commenced the organization of the Citizens Council, an arch-segregationist organization with central headquarters in Jackson. It was designed to "organize" Mississippi, from one end of the state to the other, to prevent any changes of any sort in the racial status quo by enforcing conformity in both the white and the black communities.

Although, as the Citizens Council developed, it was to make full use of the poor white in its campaign against integration, it did not seek to attract him into membership. Instead, it concentrated on recruiting the power structure: planters, urban businessmen, political leaders, lawyers, judges—even Federal judges. With an eye toward molding public opinion, it recruited those involved with mass media; with a recognition of the value of economic pressures, it signed up bankers. Crystallizing all of the traditions of white Mississippi, and certainly never ignoring the fact that a repressed black community equaled low wages and a continuation of white political power, the Citizens Council recruited so successfully at the power-structure level, and the movement spread across Mississippi so rapidly, that within a few years the Citizens Council was a major power in the state which no one could ignore, and all of the "big people" supported it in one degree or another. Also, the Council movement began to spread from its Mississippi citadel into other southern states.

In the eyes of the Citizens Council and its adherents, the Supreme Court and the NAACP were equivalent to "communism"; the Federal government was synonomous with "tyranny"; those who joined and supported the racist programs of the Citizens Council were "patriots"; those who did not were "traitors."

By late 1955, Mississippi Senator James Eastland, Congressman John Bell Williams, and Judge Brady—all, of course, devoted Council advocates—could sign a public statement which implied, in its own way, rebellion against the United States:

> We think the Southern States should carefully consider the doctrine . . . that a State has the legal right of interposition to nullify, void, and hold for naught the deliberate, dangerous and palpable infractions of the Constitution committed by the Supreme Court; infractions that are so great that our system of government is threatened.

A rash of legislation designed to bolster state segregation laws and prevent civil rights activity began to flow through the legislatures of the southern states. Again, Mississippi led the others.

Those few moderate white Mississippians who disagreed with all of this, or who even had the temerity to suggest that Federal law be obeyed, found themselves either forced out of the state or silenced—by economic threats and pressures, community ostracism, threats of physical reprisals, and some violence. To ensure that future generations of white Mississippians grew up in the proper fashion, the Citizens Council could, in 1957, with full recognition of its strength and with every realization that this would be done, set forth for elementary school teachers a teaching guide that included more than fifty items—some of the titles of which were very much to the point:

Many American Leaders Were Southerners . . . South Led the Way to Freedom . . . Our First President Was a Southerner . . . A Southerner Wrote the Declaration of Independence . . . South Still Protects America . . . White Men Built America . . . Southerners Were Kind to Slaves . . . Blacks Should Not Live Among Whites . . . Races Should Never Mix . . . God Made the Races Different . . . Birds Do Not Mix . . . Chickens Do Not Mix . . . Race-Mixers Want the Races to Live Together . . . Southern Way of Life Is Segregation . . . We Have Always Been Segregated . . . Many Differences Between Races . . . God Made the Negro Black . . . Races Have Always Lived Apart in the South . . . Race-Mixers Want to Mix the Races in the South . . . Race-Mixers Do Not Tell You Races Are Different . . .

Race-Mixers Want to Cause Trouble . . . You Aren't Told What Happens When Races Mix . . . Race-Mixers Want Whites and Blacks to Date . . . Whites Learn Faster Than Negroes . . . Races Can Only Live Peacefully When Separated . . . Race-Mixers Help Communists . . . Race-Mixers Want to Change America . . . Mixing the Races Will Make America Weak . . . Race-Mixers and Communists Want America Weak . . . Segregation Is Christian . . . America Must Not Listen to Race-Mixers . . . Southerners Won't Let Race-Mixers Ruin Their Country.

For the black community, also, there were pressures—but far more vicious, generally, than those leveled against the few white moderates. The handful of black parents in Mississippi who, following the Supreme Court decision, petitioned local school officials for the admission of their children into white schools, were speedily forced to remove their names from the petitions. When a black named Clennon King attempted to secure admission into the University of Mississippi, he found himself in an insane asylum. Another, Clyde Kennard, attempted to be admitted to the University of Southern Mississippi and within a short time found himself serving a long prison sentence for the framed-up charge of chicken-feed theft. The Rev. George Lee, a leader of voter registration in Humphreys County, was mysteriously shot and killed; Lemar Smith, another black involved in political activity, was shot and killed in

Lincoln County—in front of the courthouse in broad daylight. Again in Humphreys County, Gus Courts, a grocer, active in voter registration, was shot and seriously wounded. The youth Emmet Till was found murdered in the Delta. Mack Charles Parker was lynched in Pearl River County. These and other acts of violence, often death—and always unpunished—combined with systematic economic reprisals, destroyed most of the small scattered NAACP units that existed in the state and effectively silenced black grassroots protest.

On September 8, 1959, the governor-elect of Mississippi, Ross R. Barnett, stated at a Citizens Council banquet:

> The Citizens Councils throughout Mississippi and the Southland are rendering a great contribution to the general welfare of both the white and colored races and the maintenance of constitutional government. . . . I am proud that I have been a Citizens Council member since the Council's early days. I hope that every white Mississippian will join with me in becoming a member of this fine organization.

The ascendancy of Ross Barnett to the governor's chair completed— if, indeed, such had not already existed—the Citizens Council coup in Mississippi. By this time, total segregation was deeply rooted in every hamlet, every town, every county in the state. Every white businessman, every political official, and most of the white citizenry in general were committed to the preservation of this status quo. Virtually all of the mass media echoed the position of the Citizens Council. Whatever opposition to all of this had existed in the white community was now ended. The black community was almost silent. An institution named the State Sovereignty Commission had existed for a few years prior to Ross Barnett's election—a sort of pro-segregation public-relations agency that also functioned as a secret-police force. Once Ross Barnett was governor, the Commission's second function became paramount, and further, the state began to transfer a regular subsidy of several thousand dollars each month, through the Sovereignty Commission, to the Citizens Council, which then became a quasi-state agency itself.

Other southern states were in varying degrees defiant of the Federal government, the Supreme Court, civil rights efforts. But if the other southern states contained widespread areas reminiscent of Mississippi, they also contained, because of a measure more of industry, for one reason, areas that were not quite so negative in their approach; and their state houses reflected this diversity of opinion. But Mississippi was a total situation—total segregation, total repression, a total monolith.

For those who might look toward Mississippi's largest city and its capital for some signs of positive social change, there could be only bitter disappointment. Not only was Jackson the seat of a state government committed completely to the preservation of total segregation; it was also

the center of state activity for the Citizens Council. And every segregationist in the state informed as to the creeping progress of civil rights
in other southern states knew full well that the largest cities were always
the first to crack. As a consequence, Jackson was watched continually
and sharply for any signs of "weakening." The same conformity that
strangled the white community outside Jackson existed within the capital;
and it was known that the Citizens Council and the Sovereignty Commission had at least one watchdog citizen in every city block in the white
sections. The same fear that strangled the black community elsewhere in
Mississippi strangled it in Jackson—and it was known that the Citizens
Council and the Sovereignty Commission had their spies there, too. Backed
by the power of the business community, which was itself enmeshed with
the Citizens Council, and bolstered by a police force that was all white
and larger than that of any city of comparable size anywhere in the
country, Jackson's chief executive, a former college Greek teacher and
ardent Citizens Council member, Allen Thompson, could say, as the
Freedom Riders rolled into his city and as the police speedily carried them
off to jail, ". . . this city will not follow the course of some southern states
who have yielded to integration."

The evidences of the vicious system under which Mississippi operated
leapt out at Eldri and me from every side, from the first moment we were
in the state. There are three things that I remember from those first
few days in Mississippi, each a quiet sort of thing, as I experienced it, and
each utterly revealing.

The first was going into downtown Jackson one Saturday afternoon
and seeing several of my students there on the sidewalk. As I waved at
them and walked over to talk, they smiled at me briefly, then looked
quickly at the white people passing on the sidewalk, who were looking at
us. Then the students turned away: blacks and non-blacks did not talk
socially with one another in Jackson, certainly not on the sidewalk, not
even when they were students and a teacher.

The second thing was hearing students of mine tell me in class that
their parents believed that blacks *were* born inferior to whites and that
nothing could ever change that. Then, after that class, in a private conversation, a seventeen-year-old who had just come to Tougaloo told me
that he wondered seriously if blacks weren't born with "less of a mind than
whites."

The third thing was a small group of students casually showing me
a brief news item in a local Jackson paper, the *Jackson Daily News,*
which was buried inside the publication and which, without mentioning
the fact that the victim had been a leader in the SNCC voter-registration
effort, simply said that a Herbert Lee, a Negro, had been shot and killed
by a white man in Amite County. To the students, this was simply
something that happened with enough regularity to warrant no great
comment among themselves, only a matter-of-fact sympathy for the slain
man and mild curiosity. They had lived in Mississippi all of their lives.

2

LATE IN THE AFTERNOON of the day that Colia asked me to speak at the NAACP meeting, I picked up Eldri at the Tougaloo business office, where she was then working, and we drove into Jackson. We were living in the city because, although most of the Tougaloo faculty resided on campus, only one cottage had been available when we came, and that, all decided, should go to another new faculty member whose wife could not speak English. With some difficulty, the college had rented for us one portion of a small duplex on the "white" side of Lamar Street—a dividing line between white and black residential sections.

I told Eldri that I was going to speak at the meeting, and she agreed that that was good. She asked if she could go, and I told her that since apparently no one knew quite what would happen, she ought to stay home this time. Then we went on to discuss other things, such as her pregnancy, and as we approached our home, our talk shifted to a perennial topic: the people who lived in the other half of the duplex. They were from Philadelphia, Mississippi, a young couple, and they did not like us at all. The duplex was poorly divided and there was no privacy at all; we could hear them and they could hear us. Although we rather suspected that their animosity toward us was motivated, in part at least, by a wish to have us move out and hence to secure greater privacy, there was no question about their dislike of Tougaloo and what they felt us to be.

Some days before, the man and I had had a little discussion about voting rights. He had told me that, in Mississippi, "No niggers are even registered, to speak of. We make it just as hard for them as we can. We've got to, since they don't know their own minds." He had pointed, then, down half a block on the other side of Lamar Street, where a black family was gathered on their front porch in the cool of the early evening.

I told him that it seemed to me that blacks knew their own minds and ought to be able to register and vote as they wished.

He told me, with his blood pressure clearly rising, that I "didn't understand" and that I was "from the North."

I had told him that I didn't think that Arizona was "the North" and that, in any case, people ought to be able to register and vote.

He got up, shaking angrily, then told me, "You'd damn well better be careful the way you talk around here."

I told him that I'd talk any way I pleased. His wife, who had heard all of this, came to the door and asked him to come inside. He went— not before, however, he'd given me a long glare just before he slammed the door violently. After that, all of us had stopped speaking to one another.

Now, as we drove up to the house, talking of our little situation with the neighbors, we noticed that they had company and appeared to be having a lively time. "Well," said Eldri, "we'll be having company ourselves tomorrow night. I hope that we're quieter than they are." She was referring to the fact that we had invited two students over for supper. One, Al Rhodes, was from Jackson; the other, Charlotte Phillips, was the exchange student from Swarthmore.

I told Eldri that I didn't much care whether or not we were quiet.

The next night Al and Charlotte came over for supper. I heard Al's car outside and I stepped out of the house to greet him. Then I saw that he had parked his car up by some trees, out of sight. We went into the house and I told him that he should have parked closer. "I don't know what kind of neighbors you have," he told me, half laughing but half serious.

I told him that we had some "rough ones" on the other side of the wall, but not to let that bother him. Eldri and Charlotte were bringing food in from the kitchen.

"Charlotte's white," he reminded me.

I joked with him. "All the students say Charlotte looks Negro," I said. This was true; her skin was dark.

"I guess that's right," he answered. "But you never know what you're going to find around these white people in Jackson." He shook his head.

We were having a good dinner and a good talk when I heard a twig crack under our window, which was partly open and which had the shade slightly up. We listened. Someone was moving around outside. Then we heard a door open, slam. "It's the people on the other side," I said. "Forget about 'em." We had a fine evening.

As I walked out to the sidewalk with Al someone turned on the front-porch light. "That's your neighbors," said Al, "looking at all of us right now." We said good night, and he drove away. The porch light went off. Suddenly, it seemed very dark.

The next afternoon, as we came in from Tougaloo, our duplex neighbors were talking with a man who lived in the next house and who obviously was just getting home from work himself. They glared at us and we glared at them; they looked away and went on talking in low tones.

The next morning, Tougaloo received a registered letter from the real-estate agency from which they had rented the house for us. We were to vacate the premises, the letter told the Tougaloo administration, in no more than one week. No explanation was given, and when the college pressed for a reason, it was told only that no reason was necessary. But by that time we had decided that it must have been because Al and Charlotte had come over for dinner.

Eldri and the college began to search for another place for us, and it soon became clear that this was going to be difficult indeed. The college felt that it would be unwise for us to try to live in the black community, and frankly doubted that anyone there would even rent to us. The white people with whom Eldri talked, who had places advertised, backed away when she mentioned Tougaloo. Real-estate agencies were not at all interested, and the college decided that the Citizens Council had circulated our name.

Finally, as the week was about over, we found a very battered "fourplex" in a tough-looking neighborhood on Bailey Avenue. An old couple who lived in an adjacent house handled the rental for the owner, a woman who spent most of her time out of state. The word "Tougaloo" didn't seem to disturb them at all and, after we had paid the first month's rent, they told us that several months before, there had been a fire in one of the upper apartments; a woman had "burned all up" and this had made it difficult to rent all of the apartments. We were glad enough to get one of them.

Late the next afternoon, I rented a small trailer and moved out of the old place. Our neighbors on the other side of the wall had avoided us ever since the college had received the letter, and it was clear that they had been responsible for our eviction. Sometimes they had even used the back door rather than come up on the porch while we were sitting there. Now, as I moved our things out, I could see them looking out their window. Elsewhere, in the immediate neighborhood, people were observing from their porches, doing so, I was sure, with a great deal of satisfaction. But just as we were ready to go, a tired lady who lived behind us, and whose half dozen small children had come shyly into our house on occasion to look at a wolfskin I had which fascinated them, came over with all of her children to say good-bye. She was barefoot; so were they. And she confirmed what had happened.

"I don't care," she told us, "what they say about you all. You've been good neighbors and mighty nice to my kids. So good-bye and good luck." On that note we left, to move into an apartment in a building where a woman had "burned all up."

It was now time for the NAACP community meeting on the Interstate Commerce Commission ruling. I had dug into the background of the whole Federal involvement in interstate commerce and I had, I felt, a good little speech prepared. The church was in the Virden Addition, in the northern part of Jackson, and I was there a good half hour before the meeting was set to begin. Inside, a church service was in progress, and while I sat on the steps and waited, some teenagers came up to the church, obviously to attend the meeting, then saw me, and quietly withdrew to a point where they were not in the light.

Colia soon came up, greeted me almost as if she hadn't expected to see me, and introduced me to the teenagers, who then informed me that, when they'd seen me, they had felt that I was some sort of police officer. Colia indicated that the people in the church service would be staying over for the meeting. A few more young people came up. Then a police car drove by, slowly, its occupants staring at us, and a few minutes later it came by again. Then the church service was over and we went inside.

After the opening prayer had been given by the minister, a freedom song was sung which the people obviously didn't know, nor did I, as far as that goes. The burden of the song came to lie with the dozen or so young people who had come. I was introduced as an "outstanding authority" on the Interstate Commerce Commission, and indeed, it was implied that, although a Tougaloo professor, I had some sort of connection with President Kennedy.

I gave my talk, tracing the background of Federal involvement in interstate commerce, discussing at length the effect of the Freedom Riders on the situation and stressing that, as a result of the ICC order, the bus stations and the railroad station could no longer force a person to accept segregated facilities. Nor could the police enforce segregation in the terminals. I encouraged people to use the previously all-white waiting rooms, restaurants and restrooms in the stations.

People nodded their heads. Several said, "Amen."

When I had finished, I asked for questions, but there were none. Colia encouraged the people to use the facilities; a freedom song was sung; a very small collection was taken; there was a brief closing prayer; and the meeting was over.

People came up to shake hands. "That was a fine talk you gave, professor," said an elderly man. "But," and I thought he smiled a little sardonically, "we all know that if we use those waiting rooms and restaurants and toilets, we're going to be in city jail so fast. . . ." He shook my hand warmly and went out. It was clear that he had expressed the dominant feeling at the meeting. This was Jackson, in Mississippi, and whatever the Federal government might say, it will never penetrate down here.

Sure enough, as soon as the ICC order had gone into effect, a young Jackson minister was arrested when he attempted to secure service at the still-white restaurant in one of the bus depots. There were no marshals to escort him into the restaurant, no visible reaction from the Federal government when he was, smoothly and efficiently, carried off to jail. And down at McComb there were several arrests. No one, apparently, tried anywhere else in Mississippi; we heard of no other arrests.

Two days or so after this, Colia again waited after class. The people at the meeting, she told me, had enjoyed the talk that I'd given very much and the members of the Youth Council who had been there had enjoyed talking with me. What she wanted to know was, would I be the adviser to their Youth Council. It seemed that under the NAACP constitution, they needed an adviser, and they couldn't for some reason find anyone who would take the position.

I thought for a few moments. Then I told her, yes, I'd be their adviser, would consider it a privilege. I asked her to tell me a little about the group.

It wasn't big, she answered, because many of the kids were afraid, and even if they weren't, their parents were. It was called the North Jackson Youth Council, she went on, and there were similar groups in the city—a West Jackson Youth Council which, she thought, wasn't really functioning, and one at Campbell College, a small black junior college, which was also about defunct. Tougaloo College had its own NAACP group, but both Colia and I knew that it wasn't doing much, and some of the Tougaloo students were actually more closely identified with Colia's group.

The North Jackson Youth Council, Colia finished, was the only one really even holding meetings.

I asked about the Jackson adult NAACP, since I had heard that one existed. She told me that the adult group was very small, and I gathered that she also felt that it was rather stodgy. Apparently it did not do a great deal either. "But," she said, "we've got an adviser now and I think we'll pick up members."

We talked about Mississippi. Were there some white people involved on behalf of civil rights? I asked.

"There really aren't any white people in the civil rights groups in Mississippi," she stated sadly.

I was amazed. "There must be a few," I told her.

Then she said that although she'd heard of a white kid or two from out of state who had worked briefly in the McComb area with SNCC a few weeks before, she guessed that they had left by now. Dr. A. D. Beittel, she remembered, was involved in some way with the U.S. Commission on Civil Rights, and sometimes, she said, white faculty from Tougaloo attended NAACP community mass meetings in the black Masonic Temple, where the state NAACP offices were located, but that was about as far as it went. She mentioned Bill Higgs, a white lawyer in Jackson who was sympathetic to the civil rights struggle and who had, as a consequence, lost most of his law practice.

"But that's about it," she finished.

Then Colia sold me two tickets for the Freedom Fund Dinner that the Mississippi NAACP was going to hold in connection with its annual convention in Jackson in a few days. I said that Eldri and I would attend.

That day, I told another faculty member about the advisership to the Youth Council. He wasn't at all certain that I should have anything to do with it. "We're *all* for that, of course," he said. "But you can find yourself in jail doing that kind of thing," he went on, "and that isn't a pleasant experience in Jackson." He shook his head.

I told him that I thought I'd be the adviser—that I'd probably learn more from the members than they would from me. Much later that day, when I saw Eldri, I told her about it. She agreed that it was a good thing to do. And much later that evening, long after we'd talked about it, she again brought up the subject. Outside it was dark, and except for the traffic going up and down Bailey Avenue, it was very quiet.

"I'm glad," she said, "that you're going to be the adviser to their group. I think we'll both be much happier doing even a little directly for civil rights than simply by teaching." Her point was well taken, and I realized that I felt that way also. We were, I think, beginning to chafe in a situation where the rigidity and oppressiveness of Mississippi bore down each day, seemingly without any opposition from any quarter.

Several nights later, we attended the NAACP Freedom Fund Dinner. With some difficulty, we found Lynch Street, in a black section, on which the Masonic Temple was located, and with additional difficulty, we found the building—a large, newer type of structure that housed not only the NAACP offices but a number of black business offices as well. Cars were parked all over as we walked several blocks to the building. A number of people glanced at us, wondering, I imagine, just who we were. As we walked into the building, a number of men standing by the door stared at us. We saw a police car parked across the street, and *they* seemed to be watching.

A man was taking tickets some feet back from the front door, greeting everyone cordially as they came in and shaking hands with most. He was in his mid-thirties, seemed to have considerable zest and enthusiasm as he chatted with people, an optimism that contrasted strangely with the lines cut deeply into his face. Greeting us by name, he said that his was Medgar Evers, the state NAACP field secretary, and he told us that Colia had told him all about us. I had heard of Medgar Evers, and had heard very well of him. We talked briefly before Eldri and I went in and promised to get in touch with one another soon. We were ushered to a table and sat down, but since we were the only non-blacks present, we attracted considerable curiosity, and it soon became clear that people were reluctant to sit down by us and, instead, went over to other tables. Finally, matters reached the point that all of the other seating space was filled. Several people then approached us and, very courteously, asked who we were. I told them, said that I taught at Tougaloo, and I mentioned Colia Liddell. The ice broke immediately. They sat down, and we visited before the meeting got under way.

Colia was supposed to function as mistress of ceremonies but was somewhat late in arriving. Until she did, that job was handled by a man who we learned was Aaron Henry, president of the Mississippi NAACP. He reported on the activities of his local group, up in Clarksdale, in Coahoma County; the people from McComb gave an interesting account of the situation there; and other groups made their reports. In some areas, voter registration efforts were being made, but virtually no one was being registered; in other sections, attempts were being made to secure worthwhile employment for black people but, essentially, to no avail. There had been much violence, most of which hadn't been reported in the news media, many threats and economic reprisals; and from the reports we gathered that the climate of fear was increasing throughout Mississippi.

Medgar Evers reported on the case of Clyde Kennard, the young man who had attempted to gain entrance to the University of Southern Mississippi and who had, instead, been railroaded off to the penitentiary. As he finished his report on efforts to win Kennard's freedom, Medgar Evers wept; he was a good friend of the imprisoned man. An NAACP leader from Savannah, Georgia, W. W. Law, gave a speech discussing their struggle in that area. James Bevel, originally from Cleveland, Mississippi, and connected with the Student Nonviolent Coordinating Committee, sang freedom songs, including one which he had developed out of an old miners' song, "Which Side Are You On?"

> *Don't 'tom for Mister Charlie, don't listen to his lies*
> *'Cause black folks haven't got a chance until they organize.*
>
> *They say in Hinds County, no neutrals have they met.*
> *You're either for the Freedom Fight or you 'tom for Ross Barnett.*

Afterwards we talked with a good many people—Aaron Henry, a man named Amzie Moore who had done pioneer civil rights work in the Delta for years, and some of the people from McComb. None was optimistic about things; all felt that it would get much worse in Mississippi before substantial improvement really came; and none showed any sign of giving up.

"Hope you're with us," Aaron Henry told Eldri and me as we left.

"You'll see us again," we told him. And we meant it. Never before had we quite realized the oppression of Mississippi—not until we heard those reports from the local NAACP groups scattered throughout the state. These were brave people.

The segregationists, from what we were reading in the newspapers and hearing on the radio, were becoming increasingly busy. As small civil rights victories were won in other southern states—schools desegregated in Atlanta, parks opened up in Memphis—Mississippi became even more rigid, almost hysterical. Day after day, the news media echoed with editorials and the statements of political leaders and Citizens Council spokesmen, all to the effect that whatever else might happen in the universe, integration would never come to Mississippi.

October 26, 1961, was United Nations Day in other sections of the United States, but with the exception of a small ceremony in the chapel of Tougaloo College, it was deliberately not observed anywhere in Mississippi. Indeed, that day was proclaimed Race and Reason Day by Governor Ross Barnett—in honor of a northern businessman, Carleton Putnam, who had written a racist book that had dredged up every long-ago discredited racial myth: *Race and Reason: A Yankee View*. Almost 200 of Jackson's most influential citizens joined Congressman John Bell Williams in sponsoring a dinner honoring Putnam. At the affair, which was held under the auspices of the Citizens Council, Putnam was greeted officially by Ross Barnett and introduced by Dr. W. D. McCain, president of Mississippi Southern. Almost 500 other people paid $25 apiece to attend the dinner, which was held in one of Jackson's largest hotels. Putnam spoke for an hour on the inferiority of blacks.

A few weeks later, Robert Welch of the John Birch Society came to Jackson for another huge affair. I attended that one, accompanied by Charlotte Phillips and a Tougaloo faculty member, Dr. J. B. Hunter. Dr. Hunter, a minister who had formerly been secretary of the Arkansas Council of Churches, wore a wide-brimmed hat and looked, for all the world, like some elderly planter just come out of the Delta. We went into the Heidelberg Hotel, which was filled with people, and sitting at tables selling John Birch literature were the hard-eyed ideologues who reminded me very much indeed of the people who were coming so close to staging a take-over in Arizona. Top Mississippi officials were on hand to greet Welch, including Congressman John Bell Williams. The head of the Mississippi American Legion sat on the platform.

Our little delegation of three was enveloped by the several thousand who had turned out to hear Welch, but we soon became conspicuous by not rising for any of the several formalities that were bringing people to their feet. We could hear whispers around us, and were the recipients of curious glances and stares; but apparently Dr. Hunter's "southern look" reassured those who had become worried. Midway in Welch's speech, we had heard enough and rose to leave. Dr. Hunter's eyesight was not the best, and at the back of the room, he mistook a locked door for the entrance, grabbed its handle and rattled it with great vigor. Robert Welch stopped speaking. Many of the several thousand turned to look while frantic ushers steered us to the proper door.

Day after day, week after week, newspapers, radio, television all continually poured out the message: integration is subversion; Mississippi's segregationists are the true Americans; the Supreme Court and the Kennedy brothers are somehow involved in a communist conspiracy

—we will never integrate anything, *never, never, never*. Pages were devoted to letters to the editor in such newspapers as the *Jackson Daily News* and the *Clarion-Ledger*, many expressing the rawest kind of hatred:

> To pronounce "knee-grow" in the . . . approved manner is a helluva lot of work, and must be practiced before a mirror to bring out the full depth and beauty of the word. One must first assume a reverent and respectful attitude and draw a deep breath. Then, with mouth slightly stretched, upper lip lifted somewhat and lower lip only slightly puckered, tongue tightly against palate—accomplish the "knee" syllable while expending the whole breath. During the hyphen period, one catches another lungful of air. Next, contract the mouth and place the lips in a full, exaggerated pucker, tongue out of the way in lower mouth. Let the exhalation of the "grow" syllable be real strong, but not too fast.
>
> Smile sweetly at yourself because of this wonderful improvement and practice daily for at least six months. At the end of this time, I will wager that you will still say nigra or nigger because of the time and labor saving.

Meanwhile, our Youth Council met, usually in someone's home in north Jackson. Only about a dozen or so attended initially, but we began to pick up a few members here and there. The climate of fear was strong, though, among the youth and especially their parents, and out of that an apparent apathy had developed. Even such hardworking stalwarts as Colia Liddell, her brother Lewis Liddell, Pearlena Lewis, and Cleveland Donald, Jr., found recruiting to be tough sledding. Sometimes we held "mass" meetings, but only a few adults, usually parents, attended. Once we conducted a survey for the NAACP throughout a large portion of the black section of Jackson, taking around questionnaires and asking people such "touchy" questions as their names and addresses, whether they were registered to vote, would they allow their children to attend an integrated school, would they be party to a Federal court action designed to integrate the schools. We split into teams of two and spent many evenings carrying out this project. Lewis Liddell, who attended high school and who knew the area well, went with me, house to house. Often people would not come to the door, or when they did, they were reluctant to give any information. Most were not registered to vote, nor were they interested in trying to hurdle the high barricades that Mississippi had erected for blacks who tried to register. Most were noncommittal on the matter of schools. They did not know me, and even the fact that Lewis Liddell was with me did little, really, to ease them—nor, so far as that goes, did the word "Tougaloo." The people were afraid, with good reason, and many looked as if they expected the Jackson police to roll up at any moment. Even if it became frustrating to Lewis and me, and to the others in the Youth Council who all encountered basically the same reaction, it was understandable to all of us.

We were getting to know Medgar Evers well, and one night Eldri and I spent the evening with him and his wife, Myrlie, at their home. The three Evers children were tucked away and we had a long talk. He was a hardworking man who spent much of his time on the road, traveling into all sorts of grim, isolated areas—a quiet trouble-shooter who put about 40,000 miles a year on a car. He told us of his background: boyhood in Decatur, Mississippi, in Newton County; off to war in a segregated unit and to Normandy; attended and graduated from Alcorn A&M, one of Mississippi's two four-year state black colleges, where he tried to organize the students; worked as an insurance man up on the Delta and tried to organize NAACP groups on the side; and, in 1954, attempted to enter the law school at the University of Mississippi. Turned down there, he then went to work for the NAACP as its state field secretary in Mississippi. By that time he was married and the Evers family included one child, Darrell, whose middle name was Kenyatta.

Medgar Evers said that when he took the NAACP job—the first NAACP staff position in the history of the state—friends told him that, most likely, he had only a month or two to live at most. But he had hung on, year after year, recipient of continual death threats, carrying with him early memories of lynching and terror, and, with those, he added, as he worked on in Mississippi, new memories of violence and hate. Yet he himself was not a hater, at least not a conscious one, and told us that although at one time he'd felt that violence was the only answer to the white man in Mississippi, he credited the teachings of his mother, a strong Christian, for his ultimate conversion to a sort of nonviolence. But Medgar Evers also showed us that night half a dozen firearms which he had in his house—a supplement to bullet-proof blinds at the windows and to the training he had given his wife and children to the effect that, if they ever heard a car's brakes screech outside at night, they should immediately fall to the floor. In his backyard, he had a German shepherd. In his car, he carried a .45 automatic.

It was a grim, uphill struggle in Mississippi, he said, and most of the NAACP local organizations in the state, with very few exceptions, were quite small and relatively inactive. Many of the problems he faced were those stemming from the effect of the Mississippi system on blacks themselves, such as many of his neighbors in Jackson who, because they were school teachers, feared any involvement in civil rights—were uneasy even when he was just chatting with them. Some of the black ministers were oriented in a civil rights direction, he continued, but he didn't know how far they would actually go; and most of the ministers, he felt, were afraid or dependent upon the financial contributions of white people to, say, the church building fund. It seemed clear to us that essentially, Medgar Evers had given up attempting to organize any sort of large-scale campaign and had, instead, concentrated on functioning primarily on a one-man basis—a situation arising not only from the fear-based apathy of the black community but also from the fact that he had an entire state to try to cover.

His wife, Myrlie, was a strong pillar who was without her husband most of the time. But quietly and in a determined fashion, she stood with him all the way. She too was from Mississippi; she too had her memories; and she too had her commitment.

Around the same time that we became close friends with Medgar and Myrlie Evers, we met another embattled couple, the Rev. Tom Johnson and his wife, Marcy, of Canton, Mississippi. They were white and had come to Canton, in Madison County, almost five years before under the auspices of the American Sunday School Union, working as sort of welfare missionaries with black sharecroppers and tenant farmers. Although for several years the Johnsons had concentrated mostly on sermons and the distribution of used clothing from the North, both became increasingly oriented, as time passed, toward a more direct application of humanistic Christianity. Some months before we met them, Tom Johnson agreed to become a member of the Mississippi Advisory Committee to the U.S. Commission on Civil Rights, a sort of unofficial extension of the Federal agency. Several black people were connected with this group, along with a handful of other white people: the Rev. Murray Cox, who was a retired clergyman on the Gulf Coast, Dr. A. D. Beittel of Tougaloo, Mrs. Wallis Schutt of Jackson, and a rather conservative retired Navy admiral from Liberty. The purpose of this advisory committee was to air violations of civil rights, and although not a civil rights organization in the sense of the NAACP, it was, of course, bitterly condemned by the Citizens Council, mass media, and politicians.

When Tom Johnson's involvement with the advisory committee became known in Canton, he and his wife were subjected to immediate and total ostracism by the white community. One night a sheriff, apparently just to frighten Tom, came to tell him that a mob was coming up from the Gulf Coast to "get" him. Their neighbors became extremely hostile, and the Johnsons' small children found themselves under attack by their former playmates. Tom Johnson, too, had a gun in his house.

Occasionally the Johnsons would visit at Tougaloo, and we met them at the home of Dr. Beittel. Then we began to go up to Canton, twenty or so miles away, to see them. Apparently no one else did. The town of Canton exuded a feeling of poverty and general toughness, and during our first visits to the Johnson home, neighbors peered at us through the window and took down our license-plate numbers. Once, in a grocery store, Tom pointed out a man who had, in three or four years' time, cold-bloodedly murdered three blacks. He was an elderly little man who looked at us with much distaste as we observed him. Later, in the winter,

Tom Johnson took me along his "route," visiting at the tiny cabins of sharecroppers, all poverty-stricken, all glad to see him.

Once I helped him fix up a small building out in the pine-dotted countryside, one of several scattered through the area in which he and Marcy worked. They held church services in the building each Sunday, and it took us all afternoon to board up the gaps in the wall and the broken windows as well to make it even partly weatherproof.

The Johnsons came to visit us one afternoon on the day that we really got to know a few of our neighbors on Bailey Avenue. We had been living there for several weeks, having little or nothing to do wtih any of the people around us. Although I am certain that they all knew where I worked, they said nothing to us, and we said nothing to them. Occasionally, people would come over to see us, some of whom were black; but interestingly enough, nothing was ever said about this, perhaps because the reputation of the fourplex was such that it was feared no one else could be found to rent our apartment if we left. One couple lived upstairs, and on the afternoon that the Johnsons came over, the couple were having a terrific fight which concluded by the husband beating the wife up very badly. She left, called the police, and then returned. Eldri and I and the Johnsons watched half a dozen officers arrive and go upstairs. Then we heard a "clunk" and the police, who had obviously knocked the husband out, carried him down the stairway and presumably off to jail. The wife then left. We visited with the Johnsons a little longer. They left for Canton, and we went up the street to the grocery store.

We were there almost an hour. When we came back, we could see fire trucks and police cars and a huge crowd of white people gathered in front of the fourplex. Smoke was pouring out of it. We found a parking place, got out quickly, for just a moment thinking that we had been the victims of arson. The old couple who managed the place came rushing up to us, explaining that a cigarette had been left burning up in the apartment where the fight had taken place, and there was now "a mighty big blaze up there, although not as big a one as burned up the lady." The whole neighborhood seemed in a festive mood. Our old couple were making coffee for everyone—firemen, police, spectators—and were being assisted in this by the people who lived in the other downstairs apartment next to us and who were from Magnolia, Mississippi. People were visiting with one another and the firemen and police officers were leading groups of spectators in and out of the unfortunate building. We went into our apartment, which was flooded with water. People were streaming through our apartment, observing the damage. It was an incredible scene.

It became more so when a fireman, in our apartment, found a live mouse, which had been forced out of its living place by the water, held it up triumphantly for all to see, and announced that he would kill it for us. I took it away from him, not because I believe in mice, or was even hesitant about killing them, but simply because I was in the mood for an act of defiance. When I had returned from releasing the mouse outside, the fireman asked me where I was from, where I worked.

I told him that I was from Arizona, that I taught at Tougaloo.

He took this well enough, I suppose, but went on to try, somehow, to find a common ground. Finally, he said, without any particular malice, the only thing apparently that he could come up with, "I guess you all probably don't have much of a nigger problem out there in Arizona." He said it blithely, much as one would discuss the weather.

I told him that I didn't agree with Mississippi on any of that, and as far as Arizona was concerned, it had its prejudice and discrimination, but it was trying to get over that—trying to treat everyone alike. As I told him that, Eldri grinned, quite as aware as I was that Arizona was not that enlightened.

But the fireman, of course, didn't know about that one way or the other. "Oh, well," he said, cheerfully, "you all see it one way; I see it another." He quickly changed the subject to the fire, which he felt was a "pretty good one."

Meanwhile, a police officer had entered with a large group of tourists and, with his flashlight, since all of the power was cut off, was using our apartment as an example of "typical water damage." On our table in the kitchen was an NAACP booklet, conspicuously labeled, and his flashlight passed over that, then went quickly back to the pamphlet, the cover of which he studied for a time. He knew we were somewhere in the house, but wasn't quite certain where, so he recovered himself quickly and continued his tour. A few minutes later, as he was leaving, he saw us, nodded curtly, and went out quickly.

Outside we saw many of the Bailey Avenue people gathered around, and it seemed all of us connected with the fourplex had become quite important. People came up, asking our opinion of the fire, making inquiry as to whether we would stay on in the building, and asking, didn't we know that it had a jinx on it? Tougaloo connection or not, the Bailey Avenue fire had developed a real feeling of togetherness. It was a wild evening.

We continued living there, and gradually the damage was repaired. But a few weeks after that, bitterly cold weather came to Mississippi, and all of the pipes in the fourplex froze up tight. Again, we had contact with our neighbors who gave us water. And a few days after that, Eldri and I went out to Tougaloo for the evening, leaving on the kitchen table all of my carefully finished grade cards on which I had worked for several days. We returned late at night to find the people who lived in the apartment next to us, the couple from Magnolia, sweeping water out of our apartment and moving our furniture around—since, it seemed, the frozen pipes had burst, and now had thawed, and water was coming down from upstairs like a Gulf Coast rainstorm. They had rescued my grades, however, and had moved most of our belongings to dry places.

I talked once with the old couple about the racial situation in Mississippi. They made what was for them, I'm certain, a genuine effort in the direction of open-mindedness, but it was clear that they could never agree with me. They did feel, though, that "Mississippi will, most likely, have to change sometime." The old man, whom we had driven once out to the nearby hamlet of Pochahantas, where he had shown us, among other things, the now abandoned grocery store that he had "kept" for forty years or so, now, as we talked again, rambled on about boyhood days spent with black children. "The young colored people today aren't like they once were," he told me. "These have had more schooling and they know more about things." Then, with something of the bitterness of the elderly whom the whole world has bypassed, he finished, "They probably know more about a lot of things than I do."

And, once too, we talked briefly on this general subject with the couple from Magnolia. They were uneasy about even discussing racial matters, but they were far from rigid, perhaps because they had spent some time living out of the state. It was clear enough that they didn't agree with us. But the man said, "There's a whole lot of race talk in Mississippi right now, more than there used to be. But I don't imagine that all of the talk is going to make any difference about changing what is coming." He remarked that, in the Air Force, he had served in an integrated outfit, and "It wasn't bad at all." He felt that it would be a long time, though, before integration came to Mississippi—probably longer, as he put it, "than it'll take the state house to really fix up these sorry roads that we have to try to drive our cars over." Then his wife changed the subject to the matter of Eldri's pregnancy, which was well along by this time.

Shortly before Christmas, Medgar Evers called up the head of the Jackson Chamber of Commerce, asking about the possibilities of better jobs for blacks in the downtown stores; but the man told Medgar that "it isn't time yet for cash-register jobs for nigras." As a consequence, the small Jackson adult branch of the NAACP had a rather sparsely attended community meeting at which it was announced that there would be a boycott of the downtown Jackson stores. Medgar had gotten several hundred boycott leaflets printed, which were distributed at the meeting and were also passed out in neighborhoods by our Youth Council. I asked about the possibilities of direct action downtown, such as picketing, but it was felt, apparently, that no bail-bond money was available. I then learned that there were no black bail bondsmen anywhere in Mississippi and that no white bondsman would post bail in civil rights cases. Although the court authorities would accept property as bond, such as real estate, if it were unencumbered by a lien or mortgage, most of the blacks in Jackson who had such property either wouldn't put it up for bond or had already done so in previous civil rights arrests.

We boosted the boycott as hard as we could, but few of the adult leaders in the NAACP really felt that it would work. As a consequence, no more leaflets were printed and the lack of those, plus the absence of direct-action demonstrations downtown, made the boycott more a protest gesture than a genuine campaign. But some blacks stayed away from the downtown area for Christmas shopping season, at least, although there were no resultant improvements in employment practices. After the Christmas season was over, we were told that the boycott had been, more or less, called off. But Eldri and I, who never went to any restaurants or movies since they were all segregated, now never again shopped downtown —nor did Medgar and Myrlie Evers.

But one civil rights group was having quite a boycott in Mississippi. Up in Clarksdale, Aaron Henry's Coahoma County NAACP initiated a firm campaign against the downtown stores in that small Delta city, and since the town was heavily dependent upon black trade, the boycott had an immediate effect on the economy. But the white power structure refused to come to terms with the black community, wouldn't even meet with black leaders, as far as that goes, and the boycott dragged on with Aaron Henry and others taking the position that it would go on forever unless there were constructive changes in hiring practices. Clarksdale reacted by arresting Aaron Henry and six other leaders of the campaign on the charge of "conspiring to withhold trade." The civil rights leaders were convicted in local courts but, of course, appealed, and the boycott went right on. Some weeks later, Clarksdale again moved against Aaron Henry by arresting him on a trumped-up "morals" charge, and, once again convicted, he appealed—and the boycott went on. By this time, his wife had lost her longtime teaching job in the black schools of Coahoma County.

At the same time that Aaron Henry and the others were being arrested for "conspiring to withhold trade," yet another group launched a boycott. The Mississippi State Legislature, which was distinguishing itself by publicly investigating conditions at the University Hospital in Jackson, where white and black children were leaving their segregated wards and playing together in the corridors, up and passed a resolution, with scarcely any dissent, calling on all loyal Mississippians no longer to trade in Memphis, Tennessee, just across the state line, and quite close, as far as that goes, to Clarksdale. The legislature was enraged by the fact that public accommodations and other facilities in Memphis were in the process of quietly desegregating.

And something new had been added to the struggling civil rights movement in Mississippi—a little weekly newspaper called the *Mississippi Free Press*. It was, largely, the brainchild of Medgar Evers and several of the younger people in the black community of Jackson and, in addition, received considerable help from the friendly white lawyer, Bill Higgs, and from Tom Johnson of Canton. It was a little four-page publication printed up in Holmes County by Mrs. Hazel Brannon Smith, then shipped to Jackson, where it was distributed. It was a blend of social news and civil rights, with the latter paramount, and because of this, the power structure condemned it vigorously. For a time, although eventually this ended, Jackson police harassed newsboys selling the *Free Press*, and one night investigators from the Sovereignty Commission crept to the Masonic Temple and took a picture of Mrs. Smith and Bill Higgs and Medgar, all talking together in the downstairs corridor of the building. Then the Citizens Council, apparently reproducing copies of the paper, mailed it to many of its members, informing them that this was what Hazel Brannon Smith was doing.

All of us—Medgar, Tom Johnson, Bill Higgs, myself—wrote articles for the *Free Press,* which was always in perennial need of material. But one of the best items ever to appear in the paper came in an early issue, a reprint of a letter which, on November 1, 1961, Bob Moses of SNCC— then in jail in McComb with other SNCC workers, including the chairman of the organization, Charles McDew—had written:

> I am writing this letter from the drunk tank of the county jail in Magnolia, Mississippi. Twelve of us are here, sprawled out along the concrete bunker. . . . I'm sitting with a smuggled pen and paper, thinking a little, writing a little. . . . Later on Hollis will lead out with a clear tenor into a freedom song, Talbert and Lewis will supply jokes and McDew will discourse of the black man and the Jew. McDew, a black by birth, a Jew by choice, and a revolutionary by necessity, has taken the deep hates and deep loves of America and the world, reserved for those who dare to stand in a strong sun and cast a sharp shadow. In the words of Judge Brumfield, who sentenced us, we are "cold calculators" who designed to disrupt the racial harmony . . . of McComb into racial strife and rioting; we, he said, are the leaders who are causing young children to be led like sheep to the pen to be slaughtered (in a legal manner) . . . It's mealtime now, we have rice and gravy in a flat pan, dry bread and a "big town cake"; we lack eating and drinking utensils. Water comes from a faucet and goes into a hole. This is Mississippi, the middle of the iceberg. Hollis is leading off with his tenor, "Michael, Row the Boat Ashore, Alleluia." This is a tremor in the middle of the iceberg—from a stone that the builders rejected.

Shortly after my articles, all of which I signed, began to appear in the *Mississippi Free Press,* a long white car with a big aerial began to park across the street from our home on Bailey Avenue, usually with two men, in plainclothes, just sitting in the front seat. There was little doubt but that this was the Sovereignty Commission. We ignored them, even when it became a regular practice, beginning about an hour or so after Eldri and I would return from Tougaloo and lasting, off and on, until rather late at night. When Eldri's pregnancy reached the point where she was unable to continue working in the Tougaloo business office, she stayed home. One night, when I had stayed over at Tougaloo for an evening faculty meeting, Eldri walked several blocks up to a little corner grocery store. The white car followed her, block by block, up the street and, block by block, back to our house—pulling alongside of her and then waiting until she got half a block ahead, then pulling up again.

For some reason, none of this appeared to bother either the old couple who managed the apartment building or the people from Magnolia. I'm certain that, just as they knew we had black people as guests, they knew that that was the "laws" waiting outside our home in the big white car. We never talked about this with our neighbors, but there may have been several reasons for their not turning on us. For one thing, it was certainly not going to be easy to rent an apartment in a building such as we were in, especially after the second fire; and for another, we knew them and they knew us. We'd had the fire together; we'd had the freezing pipes together, and the "flood" from the burst pipes as well; and all of this had brought us very definitely together in the face of a hostile nature. Then, too, I would not be surprised but that both the old couple and the people from Magnolia were just "anarchist" enough not to like law officers and to feel a certain measure of sympathy for those who incurred the disfavor of police agencies.

Our Youth Council was moving along, meeting regularly and continuing to pick up a few new members, trying to hold community mass meetings on such matters as voter registration and boosting the *Free Press*. And although the Christmas boycott was now long over, we were encouraging people to make application, at least, for decent jobs, especially in those white-owned stores located in black neighborhoods.

But the aura of fear was unchanged, with respect to adults especially but also as far as many of the young people were concerned. Once, a group of us went to the Masonic Temple for a small meeting, but the building was still locked and, as we waited there on a cold and empty street, a police car came slowly by, then turned around and came by again. Some of the youth became afraid and began to walk away, but Colia Liddell and I kept the group together and the police never returned. By this time, the North Jackson Youth Council was about the only NAACP youth organization functioning on a continuous basis in and around the city. The West Jackson Youth Council, and the groups at Campbell and Tougaloo colleges, had become virtually inactive.

The NAACP, it seemed, was interested essentially in a more legal-action approach toward the cracking of segregation barriers than in any sort of direct action. Several lawsuits had been filed and were moving ahead slowly. One, which had been in progress for several months, was aimed at desegregating the privately-owned bus line within the city; another, recently initiated, was an effort to open up the Jackson parks and recreational areas. Still another, filed back in May, 1961, was beginning to pick up momentum; it sought the entry of a young black from Attala

County, James Meredith of Kosciusko, into the University of Mississippi. In addition, Medgar was working with several black families in remote Leake County, who were preparing a petition to the county school board asking for the entry of their children into the white schools. But all of this legal maneuvering was taking a long time indeed: the Federal judges in Mississippi were all firm segregationists and it was necessary to appeal everything to the Fifth Circuit Court of Appeals in New Orleans—a long, time-consuming process.

A few of the people who had been involved in the SNCC campaign in McComb were now in Jackson, and these, plus Joan Trumpauer, who had been a Freedom Rider and who was now at Tougaloo, and a CORE field secretary, Tom Gaither, who occasionally came through, were endeavoring to start a group called the Jackson Nonviolent Movement. But it, too, was moving very slowly, generally in voter registration directions, and was really making no substantial progress.

But there were still tangible signs of changing times. For the first time since Reconstruction, there were blacks in Mississippi who were running for Congress in the June primary election. One of these was an elderly minister and grocery store owner in Jackson, the Rev. Robert L. T. Smith, who was opposing the racist incumbent, John Bell Williams. The Rev. Mr. Smith, after making his announcement for Congress, went to the Mississippi Capitol building and sat in the gallery of the legislature as a spectator, thus leading the legislature to pass the requirement that, in future cases, all observers would only be admitted by permit. It then made it clear that blacks would not be given such permits. Up in the Delta, Aaron Henry and James Bevel and Amzie Moore joined forces to support another black for Congress, the Rev. Theodore Trammell who died soon thereafter of a heart attack. But the campaigners then persuaded the Rev. W. W. Lindsey to give it a try. All of us in the Jackson area were busy indeed distributing campaign literature for R. L. T. Smith; and the Youth Council members, even those who wouldn't be of legal age to vote for eight years or so, were busy on his behalf, traveling house to house, block to block. No one expected the candidates to come even remotely close to victory, but it was hoped that more blacks would at least attempt to pay poll tax, register, and vote, despite the extraordinary difficulties encountered in even attempting to do those things.

Despite the fact that defeat was a certainty, the candidates made an intensive campaign effort. After a bitter behind-the-scenes struggle, with the Federal Communications Commission involving itself on their behalf, the candidates were able to secure television time—the breaking of a historical precedent in itself. Although the civil rights message was always, of course, implied at least, the black candidates devoted themselves mainly to discussions of the economic problems common to most Mississippians, black and white. The Rev. Mr. Smith talked of matters which Congressman Williams had never, in *his* career, dreamt of mentioning: legislation improving the school systems, a broader plan of medical coverage, special training facilities to develop industrial skills among the great mass of young Mississippians who lacked these completely; and he said:

> Let us here and now resolve in our hearts and minds that we will shut our ears to the shouting of outworn slogans and the screaming of epithets of bigotry that actually serve as smoke screens to hide selfishness, inefficiency and dereliction of duty from the people of the state of Mississippi.

But with the exception of their hard-won television time, the black candidates' statements were scarcely even touched in the news media. Far, far more coverage was devoted, of course, to such matters as the visit made to Jackson by Edwin A. Walker of Texas, who had recently been ousted from active duty in the U.S. Army, where he had served as major general. When Walker spoke in Jackson, he was flanked by Governor Ross Barnett, Lieutenant Governor Paul B. Johnson, Congressman John Bell Williams, and Jackson mayor Allen C. Thompson, and he told them, and several thousand others:

> To Mississippi goes much of the credit for the preservation of the Union. In standing for its own sovereignty, Mississippi has defended the sovereignty of all. The eyes upon you are appreciative of your stand and proud to claim kinship with the blood that runs in your veins. . . . We are at war. You are infiltrated and your cause starts in every home, church, school, street corner, and public gathering. Man your weapons and attack!

Up in Canton, Tom Johnson was having some real problems as winter drew to a close. In his capacity as Mississippi advisory committee member to the U.S. Commission on Civil Rights, he had issued a statement charging that, in Madison County and elsewhere in Mississippi, flagrant cheating of black sharecroppers and tenant farmers was being practiced by the white landowners. This statement had been too much for the white people of Canton. The Johnson home was receiving a barrage of "hate" telephone calls; and when Eldri and I, on occasion, drove to Canton to see Tom and Marcy, police would often drive by as we talked inside. Sometimes Tom and I would be followed if, say, we went down to a grocery store or over to see someone in the black community. The harassment of their children had increased tremendously. Hoping to be able to move into Jackson, the Johnsons had put their house up for sale, but had found no takers.

On top of all of this, Tom Johnson's car broke down completely. His church headquarters told him that if he would go up to Detroit, he would be given another car. But Marcy, for good reason, did not want to stay with her children, alone in Canton, while Tom was gone for several days, and arrangements were made for her to stay temporarily at Tougaloo. She had a good many belongings that she wished to take with her, so one Saturday a few hours after Tom had left, Eldri and I drove to Canton to help Marcy Johnson make her temporary shift. A woman who had worked with Eldri in the Tougaloo business office, Mrs. Barbara Bettis, said that she and her aunt would join us in Canton to help.

As we approached the Johnson home, we saw well over a hundred cars parked in front of a church just down the street, and Marcy told us that a prominent white landowner had died and his funeral was being held. We began to pack up those possessions that she wanted to take. About this time, a young white couple, with a mother-in-law and a small child, arrived from Jackson to inspect the Johnson home with an eye toward buying it. While they were in the house, Mrs. Bettis and her aunt, who were black, arrived. We were moving various things from the house to the cars when the mother-in-law, carrying the small child, came out to watch us. Almost immediately, she realized that the relationship between Mrs. Bettis and her aunt and Eldri and me was not, by any means, the traditional Mississippi relationship between black and non-blacks. The mother-in-law, giving us a long, hate-filled stare, clutched the child to her bosom and went over on the other side of the lawn. Then the young couple came out, not really noticing us at all; but as they got into their car, the mother-in-law was talking very fast and, as they drove off, all of them turned to give us an angry look. It seemed clear that the Johnsons would never hear from them again.

At this moment, the funeral adjourned and at least a hundred cars followed the hearse to the cemetery, passing right in front of the Johnson house. By rough count, the people in at least half of the cars in that line turned to look hard at us as they passed, and although the day was chilly and their windows were rolled up, we could see their mouths working as they apparently cursed us. One old man shook his fist violently.

Although the Sovereignty Commission had appeared to have given up watching our home, Eldri and I were preparing to move from Bailey Avenue. Another faculty family had moved into Jackson and a house was available on campus. The jinx had struck the fourplex again: a hot-water heater in one of the recently repaired upstairs apartments had exploded. Although no one was injured, it was much too much, not only for us but for the people from Magnolia, who moved out the same day that we did. We parted on very friendly terms and, shortly after we moved onto the campus, a nice note came from the elderly couple telling us that "it was good to have you around."

Spring was coming to Mississippi, and March had almost arrived when Eldri and I came to the realization that the child was also arriving. The southeastern states NAACP units were holding a convention in Jackson, and I was endeavoring to attend as many sessions as possible. Eldri, because of her condition, usually remained at home now; but we temporarily suspended this practice for one night when she accompanied me to the Freedom Fund Dinner that climaxed the NAACP affair. While we were listening to an after-dinner speech by Mrs. Ruby Hurley, southeast states field director from Atlanta, Eldri went into labor. Off we went to St. Dominic's Hospital, where a girl, whom we named Maria, soon arrived. The Youth Council gave her a membership card before she was two days old.

By this time, primarily because of my involvement with the Youth Council, I had become a member of the Mississippi state NAACP board of directors, two dozen or so individuals from around the state who met about every four months. We gathered in the early spring, in Jackson, and spent most of a day discussing the Mississippi situation. Several staff people from higher echelons were present. The Mississippi board members gave reports of things that were occurring back in their towns and counties. It was quite clear that not much was happening. The black candidates for Congress were being boosted in those districts in which they were running, but voter registration was proceeding very slowly, if really at all. Tension, violence, and fear, however, were on the increase, and it became obvious that the civil rights push was bogged down in this from one end of the state to the other. Most saw no real possibility for an intensive grassroots type of campaign—although the people in Clarksdale were moving close to this with their boycott. But legal attacks on segregation, slow-moving as they were, seemed to hold most of the hopes.

Much of the discussion centered around the Meredith effort to enter the University of Mississippi the next fall, and after the board meeting was over and we were eating in a little black café across the street, Cleveland Donald, Jr., one of the staunchest supporters of the Youth Council, looked very glum. I asked him why.

"I wanted to be the first Negro in Old Miss," he told me, "but I'm only in high school now."

One of the NAACP lawsuits won through in the spring—the suit, filed many months before, and designed to desegregate the privately-owned city bus line in Jackson. At about the time the legal victory was won, the small Jackson Nonviolent Movement pressed the bus line also, asking for desegregation and fair employment practices. When the bus line refused to negotiate, the Jackson Nonviolent Movement called for a boycott of the Jackson bus line. Our Youth Council immediately supported the effort, but the adult NAACP felt that, now that the lawsuit had been won, a boycott would make it impossible to test the effect of the legal victory. There was a brief period of intense confusion and the boycott was called off. The bus line, up to a point, adhered to the court ruling, but many of the white drivers functioned as enforcers of segregation; and in the end, fear and past traditions prevailed and most black people continued to sit in the back of the buses, although many students, such as the Youth Council members, always sat up front.

The Youth Council plugged grimly along into the spring, moving from one little project to another but mostly supporting the R. L. T. Smith campaign. However, one day a white grocer in a Negro section of Jackson short-changed a child whose mother had sent him to the store. When the mother came to the store, the white man did what was frequently done to black consumers in white business places and cursed the lady. She continued to ask for the remainder of the money, whereby he picked up a chair and, although she was pregnant, knocked her down with it. She called the police, who refused to take any action against the grocer. Immediately, we called a boycott against him, and several black students picketed his store for a few minutes until the police came by. Then by prior arrangement, the students left rather than get arrested, since there was no bail bond available.

We drew up mimeographed boycott leaflets, distributed them throughout the area, publicized the incident in the *Free Press,* and called a rather successful mass meeting at a Baptist church on Florence Street, where the woman herself gave an excellent account of what had occurred. I spoke at length on the matter of boycotts, what boycotts can do—how they directly affect businessmen, and indirectly affect politicians by forcing the businessmen to apply constructive pressures on the political structure. I suggested that the time was coming for a full-dress boycott of all of downtown Jackson.

After the meeting was over, a number of us talked for a long time at the church while the police drove up and down Florence Street. I asked again about the possibilities of a really intensive boycott of the whole downtown area. The idea was well received by everyone, but some people doubted that it would work, questioned whether the black community would support such an endeavor for the long period of time necessary to win. I mentioned Clarksdale, where Aaron Henry's boycott had held up well for several months.

"That's a small town," said one of the adult NAACP leaders. "Jackson's too big."

But I continued to press. "I think we could do it," I said, "especially if we could get some bail bond and picket down there every so often."

Some other adults said that they very definitely felt that a boycott could work, even in Jackson, if it was really seriously pushed. "Just look," said one, "at the downtown area any afternoon. Negroes are all over down there."

No one held out much hope of getting any bail bond for picketing or for anything else along those lines. Again, some reiterated that they felt that Jackson was just too big, too difficult to organize.

As we talked the idea over, though, after the meeting in the church that night, the Youth Council members and I felt somehow increasingly enthusiastic about the idea of a boycott in downtown Jackson. We felt that it could be successful, quite possibly if it were started well in advance of the next Christmas shopping season and then went on into the spring and beyond. But all of that was a far-off and long-range thing, and we devoted our present energies to the campaign against the white grocer who had beaten up the woman. Two weeks or so after it all began, he closed his doors and went out of business.

A delegation of men came to see me from Laurel, Mississippi. It developed that they worked in a masonite plant—wood processing—where the most rigid discrimination was practiced: separate entrances to the plant, separate water and rest-room facilities, the most menial type of jobs, even separate pay lines. Not only was the company, which was based up North, supporting this, but the union, dominated by segregationists, was every bit as involved. In fact, the black workers could not meet with the white workers even though they had themselves helped to organize the union a number of years before. The divided nature of the work force had had such an adverse effect on the union's strength that a floor sweeper in an Oregon sawmill made more money than the highest-paid white worker at Laurel.

One of the men in this delegation had a college degree from a black state college, had begun work at this plant almost fifteen years before, stacking boards, and had been a pioneer in the development of the union. Now, fifteen years later, he was still stacking boards, kept from any decent job by the practice of separate seniority lists. We took affidavits and filed complaints against both the company and the union with the Federal government, which was a main purchaser of the company's products. But we knew it would be a long time indeed before the complaints were even investigated.

Still nothing much was happening in Mississippi from the standpoint of civil rights. As breakthroughs against segregation and discrimination occurred in other sections of the South, closer and closer in such neighboring states as Arkansas, Louisiana, and Tennessee, Mississippi segregationists tightened their control. The mass media became even more shrill, the political leaders more adamant in their stated positions that no integration would ever come to Mississippi.

At Meridian, in Lauderdale County in the eastern part of the state, a black serviceman stationed at a nearby airbase atempted to secure service in a white restaurant. He was badly beaten and evicted, then chased by an armed group of thugs and was finally arrested and jailed by a constable. Down in the southern part of the state, in Taylorsville in Smith County, a black corporal, Roman Duckworth, Jr., on leave from his army base in Maryland to see his wife, who was in a hospital experiencing difficulty with the birth of their sixth child, was taken from a bus, in broad daylight, and murdered in cold blood by a town constable when Duckworth refused to move from the front of the bus to the rear. The constable claimed self-defense, and was not indicted by a local grand jury. The army sent an integrated color guard to the corporal's funeral, which was held in Taylorsville. In Canton, Tom Johnson investigated the case of a young parishioner who had been arrested by the Madison County sheriff's department, charged with the attempted rape of a white girl, denied the right to see an attorney and quickly sentenced to death. Tom came to the conclusion that this was simply one more in the long history of Mississippi's periodic rape frame-ups. He and I then contacted the American Civil Liberties Union, which began the long, uncertain effort to free the man.

Step by step, the tension was mounting in Mississippi.

In May, 1962, an attempt was made to form a Mississippi Human Relations Council—not connected, of course, in any way with the Mississippi government—and made up of concerned white and black citizens. Something comparable existed in every other southern state, even Alabama, and had once existed in Mississipppi but had been destroyed by Citizens Council pressures. About sixty people, almost all of them black, but including a handful of the white moderates in the state, met at Tougaloo. Police were thick at the college gate and the Sovereignty Commission investigators were everywhere—at the gate and on the campus, taking photographs of people and copying down license numbers. The human-relations group wanted no direct connection with civil rights organizations, and indeed, most did not even want a statement of purpose which attacked the Citizens Council and the Sovereignty Commission. But it pledged itself to work for freeedom of speech and assembly, equal enforcement of the law, voter registration reforms, fair employment, voluntary end to segregation laws, integration of schools, and the appointment of blacks to local and state boards of education. These were, of course, "radical" goals—for Mississippi. Dr. A. D. Beittel, who was elected president of the group, had a very forthright position, as did those black people elected to posts in the new organization. But several white clergymen, also elected to positions, were soon pressured into resigning by the Citizens Council, mass-media publicity, and pressures from their church members. Dr. Beittel and several others stood with the group, but it was clear that, at best, it was a very small beginning.

Then the school year was over and the intensely hot weather arrived. Tougaloo students began making preparations to go either North for summer jobs or home to whatever work they could find. The Youth Council met at our house for a party. Some of them, too, were going North for the summer, and others had temporary work in Jackson. Colia Liddell was leaving the area to work with SNCC.

Everything still was quiet in Jackson from the standpoint of civil rights and, as far as that goes, in Mississippi.

At the close of the school year, Eldri and I and Maria went North for several weeks, where I did some work for an AFL-CIO union, and then out to Arizona for a visit. But something had taken hold of us, inside, and when we picked up a newspaper, we looked first for the civil rights news. For although not much was happening in our adopted state, many things were indeed happening elsewhere. Late in the summer, just as we were preparing to return to Jackson, we saw on television shots of the mass arrests currently taking place in Albany, Georgia, scene of a large-scale desegregation drive. And I thought again of a city-wide boycott campaign in Jackson, and perhaps something even bigger.

As we had the year before, we traveled across New Mexico, Texas, and Louisiana and crossed into Mississippi at the river town of Vicksburg. The day was terrifically hot, but it was good to be back in Mississippi. Tom Johnson and Marcy, who had, in the middle of the summer, finally moved into Jackson, saw us the first night. They said that not much had happened at all during the summer, although it did look, maybe, as if James Meredith might get into the University of Mississippi.

Then we had a meeting with the Youth Council members, most of whom had just returned from out-of-state or had left their summer jobs in Jackson for school. They didn't feel, either, that much had happened. The Jackson Nonviolent Movement had even dissolved, we learned, and most of its people had either left Mississippi or, in several cases, were trying without much visible success to get something moving in the rural areas— especially up in Greenwood, in Leflore County, in the heart of the Delta. The Youth Council members said that they'd believe Meredith's admission to the university when it happened, and they were not at all certain that it would. Since Colia had left, Pearlena Lewis became the president of the Youth Council, and Cleveland Donald, Jr., became a vice-president. This was the beginning of a new school year, and we decided that we would make it a very active year indeed in Jackson.

A day or so later, I saw Medgar, who greeted me warmly. He confirmed, too, the fact that nothing much was happening, said that Jackson was more dead than ever. We talked things over at length, and he agreed that something ought to happen in the city. But Medgar was not at all optimistic. "Lots of fear, lots of apathy," he said. "Things may move out in the country before they move in Jackson."

We walked out of his office, down onto the sidewalk on Lynch Street. It was early in the evening and twilight was fast upon us. We talked a little more, Medgar looking at each car that passed, and he was very much on edge. Then he gave an apologetic grin. "This Meredith thing," he said. "I don't know what's going to happen, but I think we may just get him in there; and if we do, there are some people who are going to be riled up." He looked again at the cars passing up and down on Lynch Street. "We'll see," he finished.

3

EACH DAY IT BECAME MORE certain that the lawsuit filed well over a year before by James Meredith and the NAACP was, despite all of the painstaking but still almost candidly desperate legal maneuvering by the Mississippi attorney general's office and its large battery of associated lawyers, reaching the point where the Meredith admission to the university for the fall term of 1962 was practically assured.

When the Fifth Circuit Court of Appeals in New Orleans ruled that Meredith should be admitted, Mississippi went to the U.S. Supreme Court and asked that the Fifth Circuit order be stayed until the highest court could hear Mississippi's appeal. Hugo Black, as spokesman for the Supreme Court and assuming that the Mississippi appeal would contain nothing that would warrant a further delay in the matter, refused to intervene.

Like a fire burning in the scrub pine of the Deep South, the flames of defiance began to mount throughout Mississippi—higher, and higher still —from the Citizens Councils, from the white business associations, from political leaders big and small, from the mass media.

At first the question was, what will Mississippi *really* do?

Talk on the Tougaloo campus was almost completely monopolized by this question. There were some who felt that after a certain amount of wild-eyed oratory, Ross Barnett and Attorney General Joe Patterson and their Citizens Council advisers would take a carefully laid-out plan of retreat. But there were others, who had lived in Mississippi for a long time, who had watched all of the racist traditions crystallizing in the prior decade with the construction of the Citizens Council juggernaut, and who were aware of the individual and organizational reputations that had been developed and maintained with respect to the preservation of "states' rights" and "racial integrity." These were certain that a grim crisis, possibly one which would culminate in massive violence, was in the making.

Governor Barnett and his advisers were losing no time in making their position clear. On September 13, 1962, on state-wide television, the governor announced defiance, then invoked the long-treasured formula of "interposition." Terming the occasion "a solemn hour, indeed, in our nation's history . . . the moment of our greatest crisis since the War Between the States," he condemned what he held to be "an ambitious Federal government, employing naked and arbitrary power . . . professional agitators . . . un-American pressure groups." Reaching deeply into all of the conscious and unconscious paranoia that had been developing in Mississippi for generations, he said, "There is no case in history where the Caucasian race has survived social integration. We will not drink from the cup of genocide!"

On and on he went, the old man who so well symbolized racist Mississippi:

> The day of expediency is past. We must either submit to the unlawful dictates of the Federal Government or stand up like men and tell them *"never!"* The day of reckoning has been delayed as long as possible. It is now upon us. This is the day—and this is the hour. Knowing you as I do, there is no doubt in my mind what the overwhelming majority of loyal Mississippians will do. They will never submit to the moral degradation, to the shame and the ruin which have faced all others who lacked the courage to defend their beliefs.
>
> . . . No school will be integrated in Mississippi while I am your Governor! . . . As your Governor and Chief Executive of the Sovereign State of Mississippi, I now call upon every public official and every private citizen of our great State to join with me in refusing, in every legal and constitutional manner available, to submit to illegal usurpation of power by the Kennedy Administration. I especially call upon all public officials, both elected and appointed . . . to join hands with the people and resist by every legal and constitutional means the tyrannical edicts which have been and will be directed against the patriotic citizens of our state.
>
> . . . I, Ross R. Barnett, as Governor of the Sovereign State of Mississippi . . . do hereby proclaim that the operation of the public schools, universities, and colleges of the State of Mississippi is vested in the duly elected and appointed officials of the State; and I hereby direct each said official to uphold and enforce the laws duly and legally enacted by the Legislature of the State of Mississippi, regardless of this unwarranted, illegal and arbitrary usurpation of power; *and to interpose the State Sovereignty and themselves between the people of the State and any body-politic seeking to usurp such power.*
>
> . . . Let us invoke the blessings of Divine Providence. . . .

The question of school desegregation in Mississippi was no longer hypothetical. And interposition equaled rebellion.

The question now was, how many are going to be killed before this is over, and who will they be?

Now statements were being made from all parts of Mississippi, echoing the position of the governor, and the flames burned more brightly now, and faster. In Jackson, the legislature seriously took up the question of secession from the Union, rejected it as being impractical, but took a

firm stand behind Barnett's interposition manifesto. Legal maneuvering
went on and on, but it was obvious that that stage had been passed;
Mississippi authorities sought to bring various trumped-up charges against
Meredith and were blocked from doing so by the U.S. Department of
Justice. Ross Barnett appointed himself registrar of the University of Mississippi.

On September 20, James Meredith, accompanied by several top
Justice Department officials, traveled to Oxford, Mississippi, where Meredith attempted to enroll at the university. With a large crowd present,
Governor Barnett refused James Meredith entrance.

The next attempt of Meredith to enroll was to be in Jackson, at the
State Capitol Annex on September 25. About an hour before the event
was to occur, Eldri and I drove down the street leading past the buildings.
There must have been at least a hundred law officers of one kind or
another gathering in the vicinity. Newsmen were already prevalent. And,
right across the street, at least 300 people, some dressed in working
clothes, some obviously students, and some looking like bankers, were all
gathered. They were silent enough when we saw them, just waiting; but
later, when Meredith and the Federal men arrived for the second enrollment attempt, the crowd across the street screamed gutter epithets at them.
Again Governor Barnett refused to enroll James Meredith.

On September 26, in front of a large crowd, Lieutenant Governor
Paul B. Johnson blocked James Meredith once again at the University of
Mississippi.

An aura of unreality filtered through the air as September moved into
its closing days. Always the rest of the world had seemed a dimension
away; now, Mississippi even seemed a dimension removed from what it
had been. Through all the wild talk and screaming oratory, and as one
event moved into another and another, there was also an element of calm
—tense and brittle calm and utterly deadly, a feeling that, at any moment,
there could be a fearful eruption. And by this time, reports were filtering
in from all over Mississippi—and there must have been many more of
which no one heard—of white hoodlum activities directed, apparently in
blind frustration, against blacks.

Everyone in Mississippi, black and white, was being caught up, somehow, in the deepening crisis. At Tougaloo, no one could talk of anything
else, and dozens of students carried around portable radios, listening to
the latest reports. The Youth Council members were more excited, now,
than I had ever seen them. So were their parents—as were black people all
over Jackson and, from what we heard, all over Mississippi. The fear was
still there, perhaps strengthened by the increased activity of white hoodlums; but there was an element of hope in the minds of black people.
Something was happening that had never occurred in their lifetimes; all
of the sovereign, defiant power of Mississippi was itself being defied—by
a black man from Attala County.

Hysteria increased steadily in the white community of Mississippi. Most of the white-driven automobiles in and around Jackson carried stickers: "Stand With Ross Barnett—The South Will Rise Again," "Get the Castro Brothers Out of the White House!" "The Kennedys Are Rat-Finks." Confederate flags seemed to be flying everywhere. Each day the mass media poured out their stream of pure hatred and defiance. Dixie was played constantly on radio and television. The minds of many white Mississippians indeed, with old myths and legends stirring, were coming to believe that this was the resurrection of the War Between the States—and a war they would win.

One night Eldri and I went to the Evers home on Guynes Street, aware that Medgar might be, as he had been for several days, observing various episodes in the Fifth Circuit Court in New Orleans, where legal manueverings were still going on, day after day. We knocked on the door of their home, could hear rustling around inside the house. When the door opened, after the passage of several minutes, we were greeted by Medgar with a gun. He had slipped into Jackson for the weekend, he told us, to see his family, and as he put it, "We were halfway expecting the wrong kind of people." Inside, all windows were blocked by stacked furniture. Several other firearms were laid out around the house. Many threats had been pouring into their home by telephone and mail, and Medgar was taking no chances. But he was not an unhappy man.

"We're going to get him in there," he told us. "They can rant and rave all they like, but we're going to get him in there."

The atmosphere in Mississippi worsened steadily. Reports of incidents of anti-black violence were pouring in continually.

Too, it was quite clear indeed not only that the hoodlum potential of the entire state was being sparked into activity, but that thugs were pouring into Mississippi from at least half a dozen southern states.

And with the exception of a tiny handful, themselves under attack, there were no voices at all, from within the white community of Mississippi, speaking out against any of this—whether against Ross Barnett's interposition or the armed hoodlums.

On Saturday night, September 29, Ross Barnett spoke more defiance at a football game attended by thousands who waved Confederate flags, sang Dixie, and cheered their governor wildly. That night, armed students stood guard around the Tougaloo campus.

On the afternoon of Sunday, September 30, Eldri and I heard on the radio that everyone was being encouraged to come into the downtown area of Jackson. We drove there to see what was happening. On the main roads leading into Jackson were hundreds of cars, with their stickers and their Confederate flags, pouring into the city. In downtown Jackson, traffic was extraordinarily congested and several thousand cars were milling around and around the downtown area. The whole block surrounding the Governor's Mansion, in the upper part of the downtown area, was ringed by white men, sometimes half a dozen abreast. Some wore business suits, others overalls, and several openly carried rifles and shotguns and revolvers because, as we learned later, a rumor had come that the U.S. marshals were on their way into Jackson by helicopter to arrest Ross Barnett. On the streets, white teenagers were plastering the "defiance" stickers indiscriminately on passing cars while dozens of police stood and laughed. One boy, seeing that our car was unstickered, yelled at us, "Hold up a minute!" But we drove past, hearing him curse us. Across the street from the mansion, a crowd of around 1,000 was gathered, blocking traffic on the sidewalks and streets while Citizens Council leaders leaned out of their windows in the Plaza Building and harangued with loudspeakers.

The whole thing was a terrible spectacle. Although it was not known publicly at the time, inside the mansion, Ross Barnett, Paul Johnson, and others were wavering between the Federal pressures on the one hand and the skillful manipulation by the Citizens Council leaders on the other, trying, apparently, to work out a "deal" whereby everyone could save face. But even if the top state officials of Mississippi had decided, at the eleventh hour, to retreat—and, in the end, caught up in their wave of perverted glory, they did not apparently so decide—it is questionable that the resources of the state government could have exercised much positive influence over the situation. The fire was out of control.

That night Eldri and I went over to another faculty home and watched President John F. Kennedy address the nation, indicating that James Meredith had arrived on the campus of the university and pleading with white Mississippians to obey the law. And Governor Barnett was on television also, with a statement that was a strange mixture of surrender and defiance—an indication of the confusion, perhaps, that gripped the old man and much of white Mississippi. But even as these men spoke, the fire was burning on and, at the university campus, the Mississippi Highway Patrol observed thousands of students and others who, whether specifically encouraged to riot or not, were beginning to do so. The patrol pulled out, and U.S. marshals, the sole remaining law-enforcement officers, were forced finally to resort to tear gas to defend themselves. When we went to bed that night, the last word we heard on the radio was that a full-blown riot had broken loose at the university and that many thousands of Federal troops were pouring across the border from a gathering point in Tennessee. And it came, none of this, as any surprise to anyone.

The next morning, very early, we turned on the radio. Several of Mississippi's leading segregationists were giving eye-witness reports of the Oxford riot, which was by that time being brought under control by U.S. military forces after two men had been killed and many hundreds injured. There seemed to be genuine shock in the voices and words of these segregationists, as if they themselves were undergoing terrific inner confusion. In a more positive sense, several of Mississippi's leading white businessmen, most of them in Jackson, publicly expressed sharp disapproval of the defiance stand, and were calling for the preservation of law and order—and for a few hours, it seemed as if finally the "moderate" upheaval was beginning in Mississippi.

But that noon I went into the outskirts of Jackson, to a little cash-and-carry grocery store. The middle-aged white man and his son who operated the store and several customers were all standing and silently watching a television set. Over the air was coming the official Mississippi position—a complete juggling of fact to fit a preconceived orthodoxy: The marshals had, without provocation, fired tear gas at peacefully assembled Mississippi students, and this had provoked those students into counteractions which, if unfortunate, were at least understandable. The marshals and the U.S. troops had engaged in unspeakable brutality against the students. Communist-type techniques were being utilized by the Kennedy brothers to suppress proud Mississippians. But despite the military occupation of Mississippi, this proud people would never surrender.

The grocer and his son turned to one another. "That's it," said the father. Several of the customers nodded. There was no need for them to painfully evaluate their philosophy, and its logical outcome, in any way whatever.

In the days that followed, the official, orthodox position was supported again and again—by political leaders, law-enforcement officers, business associations, ministers, mass media. Those few white businessmen who had called for law and order were now silent. But James Meredith was in the university.

There were undoubtedly many in the segregationist ranks who rationalized the successful enrollment of James Meredith in such a fashion as to find considerable comfort. After all, shunned by nearly all of the other students, protected by an armed guard that traveled with him constantly and, indeed, lived with him, Meredith was, as the segregationists put it, "the world's most segregated Negro." Then too, bloody rioting had been initiated which could be used, again and again, as an "example" of what happened when integration was attempted. The Federal government had been forced into a position where it was, in a strong sense, occupying a part of Mississippi, and old hatreds of a century were being fired to even greater heights.

In a very profound sense, of course, the segregationists had lost an important round. A black was in a previously all-white Mississippi educational institution, and the Federal court orders had been enforced. The Kennedy administration had made it clear that within certain limits at least, it was prepared to go all the way on these matters. The rest of the United States had now secured its first real glimpse into the rigidity and viciousness of white Mississippi's society and culture.

Even Mississippi had been shaken internally: there were prominent white Mississippians who, although they remained silent and even continued to pay their dues to the Citizens Council, were not unaware of the immorality of the Council and the state political leaders and of the decisive power of the Federal government. Certainly, many were cognizant of the damage done to the public image of the state, impairing the attraction of industry and tourists.

Very fundamentally, another portion of Mississippi had been affected in a positive fashion by all of this: the black community. Fear was still very much present, perhaps even increasing, among adult people at least; but the nature of the apathy stemming from that fear had altered substantially. Almost every black in Mississippi knew that James Meredith *was* in the University of Mississippi, that Ross Barnett and the Citizens Council *had* lost a major round, that the Federal government *would,* in some instances at least, constructively involve itself all the way, even down into Mississippi. For the first time in their lives, Mississippi blacks had seen a very tangible civil rights victory for one of their own, and if there was still fear within themselves, there was no longer quite as much apathy. There was a new interest in the battle against segregation and discrimination, especially among the youth.

The Meredith affair was, however, only one step forward. In the final analysis, the great mass of black and white people were not much affected so far as their lives being tangibly touched by the storm which had occurred between Meredith and the leaders of the United States on one side, and the power structure of Mississippi on the other. Indeed, if there were any tangible effects on the lives of many people, it lay in a negative context—in the fact that, following the climax at Oxford, Mississippi tightened its control ever more; mass media grew even more rabid; and among other things, there was a sharp increase in the already mounting attacks carried against blacks by white hoodlums: several mysterious killings, beatings, shootings.

Certainly there was no sign of Mississippi turning in a more realistic direction. The Citizens Council monthly publication, *The Citizen,* in October, 1962, came out with an "all-Oxford issue." The cover showed a black army sergeant drilling white troops at Oxford; a Mississippi clergyman wrote an article condemning several white ministers in Oxford who had expressed shock and horror at what had happened and who had called for "repentance"; the clergyman who wrote in *The Citizen* took the position that, indeed, it was the Federal government that should repent. Another article enthusiastically discussed a "just-released" study that purported to prove the inherent biological inferiority of blacks. The publication's editorial summed up the position of Mississippi:

> The dark cloud that hangs over Oxford has a silver lining. . . . It has united our people. It has dramatized the ruthless grab for political power behind Federal might. It proves that justice for white students is not considered in this struggle. . . . It proves that if the white South is to survive, it must do so through its own resources. The white South

must unite its political and economic power in order to prevent negro political domination and racial amalgamation from becoming realities.

It proves that we cannot expect justice from politically-inspired Federal courts. Onr only salvation lies in organized, united political and economic action against individuals and organizations which would destroy us. The outcome of the struggle that lies ahead will be determined by the speed and efficiency with which we organize.

We hereby serve notice on the racial perverts and ruthless politicians who would destroy the South. *We have only begun to fight!*

And following Oxford, almost 1,000 new members joined the local Citizens Council in Jackson alone.

Not all of the hoodlum activities were directed against black people. Tom Johnson and his family found that their move from Canton to Jackson had resulted in no great change; indeed, things became worse. Tom's reputation as a stalwart of the advisory committee to the U.S. Commission on Civil Rights followed him, and did so, undoubtedly, via the Citizens Council. In addition, it was known that Marcy Johnson was working at Tougaloo in one of the offices. For several weeks matters had been reasonably quiet in the Johnsons' new neighborhood, but after Oxford there were rumors of impending trouble and continuous telephone threats. This went on for quite a while; then on the afternoon of October 31, Halloween, Tom came to our house and asked if he could leave his car there. With justification, he was afraid that someone in his neighborhood might dump sugar in the gas tank and ruin the engine. The Johnsons stayed for supper, and about 9 P.M. I drove all of them to their home.

Before we had even parked in the driveway, we saw what had happened: garbage, toilet paper, trash, covered their lawn from one end to the other. And walking past the Johnson house, barely looking at either of us or the yard, were many of the Johnsons' neighbors, out with their children, "trick-and-treating." The Johnsons went into their house and I stayed with them into the night. Nothing further happened and eventually I returned to Tougaloo.

Very late that night, several hours after I had left, Tom was awakened by rocks being thrown against his house. Looking out, he recognized a neighbor, called the sheriff, and swore out a warrant. The neighbor was arrested some hours later, and then tried in a justice of the peace court. Several friends of the neighbor then testified that the accused had been in another section of Jackson at the time of the incident. The neighbor, of course, was acquitted.

Not long after all that, Tom came to our house to say that he had just been arrested by Sheriff J. R. Gilfoy of Hinds County. The charge was perjury, stemming from the warrant that Tom had signed against his neighbor. The sheriff had thoughtfully allowed Tom to carry his children to our house and to pick up Marcy, who also was to be arrested.

With the Johnson children with Eldri, I accompanied Tom and Marcy down the road a few hundred yards, where the county line crossed the campus, and where the sheriff waited with a deputy. The Johnsons were taken to jail on a charge involving ten years each in the penitentiary. Dr. A. D. Beittel and others involved on the Civil Rights advisory committee moved fast, securing Marcy's release on $1,000 bond late that night and, the next day, another $1,000 was posted for Tom. At that point the Federal government moved into the situation, conducted an intensive investigation, and, still later, the charges against the Johnsons were quietly dropped.

But the hate calls continued and their neighbors scarcely spoke to them again.

James Meredith had secured entrance to the University of Mississippi, and there were indeed many ramifications involved in all of this; but one factor remained essentially unchanged: there was still, with the notable exceptions of the Clarksdale boycott and, more recently, SNCC involvement up in the Delta, no real grassroots civil rights activity going on anywhere in Mississippi. The various NAACP groups around the state were mostly quiet. In Jackson, the adult NAACP was doing very little; the West Jackson Youth Council was no longer alive; the group at Campbell College had almost gone out of existence; and the Tougaloo chapter was no longer active. CORE and SNCC existed in the Jackson area in name only.

But it was quite clear that our North Jackson Youth Council was by no means waning. We met regularly, at least once a week, from the very beginning of the school year onward. And very early, even before the Oxford situation reached its climax, we realized that the young people in the black community in Jackson, even though still afraid in most cases, had been stirred in such a way that a great many were now interested in doing something for civil rights. The Youth Council began to grow, and when it reached the point that there were too many for a meeting in a private home, we shifted our gatherings to the attic above the Virden Grove church in north Jackson. Still, each week new faces came drifting out of the shadows to join us. Some, like Pearlena Lewis, the president, were Tougaloo students who lived in Jackson, and some were Tougaloo students from out of the city who lived on campus. Still others, like Cleveland Donald, Jr., and the majority of the old members of the year before, were high-school students. There were many who were dropouts, ranging from their late teens into their early twenties. And there were even elementary-school children. Although some came from the other, now defunct groups, such as the West Jackson Youth Council, most of our new growth had never before been involved in a civil rights group. To further build up membership, we abandoned the idea of charging a formal NAACP membership fee—although we encouraged taking out a card. Attendance continued to climb even more sharply.

We were groping hard for worthwhile projects to undertake—projects that not only would be of importance to the struggle against racism, but would be within the ability of the Youth Council to handle. From this standpoint, the Christmas shopping season, still several months away, and a possible boycott of the downtown area were very much in our minds and in the discussions. By mid-September, we had started putting out a little mimeographed newsletter called *North Jackson Action,* which we distributed to members of the Youth Council, to potential members, and to key people in the black community. We also mailed out copies of the newsletter to a few individuals and organizations in the world beyond Mississippi—and from these we asked financial help. By October, we were launching a series of "educational sessions" which were held following each meeting of the Youth Council and to which we invited adults. In these we showed films, many of them rented from the national AFL-CIO, and our first financial contributions went to pay the initial down-payment costs on a film projector and screen. But our first real victory of the season lay in our nonviolent wrecking of the black portion of the segregated State Fair, which was held in Jackson.

As had been the case for many years indeed, the Mississippi State Fair was held during the second week in October for white people; then were scheduled three days for blacks. The year before, those few Tougaloo students who had picketed the black fair briefly, before being arrested, had created a situation in which the great majority of black people stayed away from the "secondhand fair." This year, we had no bail-bond money readily available for pickets, but our Youth Council undertook the project of launching a full-scale boycott of the black part of the fair. The *North Jackson Action* took up the cry, "State Fair Is Off-Limits!" We were able to secure about a thousand printed boycott leaflets, which the Youth Council members quietly distributed throughout Jackson—in an undercover fashion in order to avoid arrest. We gave bundles of leaflets to Tougaloo students who were going home for the weekend and asked them to distribute them around their home communities. We developed the technique of chain telephone calling: a Youth Council member would call up ten, or twenty, or thirty people, ask them to boycott the fair—and would then ask them to also call up at least ten people whom *they* knew, and on and on. Medgar issued a news release calling for blacks to stay away, and surprisingly, it wasn't ignored by the news media, as civil rights news releases so frequently were.

The white portion of the State Fair ran for its week; then the black portion began on Monday, October 15. Virtually no black people attended. The whole fairgrounds was ringed by police, who obviously expected an incident or two; and they, of course, had a frightening effect on anyone who might have thought of attending. By Monday afternoon, all of the news media in the area were calling on black people to attend the State Fair, but still scarcely anyone was showing up at the gates. Black high-school bands, under the orders from their tightly controlled schools, marched to the entrance of the fair, but once there, most of the students—all of whom had been contacted by the North Jackson Youth Council—went home immediately rather than go into the State Fair. About the only people in attendance, aside from the police and the concession operators, were some rural people who hadn't heard of the boycott and a few elementary-school children whose classes had been brought by their teachers. That night, Youth Council members posted themselves in the darkness around the fairgrounds, and quietly told all blacks coming into the area that there was a boycott.

Barely anyone showed up on Tuesday, and on Tuesday night the Youth Council members were again posted. On Wednesday the fair was deserted. The police remained, but most of the concessions and displays were being taken down—many hours before the official closing of the State Fair. I traveled around the area each day and each night that the campaign was in operation, and the whole fairgrounds appeared to me to be, with all of its police, comparable to a deserted concentration camp.

Although this was a real victory for the Youth Council and the black community, we now began to think of some other things. The "educational sessions" were fine, and a good many adults were in attendance, but none of us felt that education was the most direct route to Freedom.

There was no question about the fact that, by being in Jackson, we were in the key area of Mississippi. The state's capital and its largest city, it had a population of 150,000, and almost 40 percent were black. In addition, there were at least 100,000 other people in the hinterland surrounding the city—and here the black proportion was even higher. Jackson was the focal point of economics and politics in Mississippi; and although certainly no cosmopolitan Atlanta or New Orleans, and no Birmingham with large northern-owned industries—or any real industries, so far as that went—Jackson was still as close as one got to urbanism in Mississippi. There was even a measure of black-owned business, which lent a bit more security for Jackson's black community. The size of the city presented, of course, a serious problem because of the great number of people we would have to reach in whatever meaningful project we undertook; but we felt that we could reach them if we really worked at it. On the positive side, the size of the city made it difficult for the power structure, despite its circle of spies, to learn everything that was happening.

Clearly, whatever we did was not going to be done easily. Not only did we have thousands of black people to contact, but the power of the opposition was deeply entrenched. The Citizens Council and all Mississippi segregationists—including the white businessmen of Jackson and the arch-segregationist mayor, Allen C. Thompson, and the great majority of Jackson's white community—were only too aware that Jackson, as a large urban area, could become a target for intensive civil rights activity;

and that, if the patterns prevailing in other southern states held true in Mississippi, Jackson, again as a large urban area, could change more readily than, say, a rural community. And none of them had any intention of seeing Jackson change—ever.

But Jackson was our territory. We were stuck with it, and whether it knew it or not, it had us. The question was, what were we going to do? To really change Jackson, we needed a continuous grassroots movement that involved adults as well as youth. But the youth were still essentially largely unorganized; and the adults were not only unorganized but, with considerable justification, were afraid. We had virtually no money with which to operate. What could we do?

And we talked again of the boycott of the downtown stores.

The attempted boycott of the downtown area almost a year before had been a complete failure. Not much work had really been done on it: a few hundred leaflets had been passed around and a number of statements made from several church pulpits; and there had been the rather poorly attended civil rights mass meeting. That boycott effort had lasted only a few days and had won nothing. But the basic idea of a boycott was indeed very sound, we told ourselves over and over again. There were many white businessmen in Jackson, and they had a direct, and usually negative, effect on many black workers and many black consumers. They had an effect, too, on the political power structure of Jackson. Members of the Citizens Council they were, strong segregationists they were—but they were still, in the last analysis, businessmen whose primary interest lay in the making of money. And many tens of thousands of black people shopped in downtown Jackson.

A boycott could aim at securing improvements in the hiring and promotion of blacks and could seek better treatment of black consumers. Ultimately, it could be used to pressure the businessmen into forcing the mayor and other city authorities into making many positive changes within the city. Furthermore, from the standpoint of building a concerted grassroots freedom movement, a boycott had definite advantages: not only were most blacks workers, and all were consumers, but we wouldn't, at this time at least, be asking fear-filled people to go out into the streets to demonstrate. All that we would be asking them to do would be simply to do *nothing at all*—don't buy in the downtown area. And although no bail bond seemed to be available to us, perhaps we could scrape some up—once we really got a project underway.

Some of us remembered what we had seen on television regarding the mass arrests in Albany, Georgia, and we dreamed a little: maybe, as the Jackson boycott rolled on, we could grow into an Albany in Jackson—and a much more successful one than Albany had been. If we could just get the people with us and moving, who knew what might happen in Jackson?

On September 27, 1962, the North Jackson Youth Council passed a formal motion condemning the "extreme prejudice and discrimination against Negro workers and consumers which exists throughout Mississippi" and calling for "study and appropriate negotiations and direct action in the very near future." At the next meeting, a few days later, Pearlena Lewis appointed a committee of students to investigate in detail the various patterns of discrimination against black workers and consumers, and to sample public opinion throughout the black community in Jackson regarding potential support for a serious boycott campaign. Reports of all of this appeared in various issues of our newsletter, and the October 15 issue of *North Jackson Action* threw out some even stronger hints as to what was developing:

> The North Jackson Youth Council officers have indicated very definitely that they are fully prepared to institute non-violent direct action to correct the blatant injustices. Council members have unanimously supported this position. Many officers and members feel that a full-dress boycott may well be necessary. . . .

Preliminary reports of the committee that Pearlena had appointed indicated that interest seemed high in the black community, but in order to be reasonably certain of this, the group continued talking with people and determining the mood at the grassroots. We were starting our preliminary work well in advance, since all of us felt that the best time to launch the endeavor would be several weeks prior to Christmas, so that we could start the active phase of things by cutting deeply into the Christmas shopping season and, from that point, the boycott would roll onward as long as was necessary. Our enthusiasm and our hopes were climbing high.

The 17th Annual Mississippi State Conference of NAACP branches opened in Jackson on November 1. The winter rains were beginning in earnest as the 200 adult and youth delegates and their families gathered from the twenty or so NAACP organizations scattered throughout the state. The North Jackson Youth Council, along with the Jackson adult NAACP group, was playing the role of host, and everyone, especially Medgar, had been busy arranging housing and setting up the various workshop sessions. A number of high-echelon NAACP officials were present for the affair: Gloster Current of New York City, the national director of branches; Ruby Hurley of Atlanta, southeast states director; the recently appointed director of NAACP youth groups, Laplois Ashford, from New York City. In addition, Roy Wilkins, the executive secretary of the NAACP, came down from the New York office for a day or so. Dick Gregory, the comedian from Chicago and very much a civil rights advocate in his own right, was there for a day.

The shadow of Oxford and the hysteria being generated by the segregationists hung over the whole affair. Outside, many police were parked around the Masonic Temple, taking down the license numbers of those who attended the convention.

There were a number of workshop sessions for the delegates—community relations, voter registration, desegregation of facilities, fair employment. I had set up the session concerned with fair employment: we distributed several thousand pieces of various types of union literature, showed a film, and explained to people how to make fair employment complaints to such agencies as the President's Committee on Equal Employment Opportunity. Both C. C. Bryant of McComb, president of the NAACP branch in that embittered little city and a long-time railroad worker, and Lamar Turnipseed, a unionist from Pascagoula on the Gulf Coast who had long fought discrimination, spoke at length on the need to militantly assert one's rights. I spoke at great length on economic boycotts. But the faces of the people with whom we were speaking indicated clearly that few, if any, had any intention of challenging the system and doing any of these things. People discussed their grievances but were dubious about what they could be doing to improve matters. It was obvious that the climate of fear which pervaded all of Mississippi was reaching into the room where we sat. So it was in the other workshop sessions also.

One bright spot, however, came in the one evening session which was held for the delegates from the various youth councils. Although only four or five of these organizations were represented, those being about all that were functioning in the state, there was tremendous enthusiasm. The North Jackson Youth Council members made up the majority of those present, but there was also a substantial delegation from Clarksdale, where activity had been in progress. There was a great deal of talk about boycotts and direct action, and it was quite clear where the young people stood. Some of the adults who had seemed rather skeptical about the chances of anything really being started now caught the enthusiasm.

As the session broke up, Laplois Ashford, the national youth director, told me, "Try to get something going around here." He himself, a few days after the convention had adjourned, went down to Pascagoula, the area in which he had been born, and attempted to secure service in the "white" side of the bus depot. He was beaten and arrested.

One night during the convention, several of us gathered at Medgar's home for a party. There I met Mrs. James Meredith, who, although obviously worn from the tribulations through which she and her husband were passing, still had enough energy to try to show us all how to dance the twist. The next evening, at the annual Freedom Fund Dinner, Eldri and I, the only non-black people present, were seated with the Merediths at a table, and the whole thing was televised—in an effort to indicate that a measure of integration was occurring in Mississippi. James Meredith was extremely tense. The presence of the TV cameras prevented all of us from enjoying our dinner; mostly we talked about the dismal weather.

The convention was interesting enough, but when it was over we were all filled with a sense of disappointment. There had been a number of workshops and a good many speeches. We had had a long meeting of the state NAACP board of directors, to which I had again been elected a member. Many tough-sounding resolutions had been passed on a wide variety of issues. But in the final analysis, nothing really concrete or specific appeared to be developing as concerted grassroots action, with the exception of the people in Clarksdale and the North Jackson Youth Council. In the end, the people who attended the convention as delegates knew only too well that oratory and resolutions can fade fast, but that the day-to-day realities of a repressive, fear-filled system would continue for a long time to come, back in their grim, isolated communities. I had the feeling, as we completed the annual convention, that we had rather ritualistically brought people together and possibly planted a few seeds; but it was also clear that no grassroots revolution was going to develop in Mississippi in the near future.

It was now moving well into November. Things looked good. The Youth Council membership was still growing, and a bit of a treasury was accumulating from the fund appeal. All reports from the grassroots indicated that a boycott would, if it were really seriously attempted, secure considerable support immediately. Medgar and I had talked at length, and he was increasingly optimistic about the possibilities involved in a boycott campaign. A new CORE representative in the area, Dave Dennis of Louisiana, was now based in Mississippi and, although he was planning to spend most of his time working up on the Delta, had pledged his support. The Tougaloo students with whom I spoke sounded quite interested. Jackson talked of Thanksgiving and we talked of a downtown boycott to begin in early December.

At the Youth Council meetings we sang:

> *We're going to have a boycott, we shall not be moved.*
> *We're going to have a boycott, we shall not be moved.*
> *Just like a tree, a-standing by the water,*
> *We shall not be moved!*

One evening as I was grading examination papers in my home, Karin Kunstler, one of the new white students at Tougaloo, brought her father, William M. Kunstler, a New York City attorney, over to meet us. Accompanying them was the folk singer Pete Seeger, who, actually on his way to Louisiana, had met Bill Kunstler on the plane and had been persuaded by him to visit the college. It was the first time that we had met either of these men, although we had heard of Pete Seeger for years. Karin had told us that her father was one of the attorneys who, under the sponsorship of the American Civil Liberties Union, had defended Freedom Riders in Jackson in the early fall of 1961, and that as one of the attorneys for the Gandhi Society for Human Rights, the legal defense arm of Dr. Martin

Luther King's Southern Christian Leadership Conference, he had been active in Albany, Georgia. We visited briefly with them.

Pete Seeger held an impromptu, quite well-attended, concert at Tougaloo, then left for his Louisiana commitment. Bill Kunstler gave an excellent talk on civil liberties and stayed in the area for several days. On the afternoon that he was to leave for the airport, his transportation did not show up, and I was asked to give him a ride. We missed the plane. Bill wound up spending an extra day at Tougaloo at our home, and much of our time was spent in a discussion regarding the possibilities of getting a civil rights movement going in Jackson. It developed that he had spent several hours, a day or so before, talking with a number of adults in the black community whom he had known back in the Freedom Rider days. Although some had expressed an interest in really building an active mass movement in the city, most were not too optimistic. He agreed that "if anything is going to develop in Jackson, the kids will have to start it." I told him, in detail, of our proposed Youth Council boycott. He promised his full assistance, should we require it. Then he talked on and on of Albany, and again, I found myself dreaming a bit of a mass direct-action movement in Jackson.

In mid-November, we ran a bluntly worded statement of our case in the *North Jackson Action*—"Start Putting Your Money On Strike":

> Many know that the North Jackson NAACP Youth Council has, for the past several weeks, been conducting a study of Jackson-area discrimination against Negro workers and Negro consumers. The results of the study—still not completely finished—indicate that the situation is far worse than many had imagined it to be.
>
> We can assure you that an ever-increasing amount of North Jackson Youth Council effort is going to be aimed toward cleaning up just as many of these vicious discriminations as possible.
>
> It is hard indeed to tell just what the future is going to bring—but it ought to be very interesting.
>
> Right now, we want to remind people of the obvious: the coming-up of the Christmas shopping season. And—we'd also like to remind people of what ought to be very obvious: the buying power—in the 150,000 resident Jackson area—of its 70,000 Negro citizens.
>
> We would like to remind Negro consumers that—as they fully well know—appeals to the "nice, kind side" of most of these white businessmen are going to have absolutely no effect at all. On the other hand, speaking to them in the language that they know so well—money—will always produce a reaction. If you cut off the flow of nickels and dimes and dollars into their cash register boxes—they'll sit up mighty fast and take notice.
>
> Since almost every white businessman in the Jackson area—and in all of Mississippi, as far as that goes—discriminates against Negro

workers and Negro consumers, we frankly think that it is high time
that Negro consumers stay away from those white businesses.

We feel that Negro consumers should start patronizing only those
businesses where Negro workers and Negro consumers are treated as
they ought to be—as first class citizens. This means patronizing mostly
Negro businesses—and there is certainly nothing wrong with that.

Money is equal, isn't it? Negro dollars and white dollars "mix"
equally in cash registers, don't they? No discrimination there—no
second class dollars.

All human beings are equal—and there should be no second class
citizens anywhere. Until Negro customers and white customers and
Negro workers and white workers exist on the equal basis that is their
God-given right and due—let's start segregating that money.

Keep that money away from the white businesses that discriminate.
You'll find that this will have quite a constructive effect on those white
businessmen concerned.

Patronize only those businesses where people—all people—are
treated as people. Right now is a first-rate time to begin—with the
Christmas shopping season coming right up.

But this "selective buying" shouldn't just last the duration of the
Christmas season. It should go on and on—until the vicious discrimination against Negro workers and Negro consumers passes from the
scene.

And if you start putting your money on strike, we predict that the
passing of that discrimination will take surprisingly little time.

This statement, which was moving close indeed to being a call-to-arms,
was extremely well received by those youths and adults who read it—
probably because it implied a large-scale, really serious attack on the
status quo. There was no question now but that we were, as one Youth
Council member put it, "swinging onto the boycott road."

Boycott planning intensified in the next several days. Just before
Thanksgiving, the members of the North Jackson Youth Council assembled at our home for a party. Cokes were available by the dozens, and
we moved furniture into other rooms to facilitate dancing, but the best
portion of the affair was devoted to making boycott strategy. A number
of Tougaloo students who hadn't really been involved with the Youth
Council came in and joined us. Several students from Oberlin College,
in Ohio, were visiting Tougaloo, and they sat in on the session. On Thanksgiving Day itself, Eldri served almost three dozen meals to Tougaloo students who had stayed on campus during the brief holiday period. And
much more boycott talk took place. Perhaps because of her cooking, Eldri
was asked to become the adult adviser to the Tougaloo College NAACP
Chapter, which had been defunct. She accepted the position and meetings
of the group immediately began on an action-oriented basis.

There was no question but that the downtown area was the logical target. It was the "economic nerve center" of Jackson—the center of trade. And there was no question but that the whole downtown area would have to be involved in order for the campaign to be really meaningful. Then too, it would be easier, actually, to make it a total downtown effort and to simply ask all black shoppers to stay away from the whole downtown— rather than to pick out a few stores here and a few stores there, in which case the boycott would be difficult to enforce. Since most of the downtown businesses were along Capitol Street, we decided to specify that whole area: all of downtown Capitol Street from its upper boundary, State Street, to Mill Street, its lower border. In addition, we specified a number of chain stores that had branches in various shopping centers and whose owners or managers had been especially active in the Citizens Council. A small grocery-store chain, whose hiring practices were especially negative despite the fact that it was catering almost exclusively to a black clientele, was attached to the list. In all, there were about 150 businesses involved, some quite small, but the great majority sizable enough to hire a number of persons.

We decided not to negotiate with the businesses prior to initiating the campaign. For one thing, there was always the danger that the negotiations could be prolonged by the businessmen, if they *did* negotiate, until after the key Christmas shopping season, and then be dropped. Also, on past occasions, Medgar had attempted to negotiate with the downtown merchants, and they had refused to do so. Further, the threat of a boycott had been levied several times in the past, then never really carried through. We doubted that the businessmen, at this point, would take our threat seriously. We decided really to get it started, then offer to negotiate and, in any case, keep it moving forward until substantial victories were won.

We drew up the format of a leaflet which we took to one of the Tougaloo professors who had in his basement a printing press, and he agreed to print it for a nominal fee. We ordered 5,000 leaflets, which said, "Don't Buy on Capitol Street," and which then listed the general boundaries of the downtown area, and the other business places which were also involved, and then set forth the demands:

1. Equality in hiring and promotion
2. End of segregated drinking fountains—restrooms—seating
3. Use of courtesy titles: "Mrs.", "Miss" and "Mr."
4. Service on a first-come, first-served basis

At the bottom we listed the North Jackson Youth Council and the Tougaloo College NAACP Chapter. We also added the Jackson NAACP Branch, and although these were no longer functioning, we attached the names of the West Jackson Youth Council and the Campbell College NAACP Chapter. Joan Trumpauer was the SNCC representative on campus and was agreeable to our listing that organization. Dave Dennis, the only CORE man in the state at that time, was happy to have CORE attached. We decided that on the next batch of leaflets, we would just put "Jackson Movement."

I felt strongly, as did the Youth Council, that we ought to have some picketing in the downtown area, especially at the outset of the campaign. I talked this over with Medgar, who indicated that since we had things moving so decisively, he thought there would be no difficulty in securing enough bail, either through local property bonds or from the national office of the NAACP, to finance, say, ten pickets at $500 apiece. He said that he'd check with Jack Young, one of the three black lawyers in Mississippi (all of whom lived in Jackson) who handled civil rights cases. This was good news! Now we moved to locate some pickets.

The business of picket selection was rather touchy. Nearly all of the Youth Council members wanted to participate in a demonstration, but since the great majority of these were seventeen or under, we felt that legal complications might develop; and we knew that, in this initial direct action, the power structure of Jackson might well attempt to "make examples," and all sorts of interesting things might develop. Then too, those in the Youth Council who were eighteen or older were ruled out, since they had—as did the others, as far as that goes—parents who could easily be subjected to economic reprisals. The matter of the vulnerability of parents applied also to most of the Tougaloo students. We knew that later, after the ice had been broken, we could use anyone who wanted to demonstrate—but in the initial action, we selected with care.

I felt that I should, as adviser to the Youth Council, be one of the pickets. I asked Eldri if she would be willing to join us. She hesitated for only a moment, then agreed to do so. I asked around the Tougaloo campus, on an informal basis, and within a few days we had the remainder of the crew: Rupert Crawford, Ronald Mitchell, Walter Mitchell, and Bette Anne Poole—all of them eighteen or older, all of them with parents who resided out of state.

This gave us six pickets, enough for a start. Medgar had left town for the North on a speaking trip, but we assumed that the bail-bond situation was being worked through. Members of the North Jackson Youth Council were busy lining up boycott contacts all over the black community, and a hard-core group of Tougaloo students was ready. The boycott leaflets were being printed. We set Monday, December 3, 1962, as the picket day. On November 30, the *North Jackson Action* announced that it was all beginning with its little banner headline: THE BOYCOTT IS NOW OFFICIAL; IS AIMED AT CAPITOL STREET STORES AND OTHER BUSINESSES; IT WILL LAST UNTIL VICTORY; PICKET LINES AND MASS MEETINGS ARE DEFINITELY SET.

Everything appeared to be going very well indeed. On Sunday, December 2, we had a closed meeting of the pickets, in which we discussed our demonstration strategy. The plan we set forth was: about 10:30 A.M. the next day, Monday, we would be taken in a car driven by another student to the Woolworth store, right in the heart of the downtown area, and we would commence to picket. If attacked physically, we would, regardless of our personal feelings, function in a nonviolent fashion. When arrested, we would give only our name, address, age, and occupation to the police, regardless of any other questions that might be asked. Picket signs made out of heavy poster paper were all ready, and they called on black shoppers to stay away from Capitol Street.

A woman who lived near the campus had agreed to keep Maria until Eldri and I were out of jail. And as soon as we were all arrested, Pearlena Lewis, Karin Kunstler, Joan Trumpauer, and the Rev. Eddie O'Neal, a young minister who was president of the Tougaloo student body, would call a campus-wide mass meeting in the college chapel to announce the boycott and ask for active support and participation in the endeavor from the students. Another student quite active in civil rights, Joyce Ladner, would speak on behalf of the "free Clyde Kennard" effort—a petition campaign to get that pioneer in integration attempts out of the Parchman penitentiary, where he had developed cancer. Heavy boycott-leaflet distribution, as well as other techniques, would begin in Jackson shortly after the arrests had occurred. It was a beautful plan and it looked as if nothing could go wrong.

Medgar was still in the North, but before he had left, we had told him the day events would begin. Now, as everyone began to eat the meal Eldri had prepared, I went over to another building, since we had no telephone, to call Jack Young, the lawyer. I reached him and, in "riddle-talk," since I knew that his telephone was tapped and since we had not made our picket date public, told him that "everything is set for the party tomorrow." Then I received a serious shock.

Jack Young told me that no bail bond had arrived and that it was somewhat questionable that any would be available.

There was no point in proceeding any further over the telephone, so I drove immediately into Jackson to his home. He reiterated what he had told me: there was no money. He knew the hotel in which Medgar was staying, somewhere in New York State, and we telephoned there, reaching Medgar right away. "There is no money," he told me. "Your only chance, I guess, is to try to find some Negroes in Jackson who can post property bonds." Medgar sounded tired and strained. He suggested that Jack Young acccompany me in a search for the property bond, and the lawyer agreed to do so.

It was now late in the afternoon. Jack Young and I drove around Jackson, talking with a number of people, but could find no one who had property unencumbered by a lien or mortgage who would be willing to put it up in a civil rights situation. It was an utterly dismal turn of events.

As I drove back to Tougaloo, I thought the situation over at length.

It seemed strange, to say the least, that no bail money was available; we had had every assurance that it would be and, indeed, had even specified the date to Medgar. I knew that he had done his best. In any event, we had no bail-bond money and we were going to have to get some forthwith. If this had been during the summer, we could picket, go to jail, and stay there for a time—but this was right in the middle of the academic year. The position of Dr. A. D. Beittel and the rest of the college administration was extremely good with respect to civil rights matters, but there were many faculty—some white and some black—who felt that civil rights endeavors impaired academic matters. If we went to jail, we had to get out as soon as possible.

We had to get some bail bond.

Back at Tougaloo, the pickets had long since departed from our home. Quietly, I spread the word to them that "temporary complications" had developed, but that one way or the other, we would be picketing within the next several days. They were bitterly disappointed, as were the North Jackson Youth Council officers when I reached them. Several gathered at our home immediately.

Several weeks before, Bill Kunstler had told me that he would help us if the need arose. We asked Karin to come to our house, and she agreed to call her father immediately. We remembered that the Southern Conference Educational Fund (SCEF), one of the smaller civil rights groups, had in the past posted some of the bail for SNCC workers in Mississippi. Joan Trumpauer, whom we also called to our home, telephoned Anne Braden in Louisville, Kentucky, editor of the SCEF paper, the *Southern Patriot*; and Anne Braden, in turn, called Dr. James Dombrowski in New Orleans, executive director of SCEF. All of these people —Bill Kunstler, Anne Braden, and James Dombrowski—felt that something could be worked through for a group of ready-to-go pickets in Jackson, Mississippi, and agreed to let us know as soon as possible when the bail money was pinned down.

On Monday, the day that we would have picketed, we convened a special meeting of all those concerned and told everyone, fingers crossed, that it would "all work out." For the next several days, guarded telephone calls flew back and forth between Jackson and New York City and Jackson and New Orleans. Special-delivery letters were sent and received. When matters came into focus, about a week after our initial contacts, SCEF had agreed to put up $1,000 for two pickets. A New York attorney, Victor Rabinowitz, who was an acquaintance of Bill Kunstler, put up from a special family fund $1,500 for three more demonstrators. The Gandhi Society, with which Bill Kunstler was directly involved, put up $500. We were assured that the money would be in Jackson by Wednesday, December 12.

Now we were finally set, and we picked December 12 as the new date. Although much later than we had wished to begin, it was still not too late by any means; the Christmas shopping season in Jackson had not yet gotten into full swing. The basic plan of action still held, although we made one modification: news coverage. On December 11, according to our decision, Bill Kunstler, in New York City, informed the Associated Press and the United Press International to the effect that in mid-morning of December 12 a civil rights demonstration would take place somewhere on Capitol Street in Jackson, Mississippi—to be immediately followed by a large-scale mass meeting at Tougaloo College. We knew that we were running a risk in telling this to the news media since of course the news would immediately be given to AP and UPI in Jackson, and would then reach everyone—including the police. Conceivably hoodlums might even gather to wait for us. But we knew, too, that if we didn't publicize what we were planning to do, we ran the even graver risk of a quick arrest and a news cover-up. Our purpose was to get those "Don't Buy on Capitol Street" messages to as many people as possible, via, among other things, the local press, radio, and TV.

Right on schedule, late in the afternoon of December 11, the news about the coming demonstration began to pour forth from the radio and TV stations in the Jackson area. Early in the evening, Eldri and I drove to the outskirts of the city to purchase a load of groceries. We weren't actually certain just how long we would be in jail, and we wanted the woman who was keeping Maria to be well provided. We had the groceries and were loading them into the car when I suddenly saw Eldri staring at something. I looked in that direction. A large Jackson policeman, well over six feet in height, a huge man, was walking into the store.

Eldri said, "I'm afraid. I really am. I'm afraid of tomorrow." There was a long pause, and she went on. "But I'll go. I'll go." I was afraid too, but I pretended that I was not.

We drove silently back to Tougaloo. Dark stormclouds were coming down from the north and it was getting very cold. When we went to bed, the demonstration was still being announced over the radio.

4

WE WERE UP VERY EARLY the next morning. The stormclouds were gone, but it was bitterly cold. At 8 A.M. I began to teach my regular American Government course in which were two of the pickets, Rupert Crawford and Bette Anne Poole. It was a tense class for all of us, and when it was over an hour later, we went immediately to my home. The others were all gathered there, talking with Eldri, who looked as rigid as a statue. Two other Tougaloo students, Israel Robinson and O. B. Farrish, took my car and quickly reconnoitered the road leading from Tougaloo into Jackson; we thought that the police might be waiting somewhere along the line to block us before we got into the city. Israel and O.B. reported back that the road seemed clear. We took everything out of our pockets, stuffed them with cigarettes. The woman took Maria. Then we took the picket signs and at 10 A.M. sharp, right on schedule, climbed into a car driven by another student. We were off to picket on Capitol Street, the first time that anyone had ever picketed right in the heart of the downtown area—off to launch the long-awaited boycott of Jackson, Mississippi.

The ride from Tougaloo into Jackson takes only about twenty minutes at most, but for us it seemed like a trip across the country. There was a good deal of cigarette smoking and some very half-hearted attempts at low-keyed freedom singing; but there was generally a very tense silence. We entered Jackson, traveled along State Street past the Old Capitol building of Mississippi, then turned down Capitol Street toward the Woolworth store.

The first thing that we noted was that on each side of the street police cars, motorcycles, and paddy wagons were posted—block after block. The second thing we noticed was that scarcely anyone was on the sidewalks. The closer we got to the center of Capitol Street, the fewer people we saw—and the thicker the police seemed to become.

It was almost 10:30 A.M. when we stopped in front of the Woolworth store. Quickly, I got out with the picket signs and the pickets followed me onto the sidewalk. I handed the signs out, one at a time, and we formed a little picket line, six of us, walking as close to the outside of the sidewalk as we could without walking into the parking meters, and with about an arm's length between us. As we began, a news photographer came up, and I gave him a copy of the *North Jackson Action* that discussed the boycott and to which was stapled a boycott leaflet. Then the photographer quickly began to take pictures. Other newsmen were

62

now on the scene. We turned around and began to walk back in front of the Woolworth store, then back up the sidewalk again. I felt as if it were all a dream.

At this point a police officer, Captain Cecil Hathaway, stepped out in front of us. A wave of police—perhaps fifty or more—poured across Capitol Street and surrounded us.

To me Hathaway said, "You are under arrest."

I asked him, "Why? What charge?"

He muttered something about obstructing the sidewalk. Police took our signs, wrote our names on the backs of them. Captain J. L. Ray came up, smiled at me, and said to Hathaway, "I see you got the professor." A crowd of about 100 white people had gathered by this time. Traffic on Capitol Street was held up for blocks, owing to the large number of police standing out in the street.

It was clear that even if we hadn't been able to secure bail bond for a great big affair, the Jackson police force had at least provided the mass demonstration for us. It may have been a grim situation, really, but I could not help but smile.

Under heavy guard we were taken to the paddy wagon and then to jail. At the police station, a large number of uniformed police, plain-clothes detectives, and some somber-faced men in business suits whom we took to be connected with the Citizens Council and the Sovereignty Commission gathered to look at us. The police were verbally unpleasant and became more so when we refused to give them any information other than what we had decided, but other than being pushed and shoved, we were not physically mistreated. I was allowed to call Jack Young.

After being photographed and fingerprinted, we were placed in the segregated cell system. I drew a small, single cell in which someone had urinated, obviously just minutes before I arrived there. On one side of me, in another single cell, was a salesman who immediately told me that he had written a string of bad checks all the way from Virginia to Mississippi. On the other side was a man who informed me that he had been booked for petty theft. Although we could not see one another, we had no difficulty talking. The salesman seemed quite congenial and somewhat unrepentant. The other man, in one of the heaviest drawls that I've ever heard, asked me why I was in jail. Briefly, I explained the situation—the charge against me, the reasons why I had picketed, the fact that an NAACP lawyer would be getting me out soon. Then I waited for the racist invective which I was certain would follow all of this.

Instead, he said, and sadly, "I sure wish the NAACP would get me out."

Jack Young arrived at the jail, and I was taken out to talk with him. He indicated that only half of the bail bond had arrived, but that the other portion was expected the next day. Three could get out. Three others would have to remain in overnight. I suggested that Bette Anne Poole, Eldri, and whichever male picket was youngest be released right away. Ronald Mitchell was the third, and although he didn't want to leave jail, he was finally persuaded to do so.

About mid-morning the next day, a black trusty brought me a copy of the Jackson morning newspaper, the *Clarion-Ledger,* which he said the jailer had told him to bring to me. I was curious indeed as to why the jailer had done this, but when I glanced through the paper, I realized why. Our little demonstration had been played down—away down: simply a few lines to the effect that we had been arrested and the demonstration was, as the paper put it, "a flop." There was nothing more on the matter anywhere in the paper. It looked as if the power structure had played its cards well, from its standpoint, and that the publicity was not going to reach many via the local press.

We were out of jail early in the afternoon and went immediately to Tougaloo. At home, Eldri was meeting with a large number of students. Quickly, we were brought up to date: as soon as we had been arrested, the mass meeting had taken place on the college campus and had been enormously successful, with virtually all of the student body in attendance. Militant speeches had been given by our speakers; many freedom songs had been sung; and the Tougaloo students were extremely excited and had pledged their full support and cooperation.

But there was more good news, much more indeed.

Radio and television had been excellent! Our picket signs, the students told us, had all been visible and the "Don't Buy" messages had come through sharp and clear.

And other students told us that Mayor Allen Thompson had been on television, after our arrest, to denounce us all as agitators!

Pearlena Lewis and other members of the Youth Council had the distribution of boycott leaflets well underway in the black sections of Jackson. Hundreds of leaflets, at least, had already been distributed, despite the fact that it had to be done very carefully, since anyone caught by the police would be immediately arrested. Youth Council members had already started the chain telephone calling. And more leafleting and calling, much more indeed, would be taking place over the weekend.

And the good news continued to come.

Medgar arrived at our house with a copy of the afternoon paper, the *Jackson Daily News,* and it had a banner headline: "Allen Threatens to Sue Pickets—Declares Won't Tolerate Agitators." We read the news story.

It was fantastically good! Not only had Thompson orated at length the day before, but now, a day later, he had gone before a meeting of the city department heads and, with reporters present, had talked much indeed. Attacking "agitators, pickets, and such organizations as the

NAACP and others," he declared that "we are not going to have any picketing or such a thing in this city," and that "we are going to continue the way we always have. We arrested these people and put them in jail." He threatened to line downtown Capitol Street with "1,000 police" to prevent any future picketing. Further, he was talking about suing the pickets for one million dollars. At the end of the article, the mayor was quoted as saying that he intended to keep "cool, calm, and collected."

Furthermore, there was even a picture in the *Jackson Daily News* showing us all being arrested—with Eldri in the forefront and with the message of her sign prominently displayed: "Negro Customers—Stay Away From Capitol Street—Buy Elsewhere."

Good old Allen Thompson! Good old *Jackson Daily News!* At the rate both were going, there was no question but that everyone in the state of Mississippi would soon know, if they didn't already, that black people were being asked not to shop on Capitol Street—and with all of this talk about 1,000 policemen, they were only ensuring that a great many white people who simply didn't want to be in the vicinity of any trouble would also be staying away from the downtown area. We could have asked for no better publicity.

The next day, Friday, there was quite a report in the *Jackson Daily News* to the effect that Mayor Thompson, in addressing a number of businessmen, had again talked about his "1,000 police" and his million-dollar lawsuit based on restraint of trade.

There were also some hints in the paper that the mayor might be considering running for governor.

Friday night, Cordell Reagen and his SNCC Freedom Singers, who were touring the South, arrived at Tougaloo and we had another heavily attended boycott rally in the chapel. Following that, almost a hundred Tougaloo students gathered at our house to continue organizing and plan more strategy. We learned that Jack Young and another black civil rights lawyer, Jess Brown, had conferred with Bill Kunstler, and it had been decided that Bill and Jess Brown would handle our picket cases and, in doing so, would utilize, as they put it to us, "some very interesting techniques." Our trials in city court, on the charge of "obstructing the sidewalk"—the possible penalty for each picket being six months in jail and $500 fines—were postponed pending the active involvement of our new lawyers.

On Saturday dozens of Tougaloo students began to move quietly into the black areas of Jackson, joining the Youth Council in the leaflet distribution. Others worked on the chain telephone calls. We secured a large map of Jackson, pinned it to our wall, marking the areas where the leaflet distribution was underway. Medgar gave us a city directory, which, on a street by street basis, listed the names of Jackson residents and gave their telephone numbers as well. There was no question but that we were in business.

Late Saturday afternoon several of us drove down Capitol Street. There was a tremendous decrease in the number of blacks shopping in the downtown area. And for those who were there, we had a substantial number of Tougaloo students and Youth Council members, traveling up and down the streets, posing as shoppers and quietly telling blacks about the boycott. Although there were not "1,000 police," there were more than I had ever seen before downtown.

On Sunday, we sent student speakers into the black churches in Jackson to explain, with the clergyman's permission, the reasons for the boycott, and to ask for the support of the adult community. People were given packets of leaflets to take into their neighborhoods. The response was very enthusiastic.

The Sunday paper—a sort of combination *Daily News*—*Clarion Ledger*—ran a story under the headline, "City to Seek a Halt Here to Harassment by Agitators." The article conceded that "there is a potential damage to business firms," and it denounced the "brazenness of the NAACP in attempting to intimidate Jackson downtown business firms in a ridiculous, racially-mixed, sham pretense of picketing," and it went on to condemn "the mouthings and boasting of completely foreign-to-Mississippi and Jackson persons . . . racial agitators." Again, much was made of the mayor's threats to initiate a million-dollar lawsuit against the pickets and to line downtown Capitol Street with "1,000 police."

By the middle of the next week, it was clear that the Christmas shopping season in Jackson, Mississippi, had been dealt a very serious blow—and that the boycott had not only taken root but was becoming increasingly effective. Old hands, such as Medgar, felt that almost 60 percent of the black trade had been ended in downtown Jackson and at the other business places under boycott. There were no offers on the part of the white businessmen to meeting the demands, or even negotiating, nor had we expected any. They felt, I am sure, that our campaign would collapse. And we knew that our hardest job lay in keeping the boycott going after the initial burst of enthusiasm. Each night after school, we met with the Tougaloo students and the Youth Council members; and while Eldri cooked food for us and Maria, if she was up at the time, looked on in bewilderment at the increasingly large size of the gatherings, we planned more strategy.

And I ordered 10,000 more leaflets and began to look around for some more bail bond.

Bail bond was, of course, our scarcest item, but Medgar felt that now, since interest in the boycott was clearly mounting in Jackson, he would be able to locate at least two local property bonds. The two Tougaloo students whom I found to picket, Charles Bracey and Dorie Ladner, both with parents living in Mississippi who supported this, agreed to go to jail and count on our being able to secure the bond money to free them. And we set Saturday, December 21, as the time for their debut.

Meanwhile, up in New York City, Bill Kunstler and his associate, Attorney Clarence Jones of the Gandhi Society, were developing their "very interesting techniques." Bill drew up a removal petition, which sought to transfer our cases out of the local Mississippi courts into the Federal District Court. Jess Brown, in Jackson, was quite agreeable to this. We knew that Bill had tried this in several cases back in the Freedom Rider days, but that the Federal judge, Harold Cox, an arch-segregationist with whom the petitions had been filed, had refused to take jurisdiction and had sent those cases back to the state courts. Still, it sounded quite good to us, especially since Bill proposed filing another petition with Judge Cox, a bit later in the game, asking Judge Cox to disqualify himself from hearing our cases on the ground that he was a segregationist.

So, in accordance with this removal strategy, all of us signed petitions which, in essence, stated that the charge of obstructing the sidewalk was totally unrelated to what we were actually doing—peaceful picketing. The petitions pointed out that the arrests had denied us due process of law by giving judicial powers to the police and making any peaceful picketing subject to punishment if the police wished to do so. To sort of tie everything up, the petitions charged that our rights under the First, Fifth, Thirteenth, Fourteenth, and Fifteenth Amendments to the U.S. Constitution had been denied. My class in American Government began to take a new interest in those portions of the text dealing with the judicial system.

The filing of the removal petitions blocked our trials in the state court system, pending the outcome of a hearing which Judge Cox set for January 11.

Poison-pen letters were now arriving from many points in the South. Some were quite bitter and one, apparently with reference to the Federal troops still on the scene at Oxford, was stamped all over with "Mailed to Occupied Mississippi":

> So you're a professor, a dyed in the wool pedagog, in a socialist advocated and possibly financed naacp (and mister that stands for national association of socialist party) nigger camp.
>
> And you're going to get out with the off color tribe in sit down strikes and boycotts and youre going to get on the picket line again with your niggers there at the great institution of Tug.
>
> When you and your blacks and all radicals like you and the naacps, and cores, and kennedys and hugho blacks—all these bring about the desired situation in such minds to make the white and nigger race all one—Id bet you are going to be one of the key figures in that new order.
>
> One of the off colr radical South hating magazines like Post or Look, will, you hope, take note of your outstanding contribution to

integration of the black and white race move, and elect or appoint
you maybe to some high position as garbage collector

You'd fit in that position just fine

When you go to Jackson and it comes time to eat have you
the gall to go in a white mans eating place? I just wonder—thats all

This writer, who indicated that he was sending copies of his letter to
various Citizens Council groups, signed his name and address. We wrote
him, politely thanking him for his interest and telling him that, no, we
didn't eat in white eating places since they practiced an exclusion policy.

Since we didn't have a telephone, the college was receiving a number
of threatening calls concerning us, generally to the effect that our home
was going to be bombed and shot up. On Friday, December 20, I
announced to the wire services that more picketing would be taking place
on Capitol Street the next day. This was duly carried by all of the radio
and television stations, but the newspapers—probably under pressure
from the white businessmen who, by this time, had already suffered
quite a financial loss—played the announcement down. That night,
someone sneaked onto the campus and posted a sign on our house
which said, among other things, "Trash." The Christmas holidays were
beginning and the campus was much lonelier.

It was raining hard the next day. I drove into Jackson and picked up
Charles Bracey at his home, and then returned to the campus, where
Dorie Ladner joined us. We had made up two more picket signs carrying
messages similar to the first ones. It was our feeling that, quite possibly,
the police would attempt to arrest the pickets even as they stepped out
of a car, so we worked out another strategy. Dorie and Charles put
the signs under their raincoats and buttoned up tightly. We gave them
shopping bags. I took them to the outskirts of the downtown area and
let them off, and posing as "boycott-breaking" shoppers, they strolled,
hand in hand, to Capitol Street, then up to the Woolworth store—where
about twenty-five police waited on both sides of the street. Newsmen
were also on hand. When the two students were right up by the police,
both quietly removed their raincoats and quickly began picketing.
Apparently the officers did not even notice them until the police on the
other side of the street yelled across. Immediately Dorie and Charles
were arrested for obstructing the sidewalk.

As soon as they had been arrested, I went to the NAACP offices,
and Medgar and I then went the rounds seeking property bonds.
Times had changed somewhat: quite soon we were able to find two
people who would be willing to post property bond to the amount of
$500 each. Within a few hours both Dorie Ladner and Charles Bracey
were out of jail and eating supper at my home. Their cases went into
abeyance pending the outcome of the legal maneuvering in the cases of the
first six pickets.

A good deal of the picketing and arrests was shown on television—with the messages on the signs as clearly set forth as one could wish. But this time, Mayor Thompson was silent.

That night, very tired from all this, I turned in early. Eldri stayed up, talking with Bette Anne Poole, Dorie Ladner, and Joan Trumpauer—who were among a number of Tougaloo students staying in the area during the holidays in order to work on the boycott. About 11 P.M., a shot was fired through the window in Maria's room, passing very close to her as she lay asleep.

Awakened, I dressed rapidly and went into the baby's room. Eldri, outwardly calm, was sweeping up the glass. The students were much more excited. Maria was crying. I went outside, but whoever had fired the shot had departed. Later that night, the Tougaloo watchman said that shortly before the shooting he had seen a strange car parked on the back road that ran past our house. The next night, the watchman intercepted two cars filled with white men driving past our home. They forced him off the road with their cars but then left the college area. For the remainder of the Christmas holidays, several students and myself stood armed guard all night long—and I let this be known to the news services. The harassment stopped abruptly.

On Christmas Day, Eldri, Maria, and I went to the Evers home for dinner. It was still raining and was very gloomy: 1962 was almost over, and we all talked for a long time about the events of the year—Oxford, the beginnings of a movement in Jackson, the SNCC projects still in their initial stages up on the Delta. "Free by '63"—the Emancipation Centennial—had been a motto for the past several years, but it was obvious that, in Mississippi especially, the struggle was really only in its first stage.

But there was optimism in the discussion, too. Medgar had been a paid civil rights staff man for nine years and, in a deeper sense, had been fighting racism all of his life. Now, as he read in the newspapers of the breakthroughs coming in other sections of the South, and felt the vague rumblings within Mississippi, he felt that 1963 would see many positive changes in his home state. But he also felt that, as controversy sharpened in Mississippi, there would be negative reactions. "The white man won't change easily," he said. "Some of these people are going to fight hard. And more of our people could get killed."

Myrlie Evers said little at that point. She knew, as she had for years, who might be killed. Our talk turned back to the boycott, then to the children. But in that gloomy evening, with the rain coming down, it was difficult for any of us to escape a certain foreboding.

On December 28 we launched the attack against Judge Harold Cox—arch-segregationist, boyhood chum of Senator James Eastland, and Kennedy appointee to the Federal court. Bill Kunstler had sent down a long petition, which I signed on behalf of the pickets, and Jess Brown filed with Judge Cox. It was, in its own way, something of a precedent-setting maneuver. Judge Harold Cox was asked to disqualify himself from hearing our picket cases, because:

1. Upon information and belief, Judge Cox believes in and subscribes to the principles of racial segregation, as advocated by respondent's Governor and Legislature.
2. Upon information and belief, during the summer of 1962, Mayor Allen Thompson of Jackson, Mississippi, an outspoken advocate of racial segregation, stated, in a public address, that the people of Jackson were grateful to Judge Cox for helping preserve Mississippi traditions.
3. That Judge Cox, prior to his elevation to the federal bench, was chairman of the Hinds County Democratic Executive Committee and, upon information and belief, in such capacity invited Congressman John Bell Williams, among others, to give racist speeches.
4. Upon information and belief, Judge Cox was widely heralded as the choice of United States Senator James O. Eastland for the judgeship which he now holds, and rumors as to his appointment were current long before the appointment in question; that said Senator Eastland is an outspoken advocate of racial segregation.
5. On August 26, 1961, in deciding five other removal cases . . . adversely to the petitioners therein, all Freedom Riders, Judge Cox, with no evidence as to any of the facts surrounding the nature or the objectives of the petitioners' travel to Jackson, referred to them as "counterfeit citizens" whose interstate status was doubtful. Furthermore, despite the fact there were more than 200 such cases, including those of the petitioners therein, then pending for trial by jury in the state courts, he proclaimed, without one shred of evidence before him, that "the arresting officer promptly and efficiently and very properly discharged his duty in arresting each of these *criminals* under such circumstances."
6. When petitioners' counsel, in a letter application for a rehearing, pointed out the above facts and others of similar nature, to Judge Cox on September 5th, 1961, Judge Cox responded two days later by referring to the attorney's "publicity clients cases" and suggested that said attorney, who is of counsel to the present petitioners, had been guilty of some impropriety in seeking a rehearing of Judge Cox's decision. Upon information and belief, Judge Cox was motivated by his bias in favor of respondent and his antipathy toward those who oppose racial segregation, a feeling that will inevitably be present in the instant proceeding.

This created a great stir in legal circles in Mississippi. Judge Cox announced that he would discuss the disqualification petition on January 11, along with our removal petitions, and Bill began to lay plans for the

January 11 hearing by preparing to issue subpoenas for various police officials, the news reporters who had covered our arrests—and Mayor Allen Thompson.

The most important thing, of course, was that the boycott of downtown Jackson was holding up very well indeed. The Youth Council members, as well as those Tougaloo students who had stayed over for the holidays, distributed nearly 15,000 leaflets in the black community in Jackson by December 29. With the police making an increasing effort to apprehend the leaflet distributors, the teams of students had to function with great care: carrying folded leaflets in paper bags and under their coats and, in one case at least, in a folded umbrella, they moved quickly into a neighborhood, distributed everything they had, then moved quickly out again. The chain telephone calling, speaking at church services, and traveling as "undercover agents" up and down Capitol Street reduced black shopping in the downtown area to a minimum. We heard rumors, but were never really able to pin them down, that some white families in Jackson had stopped shopping on Capitol Street in an expression of sympathy for the civil rights cause. And we were certain that many white people stopped shopping downtown because they feared "trouble."

Some of the students who were doing the telephone chain calling had some interesting experiences. Like all southern towns, the black and white sections of Jackson are often quite close together—in some cases, almost integrated. Some streets, for example, were black one-half of the way down, and white the remainder. A student would pick out a street in our municipal directory, thinking that it was all black, but halfway down, he would suddenly find himself talking with white people. Most of them were hostile and some would curse violently. A substantial number would be simply indifferent—but a few would be surprisingly sympathetic.

In early January, with the Tougaloo students all back from the holidays, we found that we had so many boycott meetings that it was necessary to set up a tight schedule: on Monday nights, we met with Tougaloo students, on Tuesday nights with the Youth Council, on Wednesday nights with the Tougaloo students again; on Thursday and Friday nights we traveled around Jackson making contacts in the black community; on Saturdays the really big leaflet crews went out and the heavy telephoning took place; and on Sundays we all went into the black churches to discuss the boycott. Eldri cooked endless meals and pots of coffee for everyone. It made a very heavy schedule, but somehow, as I told some of the more critical and conservative members of the faculty, it was accomplished only by extending my own day.

At about this time, James Baldwin, the writer, came through and met with a large group of students at our home. He liked the idea of the boycott. Also, he talked with the students about the racial barriers existing in the North—and was the first person, I think, who was really able to convince most of the students that the North was not, by any means, a utopian situation. Indeed, he made it clear that the reverse was the case. He told Maria that he would "see you again when you have another tooth."

For the first time in the history of Jackson, the post-Christmas shopping sales did not cease in the downtown area when the old year ended but moved right on into January and displayed no signs of stopping. This was clear-cut evidence that the boycott was functioning successfully. Despite the continuing sales, the downtown stores were remarkably free of black shoppers. In the first week of January, we sent all of the businessmen a letter:

> You are fully aware that, for the past month, your place of business has been under a well organized and strongly supported boycott—a boycott designed to end discrimination against Negro workers and Negro consumers. Thus far, the following techniques have been used to push the boycott campaign: picket demonstrations, distribution of (18,500) leaflets, a thorough telephone campaign, and many meetings with interested individuals and groups. We are definitely prepared and willing to continue utilizing all of these techniques—plus others which may, as time passes, serve our purpose.
>
> Continuation of our boycott efforts may or may not be necessary—depending completely upon you. You may have been told, by those who preach relentless opposition to the development of American democracy in Mississippi, that the demands of the boycott are "blue-sky" in nature—that the movement seeks "everything." It is our position that the boycott is aimed at ending discrimination against Negro workers and Negro consumers and, in that context and taking into consideration the fact that the situation in your place of business may warrant additional demands, this is essentially what we ask:
>
> 1. hiring of personnel on the basis of personal merit without regard to race, color or creed; and promotion of such personnel on the basis of both merit and seniority without regard to race, color or creed
> 2. an end to segregated drinking fountains, an end to segregated restrooms, and an end to segregated seating
> 3. service to all consumers on a first-come, first-served basis
> 4. use of courtesy titles—such as "Miss," "Mrs.," and "Mr."—with regard to all people.
>
> There is nothing in these demands that is inconsistent with the humanistic principles upon which the Jewish and Christian religions and this nation were founded.
>
> If you are interested in meeting with our representatives, we suggest that you contact the N.A.A.C.P.—and we shall be indeed glad

to meet with you. On the other hand, we frankly wish to make it quite clear that we are fully prepared and very willing to—if necessary —continue this boycott in the most militant fashion possible until the specific demands that we have made are met.

If it is necessary in order to secure these specific demands, we shall push our campaign on a week after week and month after month basis until the boycott is rooted in the traditions of the Jackson area as a permanent institution.

It is your decision.

Their decision apparently was not to respond in any fashion, with the exception of several who telephoned Tougaloo and the NAACP offices and cursed. A segregationist lawyer in Jackson attempted unsuccessfully to get the U.S. postal authorities to arrest us for using the mails in this fashion.

But there was a significant crack in the Mississippi monolith from another direction. In early January, twenty-eight young Methodist ministers, from several sections of Mississippi, signed a statement entitled "Born of Conviction," in which they called for an "atmosphere for responsible belief and free expression" and indicated their support of the official Methodist position condemning discrimination because of race, color, or creed. Although quickly supported by several prominent laymen, the ministers incurred threats and violence and, in many cases, received these from members of their own congregations. No grassroots support from the white community came their way, and one by one they began leaving the state.

Again in early January, Mayor Thompson made a major move against the boycott when he announced that, on January 14, a large-scale affair would take place in downtown Jackson, which all black people were urged to attend and which would "honor" Willie Richardson, a noted athlete at the state-controlled Jackson State College for Negroes. Quite a program was lined up by Mayor Thompson, in association with Jacob Reddix, the Negro president of Jackson State and a quite conservative person. Immediately following the mayor's announcement, all mass media in a wide area in and around Jackson immediately launched a campaign to attract blacks into the downtown area on January 14. It was an ill-concealed attack upon the boycott. Purred the *Jackson Daily News* as it sketched out the proposed itinerary:

Special honors being planned here . . . for Willie Richardson, outstanding Jackson State College gridiron star and four-year All-American, are well deserved and typical of the respect held for this Jackson Negro educational institution. . . . Mayor Allen Thompson plans to greet Richardson at the City Hall Monday, joined by city civic and business leaders, and proclaim Willie Richardson Day. A parade from City Hall to Capitol Street and out to Jackson College will follow with appropriate honors and a climaxing dinner at the college Monday night. This occasion . . . is typical of the opportunity afforded in Jackson and the recognition accorded such ability as that demonstrated by Richardson. . . . Here is further example that Jackson works together. . . .

No one begrudged Willie Richardson his honors, but we were not going to see the Jackson boycott impaired in any way. An unsuccessful attempt was made to reach Willie Richardson and persuade him not to join this endeavor. We initiated an intensive campaign to persuade people to stay away from the whole affair. I took an extra-large bundle of our latest boycott leaflets to a Jackson State student who, with his friends, distributed them on a *sub rosa* basis on the campus—and did so at 3 A.M., since to be apprehended by the school authorities would result at least in expulsion.

Willie Richardson Day came to Jackson. The mass media were talking about the many thousands of blacks who were expected to show up in the downtown area, and the administration of Jackson State College even dismissed school for the day—with the expectation, of course, that the 2,000 Jackson State students would immediately proceed downtown. Out of Jackson's 70,000 black people, only about 350—by the count of three separate spies of ours—went downtown to hear Allen Thompson talk about the "fine race relations that our city enjoys" and to see a number of the businessmen under boycott present Willie Richardson with gifts.

While all of this was developing, our legal maneuvers were moving into open court. Bill Kunstler arrived in Jackson the day before the January 11 hearing, half expecting arrest on contempt-of-court charges stemming from the Cox disqualification petition. We were followed from the airport to Jess Brown's law office by several automobiles with long aerials at the back, but there was no arrest. Jess Brown had already seen that the subpoenas for the mayor, the top police officials, and the newsmen were being served.

The next morning, all of us left for the Federal courtroom in the upstairs of the post office building. We parked and detoured long enough to go down to the Woolworth store to measure the sidewalk in front, in order to prove that it was completely impossible for a handful of pickets to obstruct it. Bill and Jess Brown met at the post office and went up to the courtroom. We picket defendants dallied downstairs for a few minutes, then went into an elevator. Just as we had gotten in and, indeed, as the door was closing, a white man rushed up, pushed the door open, and joined us for the ride up. He turned with a sort of "Well, I made it" smile which did not quite materialize—since he was Allen Thompson and the recognition was mutual. It was a silent elevator ride and our companion was the first person out when it stopped.

The court was full of people. The segregationists had their men out in force, Citizens Council types. Aaron Henry and a delegation had come down from Clarksdale to be with us, and Bill Higgs, the embattled white Jackson lawyer, sat in. Judge Harold Cox, a large, rather fat and sleepy-looking man, came into the court and, after everyone had stood, seated himself and appeared to glare at all of us. Right behind him, on the wall, was the only segregated mural that I have ever seen, a sort of depiction of the "Mississippi way of life": all of the white people, who seemed to be relaxing, were on one side, and all of the black people, who were working, were on the other.

An indication of the seriousness with which the power structure viewed the removal effort and the disqualification petition was indicated by the presence of one of Governor Barnett's top legal advisers, Tom Watkins, and the state attorney general, Joe Patterson. The hearing lasted for only a brief period and was marked mostly by sharp repartee between Bill Kunstler and Tom Watkins. Watkins claimed that no discrimination or civil rights issue existed in the picketing arrests since the police had arrested nonblack pickets at the same time they had arrested blacks. This was greeted by a roar of laughter from everyone. Judge Cox took the position eventually that the prime issue to be decided first was the matter of whether he was going to disqualify himself, and he indicated that he would come to a decision on that later in the month. That was the end of the hearing. It was a long distance for Bill to travel for so vague and short and unsatisfactory a proceeding, but we wrote it off to typical Mississippi harassment. A week or so later, Judge Cox refused to disqualify himself and we appealed his refusal to the Fifth Circuit Court in New Orleans.

All of those on "our" side—the pickets, Bill, Medgar, Aaron Henry, Bill Higgs—came over to our home, where Eldri served a fine meal. Later we had a long talk with Aaron Henry concerning the developing situation up on the Delta. The Council of Federated Organizations (COFO), a loose federation between the NAACP, SNCC, CORE, and SCLC—spearheaded mostly by Aaron Henry and Bob Moses and Dave Dennis—was beginning to take shape. After months of painstaking grassroots organization, based mainly around voter registration, things were beginning to move in several sections of the Delta. Despite the obstacles to voter registration, which ranged the full gamut from the extraordinarily involved Mississippi registration tests to flagrant economic reprisals and overt terrorism, black people were beginning at least to come to civil rights meetings—and some were attempting to register to vote.

A steady pattern of harassment was directed against those working on voter registration in the Delta, including Aaron Henry himself; and the problem of economic destitution, stemming from economic reprisals and automation techniques in cotton growing, was becoming extremely serious. In addition, winter was the lean period in the Delta for the sharecroppers and tenant farmers, and the people were particularly vulnerable. Leflore County, a Citizens Council citadel, had some months before cut off all distribution of Federal surplus foods, in a clear attempt to penalize blacks for voter-registration activities. Other counties, which had no surplus foods programs to terminate, reduced or cut out completely their welfare payments to black families. The struggling civil rights groups had launched a campaign to secure food and clothing and medicines from the North, but there was still no special interest in the rest of the country, with regard to Mississippi, and not a great deal of relief had arrived. Then too, people bringing these supplies—such as SNCC workers Ben Taylor and Ivanhoe Donaldson—who together had driven a truck down from the North to Clarksdale, had been arrested on completely fabricated charges in that town and jailed.

Both Medgar Evers and Aaron Henry, it developed, wanted someone with a sociologist's credentials to go into two of the counties and conduct a survey concerning economic destitution among rural blacks. The national office of the NAACP had joined them in this, feeling that the material could be used in dealing with a number of Federal agencies. I was asked if I would conduct the survey, and I agreed to do it during the few days between semesters at Tougaloo.

A few days later, I was up in the Delta to survey the poverty situation, stopping first in Clarksdale at Aaron Henry's drugstore—itself a battered veteran of several arson and bombing attempts. Two men from the U.S. Commission on Civil Rights, Norman Kurland and Chester Relyea, were there, studying the general situation. Later in the day I met the two SNCC workers, Taylor and Donaldson, who had just been released from the Clarksdale jail. Aaron Henry suggested that I go first to Tunica County, forty minutes or so away and one of the poorest counties in the United States.

A black minister who knew the area accompanied me as a guide into Tunica County. We picked out a strip of rural road, and I began interviewing families at great length—probing, as delicately as possible, into all aspects of their economic condition. It was the most poverty-stricken situation that I had ever seen, and was made all the more grim by the bleak and bitterly cold weather. From time to time white people who were traveling down the road would see the clergyman and myself going into a home or coming out and would slow down to give us a long, hard look. Once, while we were in the car, the minister asked if I had a gun. I opened the glove compartment and showed him a revolver. He nodded approvingly.

One of the Tunica County families, which included twelve people living in a shack whose stove was not successfully keeping the cold air away, was eating breakfast when we arrived: one large pancake, divided among all the members, with sugar sprinkled lightly on it. The head of the family, who had lost his work on a cotton plantation because the landowner had begun using cotton-picking machines and weed-killing chemicals, had no idea what he was going to do. "I've got no money to move on and nowhere to go," he told us, "and I've lived around here all my life." He apologized for not having any food to offer us. "If you'd come a while back," he said, "we would have had rabbit. But you can hardly find a rabbit now within ten miles around. I guess we've killed 'em all out."

Nearly all of the other families in Tunica County were in generally the same position. Virtually no white people worked as sharecroppers and tenant farmers, but there were a few and, although we didn't interview them, their position—what we could see of it—appeared to be only a little better than that of the blacks. Here and there the picture of rank poverty was broken by a large plantation owner's home. Later, I interviewed families in Coahoma County, where the same situation prevailed; and still later, I traveled in rural Madison County, only about fifteen miles from Tougaloo itself. Again, it was the same dismal picture.

In all, I interviewed in great detail forty-one families in the three counties—a total of 259 people. Four of the families were living slightly above the poverty norms of their area. The others existed in varying degrees of abject economic deprivation: no employment, heavy debts, shack-type housing, ill health. More than one half of the families were receiving no welfare or surplus commodities, even though they had made application for them. The others were receiving small amounts of welfare or small amounts of commodities on a sporadic basis. Some had gotten into economic difficulties immediately after they had attempted either to pay poll tax or register to vote. Others were direct victims of automation. It was a representative picture of rural black life in the state of Mississippi.

The root of the whole situation lay in the fact that virtually all of the land was owned by a few families, who could run their operation in any way they chose and who completely dominated the black sharecroppers and tenant farmers involved. It would have been negative enough had it been even a completely voluntary economic arrangement, but the fact that it was a feudal system—backed up by police power and the Citizens Council and featuring the rampant cheating of these sharecroppers and tenant farmers, virtually enslaving generation after generation through debt and fear—made it all the more horrendous.

Automation—the mechanical cotton pickers and weed-killing chemical compounds—was seriously aggravating the whole situation by its massive displacement of black families from the plantations on which they had at least scratched out a bare existence for generations. The onset of automation was increasing in momentum, especially since it was also being pushed with great zeal by white landowners as a means of mass retaliation against the efforts of Mississippi blacks to achieve basic human rights. Those comparatively few landowners who, owing apparently to a sense of paternalistic *noblesse oblige,* had once held back on their mechanization were now finding it easy enough to rationalize by saying that "the niggers asked for it when they tried to be as good as white people."

Once deprived of employment on the plantations and possessing no academic education to speak of (through no fault of their own), and possessing no job skills (again, through no fault of their own), thousands and thousands of these displaced black people were either eking out the thinnest possible existence in the rural areas, or else were moving into the towns and what cities there were in Mississippi, where they simply joined the thousands of poverty-stricken urban blacks already living there. As matters worsened for all of these people, rural or urban, the general reprisals against the civil rights movement continued in the tightfisted and arbitrary behavior of those local officials in charge of welfare and surplus commodities.

I drew up a lengthy report on all of this for the national office of the NAACP. As well as going into the causes and effects of poverty and setting forth each case history, it also made several recommendations: substantial welfare and surplus commodities, industry, democratic unionism, Federal public-works projects, and Federally sponsored training, and voluntary relocation—and the full-scale advancement of black political rights. The NAACP made a number of copies of the study, sending them to a variety of governmental agencies, where, I gathered later, they accomplished some good. In early February, in Jackson, I testified publicly and at great length on all of this before hearings conducted by the advisory committee to the U.S. Commission on Civil Rights. But no report, whether of mine or anyone else, could even begin to compare with what was beginning in the Mississippi Delta: the coming together of black people into grassroots movements and the beginnings of a push forward. It looked as if an interesting spring was ahead in the cotton country.

As soon as the rural-poverty report had been finished, I went down to that old battlefield in southwestern Mississippi, McComb. The president of the NAACP branch, C. C. Bryant, had written back in December to ask if I could speak at their Emancipation Day mass meeting in late January. I agreed to do so and the McComb NAACP then ran off a handbill advertising the affair, with myself featured as speaker. It was liberally distributed all over Pike County, and even in neighboring Amite County. This led to some speculation that my arrival might be awaited by the "wrong people." Eldri was tired of being cooped up in our home and insisted that she and Maria accompany me to the community. The night before I was due to speak, a terrific ice storm began to move down through Mississippi from the North. We bundled up Maria and, about half an hour in advance of the ice storm, drove the two hours or so down to McComb.

The ice storm arrived about the same time we did, and with some difficulty, we found the home of one of the men active in sponsoring the meeting, Dock Owens, who operated a small garage immediately adjacent to his home. He and his wife greeted us cordially, fed us, and other people began to gather. The time for the meeting arrived and all of us stepped outside to the cars—and a car full of rough-looking white men drove up.

There was a very long and very tense moment for everyone. The white men, it developed, wanted Dock Owens to do a little work on their car, but they found it difficult indeed to take their eyes from Eldri, Maria, and me. With a flourish, Owens waved them inside his little garage, and the rest of us got into my car and off we went, as quickly as possible, to the Mount Hermon Baptist Church.

About a hundred people were gathering there, many from out in the country. The church was old and extremely cold. The people were obviously frightened, and someone told us that we were the first non-black people to set foot in the church. I had brought along the Youth Council film projector and screen and an old film, made from several newsreel shots, depicting school desegregation in Clinton, Tennessee. We felt that perhaps showing the film first would break the atmosphere of acute tension that existed. Several men hung their coats over the church windows, and with Eldri operating the film projector, we all observed the Clinton situation.

But even after the film, the atmosphere was unchanged. The coats were removed from the windows and we began to conduct the formal meeting. Those of us sitting up on the rostrum could observe the people in the pews constantly turning around and apprehensively looking out the windows at the street. Clearly, either the hoodlums or the police or both were expected at any moment. A minister gave the opening prayer, and Red Hill, a large and grizzled man, led off with an old song, "Amazing Grace." But the people were still afraid and, indeed, appeared to become even more so when I arose to speak.

Eldri and Maria were sitting in the audience, and at the point that I began my speech, Maria injected herself into the situation—with loud and continuing wails. Eldri jiggled her up and down, but to no avail. Then a woman sitting next to Eldri reached over and took Maria, bounced her around a little. For a time the baby didn't cry, but then began again, and the woman passed her down to the next person. During most of my speech, Maria traveled up and down the rows of pews, and by the time she had reached the second row she had stopped crying. Much more important, the tension was now completely gone from the church.

My talk, based mostly around community organization oriented in the direction of boycotts and voter registration, went well. When it was over, many people, warmly responsive, rose from the floor to speak. It was a wonderful meeting. As we left the church, a man told me that he thought that I had given a good speech but that they should have billed "the baby as the main speaker."

It was now very late in January. Night after night, we met with the

Tougaloo students and the Youth Council members. The printing press in the faculty member's basement was working overtime and the black sections of Jackson were being continually blanketed by leaflets. Chain telephone calling and church visits were moving full steam ahead. We had, by this time, an intricate network of boycott contacts sprinkled throughout Jackson. Some were people such as those belonging to the Jackson adult NAACP whom we had known for some time; others were persons who had come up after a church service to indicate that they would like to take leaflets to their friends. An increasing amount of our time was spent carrying bundles to contacts over the whole area. In addition, we had contacts who took leaflets and distributed them in such areas as adjoining Madison and Rankin counties, and even into such closed citadels as Yazoo County.

Each time that we put out an issue of *North Jackson Action,* we ran off more copies than before, and we were now sending out about 150 of each issue to individuals and organizations throughout the United States. Small amounts of money would come in from the outside world in answer to our fund appeal—with the most dependable source being $50 each month that Harry Stamler, a watchmaker in Scottsdale, Arizona, would send regularly. Sometimes a black church in Jackson would take up a collection. We were able to meet the monthly payments on the film projector and to pay the leaflet costs.

The boycott itself was proceeding very well. Our "spotters," who wandered up and down Capitol Street, felt that the campaign was becoming increasingly effective. Although the mayor appeared to have given up his idea of a million-dollar lawsuit, police were still very thick in the downtown area, walking up and down the streets themselves or standing on corners. The "post-Christmas" shopping sales were still continuing, unabated, and another indication of the boycott's effectiveness came when, about this time, Allen Thompson announced that the city would waive the annual property taxes for any Capitol Street businessmen who could not afford them. Recalcitrance was still the rule as far as the mayor was concerned, and he made this clear in a speech addressed to the Bessemer, Alabama, chamber of commerce:

> We must have the courage to resist the efforts of those who would take over our businesses by picketing, by boycotts, by harassment. We know that for a little while our profits will not be as good but that the money we do make will be free of the growing fear of what more will they demand. There is no satisfying a conqueror.

It was quite clear that by this time we were facing some serious problems. The downtown businessmen, backed by the whole Citizens Council-political-economic complex were not, no matter how much money they might be losing, going to sit down and constructively negotiate. This was true even with the little grocery-store chain which we had under boycott and which, because it served an essentially black clientele, was losing a tremendous amount of money. And there was no bail-bond money available for the sort of large-scale direct action which might bring matters quickly to a head. Indeed, there was no bail bond available of which we knew for even a few more pickets. We faced a very long and a very tough haul.

It was also clear by this time that the national office of the NAACP was not much interested in our campaign in Jackson. Although it had been kept informed of developments, through the *North Jackson Action* and other communications, to say nothing of Medgar, not a word about the Jackson boycott endeavor had appeared in any of the national NAACP publications such as the monthly magazine *Crisis*. We had never quite understood our difficulties in securing bail bond prior to the initial picketing in December. Other groups had lent a hand at various points: SCEF and SCLC's Gandhi Society, for example. But the home office of our parent organization had been silent even though, again and again, we had wistfully written in our own publications that the boycott was being backed by the NAACP "at all levels."

Our problem appeared to be directly related to the whole matter of relationships between the Mississippi NAACP groups and the national office. We knew, for example, that Aaron Henry had frequently felt that the national office was being slow to assist the struggle in Mississippi; and we knew that Aaron Henry himself had been criticized by the national office for his friendliness and cooperation with such groups as CORE, SCLC, and SNCC. In early January at a meeting of the Jackson adult NAACP, Medgar had publicly indicated his feeling when he had said that the Jackson school-desegregation suit had not yet been filed by the NAACP, even though the lawsuit had been essentially prepared for some time. Medgar, who had children as plaintiffs in the proposed school action, said that he had written a strong letter to the national office asking that the process be speeded. We had heard, too, that the national executive board of the NAACP was split on such matters as the desirability of direct action in general, as well as on the issue of involvement in Mississippi, and that many of the top NAACP staff people were also divided on these issues. It seemed to us to be a very strange world, up there in New York City.

But it was a strange world in Mississippi, and a bitterly harsh one at that, and we had no intention of letting the boycott of Jackson slow down in any fashion. Indeed, we intended to bolster it in every possible way.

In late January, at the regular board meeting of the Mississippi NAACP, I made a resolution to the effect that a state-wide bail-bond committee be set up to develop a reservoir of property bonds. The proposal was unanimously approved, and a committee was appointed, of which I was a member; but it was clear that the geographical separation between the committee members and, more fundamentally, our old problem of unencumbered black property in the state, made this project, at best, a long-range attempt.

For the past several months, the head of the Tougaloo social science division, Dr. Ernst Borinski, had been spearheading a pioneer student exchange project: several Tougaloo students would go up to a northern college or university for a week or two, and "yankee" students would come down to Tougaloo for the same period of time. Always, these northern students, such as the Oberlin contingent that had arrived just prior to Thanksgiving, had expressed considerable interest in civil rights matters in Mississippi. We had kept in touch with all of these student groups, through correspondence and our *North Jackson Action* and very good relationships had developed. Now we began to wonder just how they, and others beyond Mississippi, might help us.

Seventeen of the stores under boycott in Jackson were connected with either regional or national chains. It occurred to us that the time had come to build pressure against those chain stores outside of Mississippi—sympathetic boycotts. This, of course, would serve to apply pressures directly to those chain stores in Jackson, would help publicize our campaign, and might bring the situation more forcefully to the attention of the national office of the NAACP.

In the last days of January we drew up a long letter, which we mimeographed on Youth Council stationery. It discussed the background and development of the Jackson boycott movement, set forth the goals, listed the seventeen chain stores, and asked that people and organizations "boycott them, tell your friends to boycott them, write the stores letters telling them why you are boycotting them, picket them if you possibly can."

We sent these letters to almost 200 individuals and organizations. In addition, I attached personal, covering communications to several of them. To Gloster Current, national director of branches of the NAACP, I wrote:

> The attached mimeographed letter indicates the nature of our prob-
> lem. Would it be feasible for you to contact the various N.A.A.C.P.
> branches across the nation with respect to the situation here in
> Jackson—and with a mind toward their supporting us? The boycott
> movement here is primarily an N.A.A.C.P. project—and the help
> of the affiliated local organizations would be of great value to us.

At the same time, I sent an almost identical letter to Laplois Ashford, national youth director of the NAACP. We did not receive an answer from either of these officials.

But the response was generally positive from other quarters. James Farmer, the national director of CORE, wrote that "CORE is intensely interested and will want to help." SNCC pledged to publicize the matter of the seventeen stores and the Jackson boycott in general. The National

Student Association wrote indicating that it would put forth a "request for support and action on the part of our member schools." A number of the college students from the North agreed to do everything they could. In addition, Tougaloo students going north for a week or two, for a sojourn on other college campuses, carried the word to those areas. Anne Braden, the editor of the *Southern Patriot,* the monthly publication of SCEF, asked me to write a story on the Jackson situation, which I did, and it was published, along with a list of the seventeen stores. Several other liberal publications, such as the bulletin put out by the Student Peace Union, reprinted our letter asking for pressure on the chain stores.

Slowly at first, but with increasing frequency as February moved onward, we began to hear from those faraway contacts to the effect that letter-writing campaigns, and even picketing, were being applied to a number of the business concerns. It was a tremendous morale boost to all of us.

Each night Tougaloo students came over to our house to discuss the boycott and to work on various phases of the campaign. We bought two new coffeepots, and the number of meals that Eldri served increased steadily. In Jackson itself, the Youth Council was still growing and we found a building, sometimes used as a day nursery for children, which its owner, a former teacher, allowed us to use as a meeting place. In several sections of Jackson, we were meeting regularly with groups of adults who, although still very much afraid, were quietly assisting us. By this time, the network of youth and adult contacts throughout the whole region in and around the city had reached the point that, for example, we could split up a bundle of 5,000 leaflets into a hundred packets and give them to as many individuals, and within three or four days at most everything would be distributed. At the same time, the student leaflet crews went out again and again; and every ten days at most, I would take a large bundle of leaflets and travel the black laundromat circuit, leaving a packet in each. Chain telephone calling was becoming a very elaborate endeavor, and now, having covered a tremendous territory, students were beginning to go back over their telephone lists, talking with people whom they had initially telephoned back in mid-December. Most of the churches by now had a boycott speech every Sunday with regularity, either by a student speaker or by an adult member of the congregation.

And the effectiveness of the downtown boycott in Jackson continued to climb.

Clyde Kennard, who had attempted to enter the University of Southern Mississippi and who, instead, had entered Parchman penitentiary, was suddenly pardoned by Governor Ross Barnett—an action due in part to a petition campaign launched by Mississippi black students, as well as tedious and dedicated efforts by Attorney Jess Brown, and by a realization on the part of the Mississippi authorities that Clyde Kennard was dying from cancer.

Things were really beginning to move forward up in the Delta, especially in ever-recalcitrant Leflore County, where SNCC workers had been organizing for months. An intensive national campaign was finally beginning to secure tons of food, medicine, clothing, and books for the poverty-stricken blacks of the region, and in retaliation Mississippi segregationists were utilizing their traditional techniques. In late February, several buildings in the black section of the county seat of Greenwood, not far from the SNCC office, were set afire. When Sam Block, one of the SNCC workers, denounced this, he was arrested and charged with making a statement calculated to "breach the peace." Blacks began turning out by the dozens to embark on the frustrating endeavor of attempting to register to vote, and almost always turned down, they returned to try again and again.

A few days after the arson attempts, news came from Greenwood that a former Tougaloo student and now a SNCC worker, Jimmy Travis, had been shot through the neck and very nearly killed. He had been driving a car in which Bob Moses and Randolph Blackwell of the Atlanta-based Voter Education Project were riding. Thirteen shots had been fired by white men into their car.

Taken to the University Hospital in Jackson, Jimmy Travis eventually recovered. But matters moved fast in Leflore County after that: more attempts to register to vote, more shooting incidents, more trumped-up arrests. Civil rights people from much of the South began to enter this Delta county where the people were not retreating from terror but were moving forward. And what was happening in Leflore County began to send some very positive and encouraging shock waves through the entire state of Mississippi. A good many Tougaloo students who had, mostly because of fear, remained apparently oblivious to civil rights efforts now found that the shooting of Jimmy Travis and the new militancy of Delta blacks was forcing them to become involved. In the year and a half that had passed since the murder of Herbert Lee, down in Amite County, some things had changed.

At about this time, I found myself under rather heavy fire at Tougaloo. A minority of the faculty, but a substantial number, had become increasingly vocal in their criticisms of student involvement in civil rights matters, and this had led to some sharp criticism of me. Generally these faculty, most of whom were from the North, put it on the basis that too much time was being taken away from the academic work of the students. To this I would reply that a great era was upon Mississippi and that if ever students had a historical role anywhere, it was here and now. In any case, I pointed out, those students who became involved in civil rights activities soon found themselves "sparked" in such a fashion as to lead toward a new awareness of many sorts of issues: motivation for learning was being tremendously increased. But the faculty critics became ever more vocal because, I think, it was primarily a matter of fear—fear that their comparatively calm world at the college would be caught up in the new and initially harsh winds that were blowing ever harder through Mississippi. Once, students came up to me and told me that they had heard another faculty member state that I would not be hired for the coming academic year. That was unfounded. Dr. A. D. Beittel, the president, and other officers of the administration were, to use student terminology, "with it." They understood in a very positive way what was going on.

New allies arrived in mid-February. After an interlude of almost a year without any formal chaplain, a new minister and his wife came to Tougaloo—the Rev. R. Edwin King, Jr., and Jeannette King. Both were in their mid-twenties and both were, to say the least, unusual additions to the college. They were white Mississippians, he from Vicksburg and she from Jackson. Both were graduates of Millsaps College, a Methodist school in Jackson, and several years before, Ed had been arrested in a civil rights demonstration in Montgomery, Alabama, and had been beaten in jail. Later, they had gone up to Boston University and now, early in 1963, they had returned to their native state. Eldri and I immediately became close friends of the Kings. Unlike many of the faculty from the North, both Ed and Jeannette knew only too well what had to lie ahead for Mississippi—and what would be required to bring this about.

There were other allies. One day Mrs. Julia Bender, who worked as a librarian and who had been at Tougaloo for decades, came up to me and, with no preliminaries, spoke at length of her husband, the Rev. Jonas Bender, who until his death a few years before had been chaplain at Tougaloo. She told me that he was the first black in recent times to register and vote in Madison County and that on several occasions he had been forced away from the polls by white men with drawn guns— but that he had always tried to vote. She said that once a carload of armed white men had come to their home on campus and had called out the name of the Rev. Mr. Bender and he, in turn, had emerged from their back door and, carrying a gun, had come around the side of the house and had confronted the armed white men. They had immediately driven off.

"My husband was almost alone in these things most of the time," she told me. "And I am with you." And this meant a great deal.

While this difficulty with many of the faculty was brewing, the students injected themselves into the situation. One day I was told by some smiling students who knew that I had often missed the regular school assemblies held in the chapel that I should definitely come over to the chapel on that particular morning. I asked why, but the students were noncommittal. So I went and learned that I was being presented with the annual Faculty Citizen of the Year plaque, and that Joyce Ladner, who had taken an active role on behalf of civil rights, had been picked as the Student Citizen of the Year. Again, it was a morale boost for our civil rights faction.

5

It was well into March. Spring once again was coming to Mississippi. Three months had passed since the boycott had been initiated against the downtown shopping area in Jackson. And the campaign was holding up well.

More than 40,000 boycott leaflets had been distributed, and many thousands of telephone numbers had been called. Youth Council members and Tougaloo students had covered all of the black churches again and again to speak on behalf of the boycott—even those that featured conservative clergy. Informal boycott committees, composed of adults, were scattered throughout the black community of Jackson. Youth Council members had organized comparable structures within all of the black high schools of Jackson—Brinkley, Lanier, Jim Hill. When the Mississippi Teachers Association, an all-black affiliate of the National Education Association, held its annual state-wide convention in Jackson, the white businessmen, whose "post-Christmas sales" were still continuing, ran many advertisements in the mass media in an attempt to lure the black teachers downtown. But we had secured a list of all of the black elementary and high-school teachers in the Jackson area; and since we didn't have postage money with which to contact everyone, we were able to mail out specially prepared, mimeographed boycott letters, to each of which was attached a boycott leaflet, to 1,000 Jackson teachers, asking them to tell their out-of-town colleagues please to not shop in the downtown area. When the MTA convention came, virtually none of the Mississippi black teachers went down to Capitol Street.

In addition, we were receiving letters from faraway places which indicated that sympathetic action against the branches of the seventeen chain stores was either actually underway or was due to begin shortly in such large urban areas as Chicago, Denver, Indianapolis, Los Angeles, and New York—as well as in towns in Arizona, Indiana, Iowa, Ohio, and Wisconsin. Northern college students were still coming down to Tougaloo and returning North with a desire to assist us—and Tougaloo students were still going North and doing the same thing. Bob Zellner of SNCC, who ranged a wide territory, came through one day to leave some cartons of books at our home for Greenwood, and he promised to spread the word about our boycott through the areas in which he traveled.

For years a small number of white students at Millsaps College in Jackson had been coming out to Tougaloo to various evening lectures— much to the distaste, of course, of the Citizens Council and associated elements, including some of the Millsaps officials. A number of these Millsaps students were from other southern states, but some indeed were from Mississippi. Often they stopped at our home, and one evening several of them listened to Tougaloo students singing a very beautiful freedom song that had been written in commemoration of the slaying of Herbert Lee in Amite County—"We'll Never Turn Back":

> *We've been 'buked and we've been scorned;*
> *We've been talked about sure's you're born.*
> *But we'll never turn back,*
> *No, we'll never turn back—*
> *Until we've all been freed,*
> *And we have equality.*
> *We have walked through the shadows of death,*
> *We've had to walk all by ourselves. . . .*

That night the Millsaps students said that they would like to distribute boycott leaflets on the campus of their college. Two of them, who were from South Carolina, even said that they would like to picket sometime in support of the boycott. This came as an extremely pleasant surprise—marking, to the best of our knowledge, the first time that white students in Mississippi had ever even seriously considered doing this. We gave them the leaflets immediately and told them that we would be happy indeed to have them picket with us the next time a demonstration rolled around.

As it turned out, one or two did, very quietly, pass out some boycott leaflets on the Millsaps campus. But not very many were distributed. Fear arose out of the mists and traditions of their surroundings and strangled the effort even before it began—and even before one of the Millsaps officials called them in and told them never to do *that* again. When they failed to show up at a meeting which they said they would attend, a Tougaloo student and I went over to the apartment where two of them lived. Apparently they were not at home, but the door was open. On the table, face down, were the boycott leaflets we had given them. There was also a bag of groceries that had obviously just been purchased—and on the bag was the name of one of the stores under boycott. We never again attempted to contact them.

That we could understand, though, up to a point anyway. We were far less able to understand an official of one of the older pacifist organizations who came down from the North to spend a few days on a quick tour of the South. We asked him if he could help support our boycott in the North, but he seemed disturbed by the militancy of the campaign, and was noncommittal. Later, I received a letter from him in which he said, "I could not support your boycott. . . . My main reasons for not supporting it would be that it does not open any paths of reconciliation and is premised on the fact that all Whites are segregationists and enemies." He did not know Mississippi.

But more importantly than anything else, the boycott itself was continuing to go very well indeed. Although it was difficult to measure with precision the effect of the campaign, many long-time black residents of Jackson indicated that they felt that it was at least 70 percent effective in curtailing black trade in the downtown area. Around this same time, a few of the more liberal white clergymen in Jackson passed the word to us, through very devious channels, that they had learned from some of their parishioners that the economic strike was really being felt, and that the mayor and the Citizens Council and the more conservative business elements were devoting a great deal of time and effort to keeping other businessmen from reaching the negotiation stage. We noted, too, that some new business establishments, built in the outlying sections of Jackson at about this time and not under the boycott, were using courtesy titles to black customers; hiring several black clerks; installing two drinking fountains but leaving off the racial signs; and serving people on a first-come, first-served basis.

The police were still conspicuous on Capitol Street, and the businessmen, regardless of loss in trade, were still continuing their post-Christmas sales and were making no effort to negotiate constructively. Looking ahead a bit, we could see another crisis approaching: the key Easter shopping season, which, important in any section of the United States, certainly was in the South. There was no question but that, soon, it would be time for some more pickets, and I began to put out some feelers with respect to bail-bond money.

At this time, too, the Youth Council began to undertake the task of getting some of the people, especially the young people, together in the town of Canton. It was a project that was certainly close to my heart. Almost a year had passed since Eldri and I had made our little trips to that bastion of hatred to see Tom and Marcy Johnson—now free of their perjury charges and still living, uneasily, in Jackson. As the first rural Mississippi community that I had known, I was definitely interested in doing something there. At the same time, the Youth Council members, flushed with success in getting black students together all through the Jackson area, were now interested in extending their organizational efforts. Medgar was interested in rejuvenating the adult NAACP branch, dead for many years. All of us, of course, were interested in spreading boycott leaflets into the Canton area on a really continuous basis—since many of the Canton people had, traditionally, done much of their shopping in Jackson. And finally, Canton was clearly getting worse: in early January, a black had been found dead there, horribly mutilated.

Medgar contacted some of the people whom he knew in the area, and Tom Johnson helped spread the word. I talked with several of the Tougaloo students in my classes who lived in and around the town and who had already been instrumental in distributing boycott leaflets for us.

Our first meeting in Canton was the most terror-stricken situation that I had ever seen. No more than about four adults and half a dozen young people were on hand in a small room of an old church. The very night breathed menace, and each time a car passed, everyone stopped talking. Several of the people felt that the ring of spies operating under the Citizens Council and the sheriff had most likely got word of the meeting and that something was going to happen. Medgar, I, and several of our Youth Council members spoke at length on the necessity of community organization. The Canton people, those few who were there, agreed to distribute our Jackson boycott leaflets and to bring more people to the next meeting.

From that point the meetings grew larger. The adults reorganized their defunct NAACP branch and we organized a youth council. The atmosphere of terror waned somewhat, but never completely. Once, while meeting, we heard a firecracker go off a block or so away, and everyone jumped. Another time, following the close of a meeting, a man's car would not start and Medgar and I gave it a push with our hands, since the bumpers of our car and his would not fit. While we were pushing him, several cars with white men passed along the street, then turned around and came back. Our man's car suddenly coughed and started, and off he went. The white men by this time had passed us again and were down at the other end of the street, turning around. Medgar and I stood and watched them go by, then got into his car and left, driving slowly and, I think, defiantly.

We were now well into March and spring vacation was at hand for Tougaloo. Many of the students, however, stayed over during the holidays to work with the Youth Council on the boycott. Up in the Delta, the SNCC movement in Greenwood and in Leflore County was continuing to pick up steam. Early one morning, Medgar and I went up to Greenwood to attend a large mass rally that was scheduled for the evening and was featuring as its main speaker Dr. John Morsell, administrative assistant to Roy Wilkins. Traveling with us were Miss Mary Cox, an elderly but spirited woman quite active in the Jackson NAACP; Steve Rutledge, a white student from New York who had transferred down to Tougaloo in late January and who was playing an active role in the Youth Council; and a young woman almost out of Yale Law School who was going to be spending several days in Greenwood.

We arrived in town shortly after noon and went to the large church that SNCC was using as headquarters. The upper floor was loaded with food, medicine, clothing, and books that had come down from the North. An old student of mine walked in and greeted me. His name was Lawrence Guyot. At Tougaloo the year before, he had incurred the wrath of a rather puritanical chaplain who had, for a couple of minor infractions of school rules, hauled him before the college discipline committee. The chaplain had made a serious effort to get Guyot expelled. On two occasions, I had defended the student at meetings of the discipline committee which had lasted hours, and had been able to prevent Guyot's expulsion. Guyot had graduated, and the chaplain—not at all in tune with the spirit of Tougaloo—had not been rehired; but before the chaplain had left, he had made a point of telling me, "Guyot will never do anything worthwhile, anywhere." At that point we had had another heated argument. Now, as I saw my former discipline-committee client in the upstairs of the old church in embattled Greenwood, now a SNCC worker, it seemed to me that Lawrence Guyot was doing far more "worthwhile" things than most college graduates ever did. He was extremely enthusiastic about what was happening in the Delta.

He had every reason to be. Almost 1,500 people crowded into a church where the meeting was held that night, and at least 200 more were outside. Police cars were constantly circling the area but no one appeared to pay them any attention. The affair lasted for well over four hours and featured a tremendous amount of freedom singing. All the SNCC workers—Bob Moses, Sam Block, Willie Peacock, Frank Smith— and CORE's Dave Dennis seemed especially in tune with the people. Dr. John Morsell gave a good talk. It was the most enthusiastic meeting I had ever seen. Long as the road ahead might be for the people of the Mississippi Delta, those in Greenwood and Leflore County were, it was clear, well started—a long, long way from a year before when civil rights activity in the cotton country was, with the exception of Aaron Henry's movement in Clarksdale, practically nil.

Claude Sitton and another reporter from *The New York Times* arrived. I stepped outside and saw Jim Forman, executive director of SNCC, lumbering up to the church burdened down with cameras. He had just arrived from Atlanta. Bob Moses was sitting outside, looking as if he hadn't slept for months, but he looked happy. He asked how the Jackson boycott was going. I told him it was holding up well, but that it was taking a great deal of work and it looked as if it would be a long time in being won—but that we were going to keep right at it. "Maybe," I told him, "we can get it to the point in Jackson where we really have a big thing going." Again, I was thinking wistfully of Albany, Georgia.

He agreed that that was needed and wished us well. But I caught a feeling of pessimism in his voice as far as Jackson was concerned. He had spent some months living in the city a year or so before, working on the R. L. T. Smith campaign for Congress, and he knew the fear and the fear-based apathy that plagued the area.

Although I tried not to show it, especially to Youth Council members and Tougaloo students, I was somewhat depressed after that trip to Greenwood. What was happening up there was certainly invigorating; but despite the effectiveness of our boycott, matters were much too quiet in Jackson. The young people were definitely with us, all the way, but most of the adults—in fact, nearly all of them, including those who were carefully and quietly helping us boost the boycott—were still extremely afraid. Still, the events developing up in the Delta and in some other sections of the South were being featured daily in the mass media in Jackson. Somehow one could, if one were really perceptive, detect a stir at the grassroots in Jackson: in the churches in which we were speaking on Sundays, at the homes we were visiting. It was a kind of restlessness, and in my more optimistic moments I viewed it as being the vague beginning of an awakening. It was very difficult to tell.

Now the Easter shopping season was close and we needed pickets—and there seemed to be no signs of any bail bond anywhere around. Just before our visit to Greenwood, I had written Bill Kunstler:

> . . . the NAACP has given us no tangible aid of any kind. Medgar is certainly with us but, for several reasons, is unable to give us the help that we need or get it for us. Dr. Henry is too far away—and is, of course, tied up in his own very worthwhile battles. At a meeting of the state NAACP board in January, I moved that a state-wide bail-bond committee be set up to deal with this problem of bond. The motion was adopted and a committee duly appointed—but it has gone no further. The whole thing is pretty damned disheartening. . . . Briefly, then, we can expect no help—from the bail bond and other standpoints—from NAACP. It is going to have to come from elsewhere.
>
> I've seen a lot of situations, Bill, but this one strikes me as really being on the verge of accomplishing something extremely worthwhile. Something good is on the verge of happening—if the cards are played in the correct fashion. It is definitely the time for pickets. . . .

Within a few days after the Greenwood visit, a morale booster arrived in the mail. Victor Rabinowitz, the attorney in New York who had put up some of the bail bond for us in December, now agreed to put up $1,000 more. Shortly after this, word came from the Southern Conference Educational Fund to the effect that it would post an additional $1,000. This, then, gave us four pickets, and four were better than none. I indicated that we could use some volunteers and found that a great many young people indeed were ready to demonstrate. Four were selected and we picked April 4 as the day.

With the bail-bond situation temporarily in hand, we now sent another letter to all of the businessmen involved. Reviewing the history of the campaign, we once again set forth our goals, and stated that the boycott "has grown stronger each day and will grow stronger still." We asked for negotiations, and then went on to say:

This is not a fight of race against race—but let us tell you that it is a fight between humanitarian democracy on the one hand and, on the other, a strangling racism which even many of you must sometimes wish were gone entirely from the Mississippi scene.

The letter was publicized in the Jackson newspapers and the articles implied that the boycott's effect had not been felt. There was, of course, no mention of such matters as the city offering to waive the property taxes for those businessmen who could not afford them, to say nothing of the "post-Christmas" sales which were continuing right along.

A day later, Medgar received word from one of the more liberal white clergymen that there were several businessmen on Capitol Street who were rather desperate and wanted to "work something out." The minister was uncertain just how far these businessmen would go, but said that he would find out for us. We talked it over with the Youth Council and the Tougaloo students, who felt, as did we, that the businessmen should meet all of the goals of the boycott, and that they should certainly sit down with a democratically chosen negotiating committee of blacks. When the clergyman called the next day, he was apprised of this. He said that he had discovered that the businessmen involved were not prepared to make any changes, but simply wanted the boycott called off on their vague promise that, over a period of time, some changes would be quietly put into effect. This was, of course, unacceptable.

We had the bail bond and we had the four students who would picket on April 4—a date which, for the time being, we were saying nothing about publicly. Another crisis was fast developing, the matter of money for the day-to-day operation. The film projector was taking a healthy amount each month, and the leaflet expenses and such other boycott costs as postage were mounting rapidly. Harry Stamler, out in Arizona, still sent his fifty dollars a month with regularity, and other fund-appeal responses were trickling in, but although Eldri and I had put a good deal of our own money into the campaign, the treasury still threatened to expire at any moment. Word came from Steve Rutledge's father in New York that he would soon be in Washington, D.C., for a meeting of an organization in which he was especially active. It was called the National Civil Liberties Clearing House, a loose federation of groups interested in civil rights. Steve's father suggested that we send a copy of our fund appeal to the hotel at which he would be staying, and said that he would be happy to read it before that group.

We sent him the fund appeal immediately. He made good use of it, and it was immediately acted upon from one quarter: Roy Wilkins, although we hadn't known it, was present at the meeting and was one of the key people in the federation. He took the position that the national office of the NAACP would make a financial grant—possibly $500— to the Jackson NAACP youth. Congressman Adam Clayton Powell had recently attacked the NAACP for having non-black officers and members, a position that he later retracted, and Roy Wilkins took occasion at the gathering of the National Civil Liberties Clearing House to point out that the NAACP youth movement in Jackson had some non-black involvement, stemming from Tougaloo, and that this was the NAACP's answer to Congressman Powell.

I wrote once again to Laplois Ashford, the national youth director of the NAACP, mentioning the fact that, back in January, I had written asking for support concerning the Jackson boycott. I reviewed what we had been doing in Jackson and asked again for his assistance.

At this time there came brewing up from the southern scene, not far to the east of us—Birmingham.

There had been, of course, a few rumors drifting around, like smoke in the wind, regarding a major campaign that the Southern Christian Leadership Conference might be launching in Alabama. Now, listening to the radio at home, we heard of the initial indication of what lay ahead in Alabama's largest city. We were to hear and read in the days and weeks ahead of massive demonstrations unlike any ever held before in the United States, and massive fire-hosings, massive use of police dogs, and massive arrests.

Birmingham was just barely beginning when April 4 came and it was time for another of our little confrontations on Capitol Street. The bail-bond money had arrived. Jess Brown was ready. The picket signs were made up. In the early afternoon, I took the four pickets—Arverna Adams, Jimmy Armstrong, Frank Dickey, and Austin Moore III—out from Tougaloo and down to Farish Street on the edge of the downtown area. According to the strategy that we had developed, the students carried their picket signs in paper bags; then, two in one group and two in another, they went to the Woolworth store. Seventy-five to one hundred Jackson police were waiting, and across from the Woolworth store, in front of the restaurant owned by Aleck Primos, an official of the Jackson Citizens Council, about 200 spectators were gathered. A large number of newsmen were on hand. When the students were in front of the Woolworth store, they quickly took the picket signs from the paper bags and put them on, formed a little picket line—and were immediately arrested for "obstructing the sidewalk," a charge which later, with no explanation, was changed to "breach of the peace." The police did not take the signs immediately from the students. As the pickets were being driven off in police cars, they pressed their signs, face out, against the windows, thus advertising the boycott for longer than we had thought possible. We had them out of jail later that afternoon.

Late that night, Jess Brown and I got together in his little law office on Farish Street and drew up a removal petition for the four students, part of which Bill Kunstler dictated to us by phone from New York City. Once, Jess thought he could hear someone coming up the steps in the now deserted building. Matter of factly, he reached into his desk, took out the largest .38 revolver that I've ever seen, laid it by his typewriter, and continued working on the removal petition. No one came in, however.

Mayor Thompson was silent on the matter of the four pickets. But the sensation-oriented Jackson news media, especially radio and television, rose again to the occasion and publicized the whole matter far and wide. The next day, we mailed out almost 1,000 special boycott letters to key members of the black community, again asking for their assistance in supporting the campaign. A few days later, we mailed to the Jackson area 1,000 special issues of *North Jackson Action,* which contained an underlined statement on our part: *"There will definitely be more picketing in the near future—and matters, from this standpoint, will become increasingly interesting."*

Birmingham was now much on the minds of everyone. Marion Gillon, a Tougaloo student, would come over to our home after classes to talk about it. He was from that section of Alabama and was very excited. We were all enveloped by the electricity generated by Birmingham, as was the whole South, the nation, and the world. And there was more than just a little jealousy in our makeup, too—friendly jealousy. Just as we had once talked of an Albany as the best thing that could happen in Jackson, now we talked of a Birmingham. *Birmingham!* It was what we all wanted— and we wanted it in Jackson.

On April 9, Laplois Ashford telephoned me from New York City. Roy Wilkins had discussed the Jackson boycott with him. He was extremely interested in what we were doing in Jackson, hastened to assure us that at least $500 for boycott expenses would be on the way soon from the national office, indicated that NAACP headquarters might be able to build pressure against the seventeen chain stores, and thought that perhaps we could be given wider publicity than we had been receiving. He was interested too, he went on, in developing an NAACP "freedom youth corps" in the South. Although we had, each time it was published, sent copies of the *North Jackson Action* to the national office, as well as such other material that we had, Ashford now asked for a complete file of the publication as quickly as possible.

I mailed him the copies of *North Jackson Action* and a great deal of other material as well. It had been good to talk with Ashford, and it looked as if our long isolation in Jackson might indeed be over. About a week later, I received a letter from him, to which was also attached a letter to me from Roy Wilkins and a check for $500 for the Youth Council treasury. Laplois Ashford indicated that he and the new southeastern region NAACP youth field secretary, Willie Ludden, would arrive in Jackson within the next week or so to survey the situation and to see what could be done to help us.

Roy Wilkins's letter indicated that he had not been aware of our financial situation and expressed "surprise that no direct appeal had been made to this office for financial assistance either at the beginning of the campaign or after the treasury became low." He went on, "It might seem to many persons . . . that the National Office of the NAACP was indifferent to the needs of its college chapter and unwilling to contribute financially to the campaign being waged by it." But his letter was cordial in tone, and he assured us that "we stand ready to assist in any way until success has been achieved."

This was indeed good news! But now we were bewildered. Medgar, we knew, had done his best to secure help for us, but to no avail. We had always sent copies of our publications and other material to the national office of the NAACP, and we had written various individuals at that level, not Roy Wilkins himself, but other top men. We had never received replies. Not one word of our boycott campaign to date, or any mention of the Jackson picket arrests, had appeared in any NAACP publications that we had seen.

As I looked at Roy Wilkins's letter I felt that he himself, an extraordinarily busy man, had not known of what we were doing in Jackson. But others had. Why now the sudden interest?

One possible reason, of course, lay in the fact that Roy Wilkins had now learned personally of what was being done in Jackson. Possibly the fires of Birmingham—the most massive campaign against segregation ever waged in the nation and one that was being led by another civil rights organization, the SCLC—had put the NAACP in a position where it had to devote more attention to the support of direct-action approaches in the cracking of Deep South racism.

There may well have been another reason too. Rumors were rife within the civil rights movement that after Birmingham had been broken, SCLC might well come into Mississippi, perhaps to the embattled Delta, perhaps to Jackson. We had certainly heard nothing more than vague rumors. However, Aaron Henry was usually referred to as the president of the Mississippi NAACP, but he also happened to be the Mississippi board member of SCLC. Our whole legal defense in Jackson was being handled by Jess Brown, who was not a regular NAACP lawyer, and by Bill Kunstler, attorney for SCLC's Gandhi Society. Much of our bail bond in Jackson had been put up by the Southern Conference Educational Fund, whose president was the Rev. Fred L. Shuttlesworth of Birmingham —and president of the Alabama state SCLC affiliate and national secretary of SCLC.

We put aside our speculation and let the matter pass. Things seemed to be working through in a constructive fashion.

Our legal situation had been quietly moving along. The Fifth Circuit Court in New Orleans had upheld Judge Cox's refusal to disqualify himself in our picket cases, and the judge had set a new removal hearing for April 26. Bill Kunstler had sent down another petition to strengthen our case for removal some days before and Jess Brown filed it. The new petition charged, in effect, that Mississippi's discriminatory jury system, its segregated system of justice, the prejudicial atmosphere created by newspaper publicity and public statements of Jackson officials, would deprive us of an impartial jury. In conclusion, the petition stated:

> The maintenance by the State of Mississippi on both an official and unofficial basis of a system of laws calculated and intended to separate the Caucasian and Negro races and to segregate the latter in every aspect of life will make the enforcement of petitioners constitutional rights utterly impossible in the state courts.

This created a stir. To bolster our case, Bill, who was in Birmingham, had subpoenas issued a few days before the April 26 hearing for Governor Ross Barnett, Lieutenant Governor Paul B. Johnson, Mayor Allen Thompson, County Judge Russell Moore III, Police Justice James Spencer, a number of police officers, and several newsmen. This created an even bigger stir—although Ross Barnett and Paul Johnson took advantage of their executive prerogative to refuse the subpoenas.

Bill also had drawn up a sweeping lawsuit which he intended to file. This was aimed against the City of Jackson, Mayor Thompson, Chief of Police W. D. Rayfield, Judge Spencer, and Captain Cecil Hathaway of the city police. It asked for the appointment of a three-judge Federal court to enjoin Jackson from any further picketing arrests, damages of $10,000 each for the pickets, and a "judicial" construction easing the removal of civil rights cases into Federal courts. Even though everyone knew we would never really be able to collect financial damages, this created a good deal of comment.

On April 25 Bill flew into Jackson to handle these legal affairs. He was unshaven and haggard from having spent many days and nights in Birmingham, but more excited than I had ever seen him. With him was a man named Bob Stein from New York City, who was connected with both the Ethical Culture Society and the American Civil Liberties Union. We went immediately to Jess Brown's law office and then to the office of the Federal clerk of court. Police tagged along, following us. The next day, all of us were in Federal court together—the pickets, our lawyers, the various subpoenaed officials (minus Barnett and Johnson), observers from the Citizens Council, students, and newsmen. Judge Harold Cox was not present. Tom Watkins, the attorney for Mississippi, came in just minutes before the hearing was due to begin. He informed Bill that Judge Cox was in Hattiesburg, would not be able to make it over to the court in Jackson, and that obviously the hearing would have again to be postponed.

Obviously it would, and, just as obviously, this was more harassment.

Jess Brown was much angered at some harassment aimed against him. Although not a regular NAACP lawyer, he had been involved in the

NAACP-backed school-desegregation suit against Leake County, one of the several school suits that the NAACP was backing in Mississippi. Recently, Judge Cox had announced that Jess hadn't been authorized by one of the parents involved to bring the Leake County suit in her name. It looked as if an attempt was being made to get Jess Brown disbarred—a maneuver that would reduce by one-third the number of black lawyers in Mississippi who took civil rights cases. Cox had appointed a former chancery judge in Jackson, who was quite active in the Citizens Council, to process the case against Jess Brown. But the truth was with Jess, and eventually, after an appeal to the Fifth Circuit, he was exonerated.

That afternoon Bill, Bob Stein, and I were walking past the Governor's Mansion in Jackson down to the Federal building to attend to some more of the legal matters. As we passed the mansion, a young man about thirty came walking out. I recognized him from newspaper pictures as Governor Barnett's son, Ross Junior. When I told this to Bill, he immediately gave Ross Junior a hearty wave. The governor's son looked at us a little uncertainly, then waved back. Bill waved again. Young Barnett then came over with a sort of "don't I know you?" expression. Indeed, he may have seen all of us on television that very morning leaving the Federal court. Bill introduced himself, then Bob Stein, then me. Suddenly Ross Junior remembered. He gulped, backed away, and, walking very fast, escaped to the other side of the street.

Laplois Ashford and Willie Ludden had just arrived in Jackson. Both were extremely cordial. Willie Ludden, a newcomer to the NAACP staff, was from Georgia and had just been discharged from the army. They attended our Youth Council meeting, then spent some time traveling around Jackson, talking with various people. Then we talked at great length. Both seemed quite impressed with the work that was being done in Jackson. Diplomatically, I asked why the Jackson boycott movement had been ignored for so long. I received the impression, without too many specifics, that there were many policy differences involved in the national office of the NAACP, but that the youth division was emphatically behind us.

This was excellent news. I then went on to raise another point— *Birmingham!*

I told them that in Jackson we needed direct action not only to push the boycott through to a full measure of success but to accomplish some other cracks in the wall. We needed a great deal of direct action. There was no argument. Both agreed and promised to do everything that they could, as fast as possible, to see that we had the opportunity to utilize considerably more direct action than had been available to us in the past.

That evening, just before they left Jackson, Ashford and Ludden were at our home at Tougaloo, where many students had gathered to meet them. Bill Kunstler and Bob Stein, who were there, were to head back to New York City the next day. Bill spoke at great length on the importance of Birmingham. The two NAACP staff men told the students that the national office of the NAACP was firmly behind the campaign in Jackson. It was a great evening! As he left, Laplois Ashford again promised to do everything that he could for us.

April was now drawing to a close. The weather was becoming very warm in Mississippi. Birmingham was still rolling along like a great wave, and its sparks were catching fire in many areas throughout the South. And in Alabama the white Baltimore postman, William Moore, was shot down and killed as he attempted to walk with integration signs through Alabama to Jackson. There was continuing action up in the Delta branching out from Leflore County into other counties.

The segregationists were stirring much more than usual too. Birmingham had frightened them, and each day one heard of nighttime violence in one part or another of Mississippi. A gubernatorial election was beginning to take shape in Mississippi. Since Ross Barnett could not succeed himself, Lieutenant Governor Paul Johnson had announced his candidacy, as had others, and it was clear that the issue of racism would play more of a role in this election than in any others for decades past—and that the man who screamed "Nigger!" and "Never!" loudest would win. It looked like very hot weather ahead for all of us.

The Jackson branch of the NAACP was trying to build some enthusiasm concerning voter registration in the city, having observed the high degree of interest in this developing up in the Delta. I brought Youth Council and Tougaloo students into Jackson on a number of nights, and all of us did a good deal of canvassing street by street. It was very tough work not only to explain Mississippi's incredibly complex registration procedures, or the importance of people's registering and voting, but also to persuade people actually to try to register. Medgar had lined up several cars and drivers, and when a person indicated that next day, for example, he'd be willing to try to register down at the courthouse, we would take his name, give it to Medgar, and next day the car would come around. But again there was the fear, and although most would agree to make the attempt, very few indeed actually did so. One night I was off on a side street, going from door to door along a stretch of thirty little cabins, all connected. At one of them, a girl opened the door—a student of mine at Tougaloo. She immediately invited me to meet her parents. It was an extremely small, poverty-stricken home, and one blue light bulb hung from the ceiling. Several small children were attempting to sleep in one bed. I had known that the girl was on a scholarship, but I had not known that her circumstances were as poor as this. Her parents were afraid to register to vote. With me there, she tried, rather desperately I thought, to persuade them to do so. They became very embarrassed. I changed the subject to the girl's plans following her graduation from college, and we had a very nice visit during which we dropped the matter of voter registration. Then I excused myself and went on to the next door.

We were also making an effort to locate students who would, when the time came, make application for entrance into the white universities of Mississippi. On several occasions, Medgar came out to our home to meet with various Tougaloo students who had expressed interest. The talks often became quite personal, involving childhood experiences and dreams for the future, and frequently went on for hours. But when it came right down to it, virtually none of the students would seriously consider seeking entrance. It was not so much a matter of their own well-being, although the tribulations suffered by James Meredith entered into the picture. Mostly it was fear for their parents. We finally found two students at Tougaloo who agreed tentatively to make application when the proper time arrived, which Medgar felt would be quite soon. He himself was considering entering law school at the University of Mississippi—say, in the fall of 1964.

The boycott was moving along very well—leafleting, telephoning, church visits, letters—and very few blacks shopping in the downtown area. We were all waiting to hear from Laplois Ashford. Finally he called me.

He was enthusiastic and immediately told me that he had news that I would like. Could I get a number of Tougaloo students ready for a demonstration, to take place a few days away, on the weekend of May 11 and 12? I knew that we had a meeting of the Mississippi NAACP board of directors on May 12 and that an NAACP mass meeting was scheduled for the afternoon of that day. I told Laplois Ashford that we could secure all the students needed, and that there couldn't be a better time than that weekend. Then he indicated that perhaps Roy Wilkins or Dick Gregory could make it down to participate in the demonstration. This was really sounding good! I assured him that we would line up the students immediately, then asked him how many could participate. Ashford was not certain about the specific number, but said that he would be in touch with me again quite soon.

I moved fast to recruit the students. There was no problem. Although several wondered if this might interfere with their final examinations, I pointed out that the exams weren't due to start until after May 12. Within a day or so, I had specific commitments from about forty students and could easily have gotten many, many more just from Tougaloo alone. We also had the whole Youth Council in Jackson, as far as that went, although most of its members were high-school students. Because they were not due to get out of school until about June 1, we did not want to involve them in demonstrations unless absolutely necessary. To use them before school was over would be to run the risk of their expulsion from schools that were securely under the thumb of Mississippi authorities. In any event, we had many potential demonstrators. All we needed was bail-bond money.

On May 8 Laplois Ashford called me again. He sounded bitterly disappointed; the news was very bad. Things were not going at all well, he said, and it looked as if we would not be having a demonstration the coming weekend. There were some, he indicated, who felt that any demonstration in Jackson at this time would be overshadowed, publicity-wise, by what was happening in Birmingham. These people felt that such a demonstration should be postponed, possibly for two weeks, maybe even longer. From him I received the impression that there were others who questioned the desirability of such action at any time. He was not certain about what was going to occur.

For me it was almost too much. Again and again we were going to be disappointed. But I knew that Laplois Ashford had done his best. I pointed out to him that final examinations would be going on at Tougaloo beginning immediately after May 12 and lasting for ten days or so. From that standpoint, as well as others, including the fact that the NAACP board and mass meetings were being held on May 12, we ought to have that demonstration on the coming weekend.

He said that he thought it would be impossible. I began to wonder if it would ever be possible. And I knew that we needed far more than just one demonstration—however sizable one was, and despite the prominence of some of its participants. We were going to need many demonstrations indeed.

We left it sort of hanging. He would continue to do his best. I told the students, who were quite disappointed. I sat and drank coffee for a time, then reached for my typewriter. To Laplois Ashford I wrote:

It was good to speak with you on the telephone a few minutes ago. There are a number of points—pertinent to the matter of our Jackson boycott and its direct action activities—that I should like to discuss.

I regret that it was felt that the demonstration proposed originally for this weekend was moved up two weeks or so—since we definitely need direct action here as soon as possible, and since the mass meeting set up for this Sunday would have fit in well as a public call to arms. As I indicated, we had lined up a number of student demonstrators for this weekend but, since the postponement has occurred and since final examinations begin at Tougaloo next week, it will now be necessary to wait until about May 23—at which date, the Dean has just informed me, the finals will be over. While granting the fact that Birmingham will overshadow, publicity-wise, anything that we might do in Jackson in the immediate future, it cannot be emphasized enough that we need a demonstration here—and one involving national figures—as soon as possible after May 23.

And we need more than just one demonstration. Although succeeding demonstrations need not necessarily involve national figures—although this would be, of course, desirable—we need, *at the very least,* one demonstration each week for an indefinite period of time.

Our boycott is now entering its sixth month. Twelve pickets have been arrested so far. Almost 60,000 leaflets have been distributed and we plan on putting out a minimum of 10,000 each month from now. We have mailed out literally thousands of pieces of mimeographed literature to people in the community. Our boycott workers have spoken at length in almost every Negro church in Jackson—and most of these churches have been visited many times. The enthusiasm on the part of the clergy and parishioners has been very high. The Youth Council members and the Tougaloo students, working terrifically hard on this project on a week after week and month after month basis in order to make a dream come true, have done the hard and tough spadework. While the students will, of course, continue to play a major role in the movement, there is no question but that a steadily increasing number of adults are taking active positions. Certainly, the great majority of Negro people in the Jackson area are supporting the boycott and, from another standpoint, a community—previously unorganized—is now becoming structured in a "movement" sense.

Jackson constitutes, as one authority has so aptly put it, "the worst segregation complex in the nation." Other organizations—such as ACLU, Gandhi Society, and SCEF—have helped us out greatly with respect to legal defense and bail bond—and the $500 which the National Office sent us has aided us (and will continue to aid us for some time to come) tremendously. Now we have something going here that can crack this mess wide open in Jackson—and can do it in an extremely positive fashion. But, in order to do this, we must have direct action and much of it—we have definitely reached that stage. Frankly, it is going to be extremely difficult, if not virtually impossible, to raise local property bail bonds. The only place that we can get adequate bail bond is through the National Office—either from it directly or from its contacts. We also need the participating figures of national stature and—as soon as possible—negotiations with the chain stores, sympathetic national picketing, and publicity.

We shall—no matter what happens—continue to push this boycott in every way that we can. The interests of 70,000 people are involved and a successful precedent in the Jackson boycott will mean much indeed to this unhappy state.

Can you let us know—as specifically and quickly as possible—what aids we can expect from the National Office?

I sent a carbon copy of the letter to Roy Wilkins, to Gloster Current, director of branches of the NAACP, to Aaron Henry, to Medgar, and to

Professor Allan Knight Chalmers, president of the NAACP Legal Defense
and Educational Fund.

We settled down to await the reaction, which I felt, perhaps by
intuition, we were going to receive quite soon. But we had no opportunity
to brood on that matter, since another interesting problem came to the
fore.

Some weeks prior to all of this, back in mid-April, we had learned
that the annual Southern Literary Festival, drawing people from all the
southern states, was going to be held at Millsaps College, and that one
of the evening sessions, which would be conducted in the building known
as the Christian Center, was going to feature the noted Mississippi writer
Eudora Welty as main speaker.

When that night came, I went with several students to the affair.
We were of course aware that for perhaps as long as the college had
existed, no black people had ever been admitted to any of its functions.
We parked, quickly walked up the steps of the Center, past the rather
surprised girls who were giving out programs, and sat right down in the
front of the room. With the exception of a few tough looks from several
people, we were scarcely noticed, or so it seemed to us. However, the man
from the Millsaps English department who was sitting on the stage turned
beet red and seemed so fascinated by us that he could scarcely take his
eyes from our little delegation. Eudora Welty gave an excellent lecture,
including a reading of one of her short stories—which we could follow
as she read since we had brought along several copies of her work.
When the evening was over we walked slowly outside. A group of
Millsaps students came up and indicated that they were quite glad that
we had attended. Other than that, no one appeared to notice us, and that,
in its own small way, marked a significant breakthrough in Mississippi.

We were aware, of course, that this did not necessarily mean that
the Christian Center was really open. Many of the people at the affair
were from outside Mississippi, although Mississippians predominated.
Then too, we had not been expected; indeed, this had not been done
before.

On May 9 the *Three Penny Opera* opened for the general public at
the Christian Center. Eldri and myself, Jeannette King, and several students
went to Millsaps, having secured tickets from a friend who had purchased
them for us in advance. We were stopped by the ushers, who told us
that those in our group who were white could of course enter, but
that those who were not could not. The college, it seemed, had a "policy"
to which it had to adhere, but it would be only too happy to refund the
money of those who could not attend. We informed the ushers that either
all of us entered or all of us didn't, but that by virtue of the fact that
we were all human beings and the fact that we had tickets, we should now
be admitted without any delay. At that point, John H. Christmas, dean
of the students, appeared and informed us that if we persisted in
attempting entrance, he would call the police. We had decided in advance

that if the police were called, we would leave—but not until then. By this time, a large group of Millsaps faculty, students, and members of the community were standing and watching, disturbed and shocked. The dean walked off and apparently called the police; their cars began to arrive soon. We left, and back at Tougaloo I wrote a letter to the Millsaps president, Homer E. Finger, Jr., in which I recounted what had occurred, concluding with, "No matter the elaborate character of the rationalizations erected, it remains a basic historical fact that neither genuine Christianity, nor functional democracy, nor academic health can be safeguarded and expanded by behavior such as that encountered by ourselves at The Christian Center of Millsaps College." I sent copies to Dean Christmas, the school newspaper, and the student government.

The next night, of course, we returned. Ed King, very much disturbed at the conduct of his alma mater, accompanied us. We were refused tickets even before we reached the ticket desk. Dean Christmas stepped forward, joined by a man who we later learned was one of the physical-education instructors and who carried a tape-recorder. The dean ordered us to leave and we refused to do so. Ed King then began to converse with a number of faculty that he knew. The Tougaloo students began to talk to several Millsaps students whom they recognized. I told Dean Christmas that if we weren't admitted, we might well publicly testify about this to the Mississippi advisory committee of the U.S. Commission on Civil Rights, file a complaint with the American Association of University Professors and similar organizations, and publicize the whole matter through various news media. Further, I told him that if we were arrested, we would file a civil lawsuit for damages against him and against any other agents of the college involved.

We were standing at the ticket desk and the girls behind it kept trying to move up or down the table so that they could sell tickets to the Jacksonians who were piling up behind us; but we kept shifting with them so as to be always right in front. I looked back and could see a white man behind one of our students, Austin Moore. The man looked like the very epitome of white Mississippi, right down to the hard lines on his face and the wide-brimmed hat that he carried. A ticket seller caught his eyes, motioned for him to step out of the line and come over behind her to get a ticket. He knew, I am certain, what was going on, and he smiled pleasantly at her, and at us, and said, "Thank you, miss. But I imagine that I'll just wait my turn in line behind this young man." And he smiled again at all of us.

By this time, Dean Christmas had gone somewhere. The police arrived very soon, parked, and came inside the building, some dozen or so, carrying guns and clubs. We could see the police dogs out in their cars. The Millsaps people, and the others standing around, looked shaken to their bones. We nodded pleasantly and left, the police trailing along behind us. We went to the home of President Homer Finger several hundred yards from the Christian Center. His son said that Millsaps' president was not home at the time. We then returned to Tougaloo, where I wrote another letter to President Finger, again recounting what had occurred, and again mailing copies to the dean, the school newspaper, and the student government.

The next day we mimeographed copies of the two letters and sent them to many Millsaps faculty members. A few days later President Finger wrote a brief letter to me, expressing his regret concerning "the embarrassment which was caused both to you personally and to the College," but he went on to say, "Some weeks ago I had communicated to your President the prevailing policy at Millsaps College having to do with the seating of our Negro friends at college productions."

But the students and faculty at Millsaps, disturbed by these events, began exerting pressures. A great many Millsaps students signed a petition asking that their institution's programs be opened to all. Faculty spoke out. Later it became quietly known that Millsaps productions were, indeed, open now to all people.

By Saturday, May 11, I had received no reply from anyone in the national office concerning the letter that I had written to Laplois Ashford three days before. The Tougaloo students and the Youth Council members were very restless and the feeling was growing that the national office was attempting to avoid involvement in Jackson. That morning I saw Medgar, who told me that my letter had done some "shaking up" in New York City, but he did not know any specific details. Clarence Mitchell, head of the Washington, D.C., office of the NAACP, arrived in Jackson on Saturday afternoon to speak at the mass meeting the next day. Soon after he came, he and I and Medgar, along with Bob Ming, who was an NAACP lawyer from Chicago and in town for certain aspects of a school desegregation suit, gathered at the home of Jack Young.

I assumed that Clarence Mitchell knew something of the Jackson situation and indicated that it was imperative that we receive assistance from the national office—not merely support for the downtown boycott alone, but assistance geared toward a series of demonstrations against many aspects of discrimination and segregation in Jackson. He seemed in accord with this and asked how much I felt was needed. I replied that we needed, of course, everything we could get, and that while one demonstration a week would be the very minimum that we needed to win the boycott itself, Jackson actually required much, much more. We discussed the matter further in a general way, but nothing specific was determined.

It was getting dark when we left Jack Young's home that evening. The meeting of the Mississippi NAACP board of directors was convening in the Masonic Temple in the morning. There was now no question but that I was going to raise the issue of demonstrations in Jackson and support from the national office before that group. I indicated this to Medgar before we parted that evening, and he nodded emphatically; it would be an excellent idea.

At Tougaloo, I talked with more students who wanted to know what was developing. I told them that we were going to fight to build a really active movement in Jackson and that under no circumstances should they lose hope. But they were clearly discouraged.

I thought more about the matter that night. There were things going on, the specifics of which I did not know. Obviously there were basic disagreements within the national office of the NAACP regarding Jackson. This indicated that there were those, of whom Laplois Ashford appeared to be one, who were supporting us. In any event, we needed to keep up the pressure. Very late that night, I sat down and quickly drew up a resolution. It asked the Mississippi NAACP board of directors to go on public record as being in full support not only of the Jackson boycott movement but also of a full-scale NAACP-backed campaign in Jackson aimed at ending all segregation in public accommodations and places of business and publicly owned tax-supported facilities, and aimed at securing fair employment practices at all levels of private and public employment. It was a strong resolution and mentioned not only legal action but "massive" and "intensive" direct action in the sense of picketing, sit-ins, and *mass marches*. I made several copies of the resolution for the other members of the board.

I showed it to Eldri, who approved, and I took it to the home of Ed King, who was extremely enthusiastic. Early the next morning I secured approval from a number of the Tougaloo students and Youth Council members. At 10 A.M. I took it to the Masonic Temple, where the board meeting was convening.

There was an unusually large turnout. The meeting itself had not yet begun, and Aaron Henry and Medgar and several others were listening to a radio report concerning rioting that had broken out in Birmingham the night before. Clarence Mitchell was on hand. I passed out copies of my resolution to board members so that they might read it before the meeting began, and as a courtesy gave a copy of the resolution to Clarence Mitchell. Then I left the room for a moment. When I returned, Clarence Mitchell was sitting at a typewriter, by himself, typing away at something, with the copy of my resolution laid out in front of him. Aaron Henry and Medgar were still listening to the radio in an inner office. I looked over Clarence Mitchell's shoulder. He was rewriting the resolution, including no reference to direct action.

He stopped typing and looked up at me. For a long moment, neither of us said anything. Then he indicated that he felt that the tone of my resolution was much too strong, and he pointed to the terminology dealing with "massive" and "intensive" direct action. He was rewriting it, he said, so that the national office not be "put on the spot."

For me it was too much. In a voice that was tense, although courteous, I suggested, "Suppose we let the board members determine the merit of the resolution as it stands. They can accept it, reject it, or modify it."

He stood up, visibly angry. I went on, "I'm a member of the board. You're not. What right do you have to modify my resolution, or make any resolution, so far as that goes?"

Aaron Henry and Medgar, hearing all this, came out of the inner office and stood there. Mitchell was obviously quite angry but was saying little. Quickly, Aaron Henry and Medgar poured oil on the waters and suggested that we all sit down and relax. We did so and an atmosphere of comparative calm returned to the scene. Clarence Mitchell and I apologized to each other. After some discussion, Aaron Henry suggested that I present my resolution as it stood, but that as a compromise, if it were approved, we would all work out a new version that would moderate its tone to some extent, and this would be the version we would present to the mass meeting that afternoon and then make public. Clarence Mitchell and I both agreed.

As a consequence, the board meeting, which was held in an adjoining room, was a good half hour late in starting. After the preliminaries, I arose and read my resolution. It was unanimously approved as it stood, without discussion. The meeting then moved on to other business. None of us knew then, except perhaps Clarence Mitchell, how this resolution was going to affect whatever was going on in the national office, but it was now very clear indeed that it was expected to have an impact. Later, after the board meeting, we drew up a somewhat modified version of my resolution—which, however, contained its essence and included the matter of direct action. This was presented to the mass meeting that afternoon and was also given to the news media.

That evening Medgar came to our home. It was very clear that, as he put it, "Some things are really moving." I did not press him too much, but it was obvious that what we had done that morning was having the desired impact. Eldri gave us something to eat, and a number of students, now very much excited, came by to talk. Then, with Medgar standing there and using the modified version of the resolution that had been passed only a few hours before, I typed eight identical letters— to Governor Ross R. Barnett, Mayor Allen C. Thompson, the Jackson City Commission, the Jackson Chamber of Commerce, the Jackson Junior Chamber of Commerce, the Downtown Jackson Association, the Bankers Association, and the Mississippi Economic Council:

> The NAACP is determined to put an end to all forms of racial segregation in Jackson. This means that we want to end the discriminatory practices in the businesses that now do not give fair employment opportunities to colored citizens. We also insist that segregation now practiced in the restroom and restaurant and other facilities of these establishments be ended. As the patrons who help to make it possible for these businesses to continue to operate at a profit, we know that we have the economic strength to back up our requests with effective action. A selective buying campaign is already

underway. Unless we get results through peaceful negotiations under-taken in good faith, we have no alternative but to step up and broaden our selective buying campaign to produce the results that will make Jackson a place of fair play for all persons without regard to race.

We are determined to end all state and local government-sponsored segregation in the parks, playgrounds, schools, libraries and other public facilities. To accomplish this we shall use all lawful means of protest—picketing, marches, mass meetings, litigation, and whatever other legal means we deem necessary.

At this time we wish to let the city, the state, the nation and the world know that we want to meet with city officials and community leaders to make good faith attempts to settle grievances and assure immediate full citizenship rights for all Americans. We earnestly hope that those who have the best interests of the city at heart will accept our offer to reach a speedy and orderly settlement. We call upon President John F. Kennedy and any other national leaders who share our love of freedom to use their good offices in helping to get these discussions started.

At the bottom of the letter, we put three names: Medgar, as field secretary; Mrs. Doris Allison, as president of the Jackson NAACP adult branch, to which she had recently been elected; myself, as adviser to the Youth Council. There was silence as Medgar and I signed each letter. Those students who were present were now very quiet. Then one asked, "Is this it? Do you think that this is it?"

We told him that we thought that it was. There was little doubt in our minds that neither the mayor nor the businessmen, integral parts of the political-economic-racist complex that had dominated Jackson since its inception, would constructively negotiate. And even if they wanted to, there were all of the other forces of Mississippi, throughout the entire state, to prevent them from doing so.

Perhaps more than any of us, Eldri, who had been somewhat removed from the continual intra-organizational maneuverings of the past several days that had buoyed the rest of us from one step to another, perceived the gravity of the occasion. "This seems almost too quiet," she said, "too matter-of-fact for what's being done right here. This is history."

It was by now very late. Medgar left for Jackson to get the signature of Mrs. Allison on the letters so that he could mail them, certified, first thing in the morning. As I went to bed that night, I realized that almost a year and a half had passed since Colia Liddell, following that American Government class, had asked me to speak at the meeting on the ICC ruling. An even five months to the day had elapsed since the first picket demonstration on downtown Capitol Street. Suddenly, I felt no longer calm but in the grips of a high, almost ethereal hope and excitement, one that was laced with vague feelings of unease. We were now moving, headlong, into a new dimension.

6

MAYOR ALLEN C. THOMPSON carried the cry.

On Monday morning he met with various business leaders and at 3 P.M., addressed a quite large gathering of business representatives from throughout the Jackson area. Flanked by his city commissioners, D. L. Luckey and Tom Marshall, Thompson stated that there would be no negotiations of any kind with "agitators" and there would be no compromises. "Nobody is going to come here," he said, "and tell our businessmen what they must or must not do." Once concessions were made to "agitator groups," the mayor continued, "there is no stopping it." He denounced the concept of bi-racial committees: "The only thing that can come of such a committee is complete compliance with the demands of racial agitators from outside." And he pledged that "I will not talk to any member of the NAACP, CORE or any other racial agitator." He expressed the hope that local blacks in Jackson would join ranks with the white community to "give these agitators the worst beating they have ever had." He expressed doubt that any local blacks would join a civil rights movement in Jackson, because "we don't have the situations here that cause trouble in other cities."

He told the businessmen that "we have 300 policemen, 300 firemen, auxiliary police, state highway patrol, sheriffs' officers and other peace officers. . . ."

The mayor announced that he would go on all television stations that night to personally address the citizens of Jackson.

And he received a huge, standing ovation from the assembled businessmen when he finished.

Excitement was tremendously high on the Tougaloo campus, and a steady stream of students poured into our home. We told them to "get ready"—that at last it appeared as if we were going to have what we had hoped for so long: a full-scale desegregation drive in Jackson, Mississippi. That afternoon, as the *Jackson Daily News* hit the streets with its headline, "Mayor Plans Preventative Actions Here—Takes Firm Stand as Demonstrations Are Threatened," we traveled throughout Jackson, spreading the word to Youth Council members and to those adults who had quietly been assisting us in the boycott campaign. The young people were afraid and at the same time extremely enthusiastic. The adults were afraid and cautious, but hopeful. The stirring at the grassroots that had begun during the Meredith affair and had grown a bit through the Greenwood and then the Birmingham developments was now beginning to be readily detectable.

Early Monday evening, about a dozen of us gathered in Medgar's office—Medgar, I, Mrs. Doris Allison and her husband, other leaders of the Jackson adult branch of the NAACP, Youth Council leaders, and Tougaloo students. We listened to the speech of Allen Thompson, who began with a reference to the fact that he had once been president of the American Municipal Association:

When I was president of all of the mayors in the United States, I had an opportunity of observing cities all over the nation. And I became firmly convinced then that Jackson was the greatest city in the country. . . . During the last few weeks, all of us have been greatly worried, of course, about the terrible trouble in some of our neighboring southern states. Tonight, I want to try to reassure each one of you that we are going to continue our way of doing things, and although we are going to have turbulent times, when all of the agitation is over, maybe next year, maybe the next, but someday, Jackson will still be prosperous, people will still be happy, and the races will still live side by side in peace and harmony. I want each of you to know that you, your family, your home and your businesses will be protected from any harm, and from all law violators. This is a pledge to you.

Two years ago, you remember the so-called Freedom Riders, outside troublemakers, came into our city to tear it up. There was no violence and every one of the 350 cases are in the courts today. Two years later, all have been disposed of through legal action. Any agitator who comes to this city will be prosecuted without any exception whatsoever. And it will continue to be the policy.

. . . We have some of the best facilities you can find anywhere. Beautiful, wonderful schools, parks, playgrounds, libraries, and so many, many other things. Next, there are no slums. Have you ever thought about it? You can go into practically any other large city and you will find slums but you won't find them here. You will not find anything that will breed discontent. Then we have a spirit of unity, with everyone trying to work together to work out our problems peaceably. Probably most important of all, we have good people. Good white people, good colored people. We do not tolerate law violations of any kind, and we do not tolerate any intimidation by any person.

. . . This appeal to our Nigra citizens I think is very appropriate at this time. All of this is being said in a way so as not to worry anybody, to create any agitation, but to get over to you some of the things that are in my heart, that I believe must be said. . . . You live in a city, a beautiful city. . . . You have twenty-four-hour protection by the police department . . . or suppose you need the fire department. . . . You live in a city where you can work, where you can make a comfortable living. You are treated, no matter what anybody else tells you, with dignity, courtesy, and respect.

Ah, what a wonderful thing it is to live in this city!

. . . Now, with these privileges that you have there are certain responsibilities you must assume . . . do not listen to false rumors which will stir you, worry you, and upset you. Refuse to pay any attention to any of these outside agitators who are interested only in getting money out of you, using you for their own selfish purposes, and who will advocate destroying everything that you and the white people working side by side have built up over the last hundred years. . . .

Now, let me say here and now . . . there is no change in our policy whatsoever. But there will be no meeting with the NAACP or with any such group.

. . . we will not permit any unlawful demonstrations or actions . . . we will continue to resist undue pressure from the Federal government, from agitators and from those who would completely destroy all that we have through their desire for political power, for their own enrichment. . . .

Even those in our little group, who had listened to a great deal of southern hyperbole, found Allen Thompson's reference to "beautiful, wonderful facilities" and the "absence of slums" and "twenty-four-hour police protection" incredible. Medgar immediately indicated his intention of attempting to secure equal time on television in order to reply to the mayor.

There was no question but that a showdown was coming. Medgar was certain that the national office of the NAACP would back us to the hilt. We now prepared to organize a strategy committee. Medgar suggested that since all of this was growing out of the boycott, I be chairman of the group. I accepted, but on the condition that Pearlena Lewis, president of the Youth Council, serve also as a chairman. Solemnly, Pearlena accepted. We agreed to continue, as our first priority, the mobilization of the community by preparing people to move forward in the direction of action, which obviously lay in the immediate future. Conscious of the fear that plagued the adult community, we felt that every conceivable effort should be made to persuade people to join with the youth in taking an active and open role as quickly as possible. Medgar indicated that he had already talked with a number of the ministers, some of whom had been quietly active in behalf of the boycott, and that he would see other clergy. Mrs. Allison and others active in the Jackson adult NAACP said that they would immediately make contacts throughout the adult community. There was no question in anyone's mind about the willingness of the young people to participate actively.

There was no laughing or joking as we left the meeting that evening. *Birmingham! And now Jackson!*

The people were stirring in the black community. Unquestionably, they were also stirring in the white community. The sensation-seeking Jackson news media, apparently afraid that not all white Jacksonians would approve of the position taken by the mayor and indeed might be tempted to negotiate, were becoming hysterical. The Tuesday-morning *Clarion-Ledger* carried a banner headline: "Thompson Pledges City Won't Permit Violence—Says Race Agitators Won't Dictate Terms," and it ran a front-page editorial supporting Thompson's recalcitrant stand, "Resolute Unity of Our Leaders Helps in Racial Relations Here."

Somewhat more venomously, the *Jackson Daily News,* later on that same day, editorialized:

> Jackson is not going to have any anonymous bi-racial committee to peddle away the rights of this community. That statement by Mayor Allen C. Thompson was greeted with an ovation and a standing, unanimous vote of endorsement by an overflowing crowd of business leaders here yesterday. Some self-appointed bi-racial committee in Birmingham that entertained the demands of wild-eyed outside agitators helped provoke trouble in Alabama. They were termed "a bunch of quisling, gutless traitors." Any ambitious pseudo-dictator who wishes to bypass the duly elected officials of Jackson and negotiate with hate groups might as well set up shop in Hong Kong or a more distant city.

That same day, Tuesday, the Executive Committee of the National Board of Directors of the NAACP, meeting in New York City, passed the following resolution:

> We pledge the support of the national organization to the Mississippi state NAACP board of directors in its announced intensified program against racial discrimination and segregation in Mississippi and specifically we authorize the Executive Secretary to secure from whatever sources available the necessary sums to take care of the costs that may arise in connection with aiding the current selective-buying campaign of our North Jackson Youth Council and the general drive toward the objective of putting an end to all forms of racial discrimination and segregation in Jackson.

We had, indeed, come a long, long way.

Our strategy committee met Tuesday night, grown somewhat larger. More students were in attendance and there were a few more adult leaders, although we learned from those who had been making contacts in the adult community that a number of the people were still reluctant to become too openly identified with us. The youth leaders and I also encountered this with a number of the adults whom we knew. People were afraid. A woman who operated a little restaurant in which our boycott leaflets had been continuously distributed had told us earlier in the day, "I'm certainly with you all the way, but I'm going to have to be careful or they'll take my business license." She had gone on to say, "I'll help you every way I can, quietly, and maybe can do more later." We felt that when matters began really to move, many people like her would take open and active positions of support. We could understand the position she was in—and her position was, indeed, infinitely more "free" than that occupied by the great majority of black people in Jackson, or in all of Mississippi, who were, as Judge Brady had pointed out so long ago in *Black Monday,* directly employed by white people who could terminate that employment at any moment they wished.

Mrs. Allison and other older leaders also felt that once the action began, an increasing number of adults would definitely join with us. Medgar was optimistic about many of the ministers, feeling that, very soon indeed, they would be playing an active role.

In fact, from everything that all of us had seen, a general enthusiasm was building at the grassroots, and if the adults were still reluctant to commit themselves beyond genuine expressions of quiet support, there was no doubt whatever but that the young people were with it all the way. Every report, everything we had seen and heard, indicated that large numbers of students were prepared to participate with us in direct action: the high-school youth involved with the Youth Council, those at Tougaloo, many at Campbell College. And even students at rigidly controlled Jackson State had indicated that, once matters began in earnest, they would be joining the effort.

And other allies were coming. Medgar indicated that Laplois Ashford and the NAACP director of branches, Gloster Current, were expected in Jackson the next evening.

Then, just as our strategy session was drawing to a close, word came that a number of adult members of the black community were at that moment meeting at the Farish Street Baptist Church. Those attending the meeting were not known. This was news to all of us. The first possibility that came to mind, voiced by Medgar, was that this was a conservative gathering, perhaps even "Uncle Tom" in tone, maybe even a group that was trying to conclude a "deal" with the mayor and the white businessmen. But this didn't quite fit, since we knew that the Rev. S. Leon Whitney, pastor of the church, was a supporter of civil rights. Medgar, I, and Jess Brown, who had sat in on our session, went immediately to Farish Street Baptist. We walked in, not certain of what we would find.

As soon as we saw the faces of many of the three dozen or so men assembled, we knew that, whatever it was, it was not an Uncle Tom affair. I. S. Sanders, a well-known businessman, was presiding. There were many other prominent figures, some of whom had quietly, in the past, assisted in our boycott campaign. Some were ministers. All of them were men who, because of a comparatively high economic position, enjoyed more freedom of movement, within the context of segregation of course, than did the great majority of Jackson blacks. The only pro-segregation individual in evidence was Percy Greene, editor of a small Negro paper, the *Jackson Advocate* and, we all knew, a recipient of Sovereignty Commission money and a prominent advertiser of many of the businesses that we had under boycott. He was sitting by himself.

Briefly the situation was explained to us. These men had met at the request of I. S. Sanders, among others, in a rather hastily assembled group, to determine how they could best function in the approaching crisis. It soon became clear that most of them did not share our view that the power structure would not negotiate, but they told us that they were not setting themselves up as a negotiating committee. Their main interest, they continued, was in assisting us in building community support. That certainly sounded all right to us.

Percy Greene was silent as we came in but soon embarked on a heated condemnation of any sort of direct action. Then he announced that Mayor Thompson had told *him,* that afternoon, that if no direct action took place in Jackson, the city might well hire a black policeman or two, and possibly even several blacks as crossing guards for school-children at street intersections. Someone laughed at that, and someone else pointed out that in Jackson and in the rest of Mississippi, "Negro police-men" meant that they couldn't arrest white people. No one was paying Percy Greene any attention.

The group then organized itself into a Citizens Committee for Human Rights in Jackson. I. S. Sanders was elected chairman. The new group agreed to maintain a very close liaison with the NAACP and would indeed work actively within the movement. A resolution was approved that the group "resents and rejects the position stated by Mayor Thompson, who claims that Negro citizens of Jackson are satisfied with the status quo . . . we are extremely dissatisfied with the status quo and we hereby call for an immediate end to segregation and discrimination in our community." Subsequently, the statement received wide publicity.

Following that meeting, a number of us walked across the street to a well-known black restaurant to have coffee. I had never been there, because it was known that the owner, because of city pressures, did not serve the few non-blacks who, usually connected with Tougaloo, occasion-ally sought service. We had just come up to the door when Jess Brown asked Medgar what we'd do if "John isn't served."

Medgar immediately said we'd walk out and call for a general boycott of the establishment. But, indicative of the shifting pattern of things, I was served without any question. Percy Greene came in and another heated argument developed that lasted almost an hour. He had no following. Once, many years before, he had been a quite outspoken advocate of black rights; then, for reasons that were not too difficult to guess, he had shifted his position. But it was quite clear that his era was drawing very fast now to a close.

Wednesday, May 15, arrived. Governor Ross Barnett praised Allen Thompson for his recalcitrant stand: "I am indeed grateful to you," said Barnett to Thompson, "for the stand you have taken with reference to agitators and trouble-makers. You have my whole-hearted cooperation at all times. . . . I offer you any and every facility at my command and assure you that I shall be glad to have you call on me at any time."

The Women for Constitutional Government, a sort of Citizens Council ladies' auxiliary, issued an appeal, as they put it, to "the responsible citizens of both races to conduct themselves with dignity and composure through any racial crisis that may be illegally stirred up among us."

Reports were rife that the Citizens Councils of Mississippi, including the 6,000-member Jackson Council, were planning a series of meetings.

That evening Medgar and I went to the airport to pick up Gloster Current and Laplois Ashford. The terminal seemed to be full of detective types, and one man, who watched us very closely, we recognized as a member of the Jackson plainclothes force. We picked up a late issue of the *Jackson Daily News*. Earlier, Medgar had issued a statement indicating that Ashford and Current were coming, and the newspaper set it forth: "Officials Plan Talk With Negroes Here—NAACP Agitators Coming In, Not Included in Conference." Buried in the news story was an indication that the mayor expected to call in several "responsible Negro representatives" to talk with him in the near future. We knew, of course, what he meant by "responsible."

As soon as the NAACP staff officials arrived, we went to the nightly meeting of the strategy committee, followed by at least one car which we were certain contained detectives. Gloster Current told us that he was going to be in and out of Jackson for at least several days. Ashford was on a trip through the South and would be staying in Jackson only a day or so. He was elated at what was occurring, not only in our city but everywhere that he had been. Demonstrations, he said, were breaking out all over in the wake of Birmingham. He indicated that Willie Ludden would soon arrive in Jackson to assist us.

At the strategy committee meeting, Gloster Current, perhaps noting our impatience, voiced the hope that negotiations would take place in Jackson, and said that he felt that sufficient time should be allowed for that to occur. He assured us, however, that the national office of the NAACP would back up a Jackson campaign and was busy assembling money with which to finance the effort. We had, of course, been thinking in terms of mass demonstrations, like those of Albany and Birmingham, and this was possibly what Medgar had in mind when he asked Gloster Current "about how much" money would be available from NAACP headquarters. The director of branches declined to give a figure but made it very clear that there would definitely be adequate financing.

Indeed, this sounded good to all of us! And we gave Gloster Current firm assurance that the people of Jackson were behind the movement all the way. "We'll win," we said, and we meant it.

On Thursday morning, with reference to Mayor Thompson's hints the day before about the matter of "responsible" Negro leaders conferring with the city, Medgar issued a very strong statement accusing the mayor of attempting to handpick "yes men," and warning that "we consider Negroes who would sell out our program as being Uncle Toms of the first order and we will deal with them economically as we are dealing with those downtown."

A little later that day, Mayor Thompson conceded that so far no blacks had come to see him. The *Jackson Daily News,* however, ran a front-page editorial entitled "No Hate Mobs for Jackson," in which it denounced "outside mobsters who are directed and controlled out of New York and Washington as if they were marionettes . . . As far as bettering the conditions of local Negroes one of Martin Luther King's mobs or mass demonstrations will be about as useless as a reading lamp in a coffin."

The editorial went on to commend Sidney R. Tharp, a Negro attorney who had written the mayor. Tharp's letter, which was also printed on the front page of the newspaper, praised Thompson for his "sensible and logical speech," and went on to attack "immature mental midgets who have brought outside agitators into our great city and abrogated unto themselves with their Communist backing powers that are not rightfully theirs and we are not going to follow them." Tharp had assured the mayor that "there are thousands of Jackson colored citizens who feel the same way I do."

By now, only a few days after the call to arms on May 12, our strategy committee meetings were reaching the size where, with about thirty in attendance, we shifted the gatherings from Medgar's office to the adjoining conference room. The Youth Council leaders and key Tougaloo students were much in evidence. A number of men from the I. S. Sanders group were now coming, and there were ministers from the Baptist Ministerial Union and the Interdenominational Ministers Alliance. Ed King of Tougaloo was now attached to the group, as was the chaplain at Campbell College, Dean Charles Jones. The Jackson adult NAACP was represented primarily by Mrs. Doris Allison and its vice-president, an insurance man, Sam Bailey. Dave Dennis, the CORE representative and an old friend, sensing action in Jackson, had come down from the Delta, where the Mississippi SNCC contingent was now working, and was entering our situation.

The meetings of the strategy committee were informal. Pearlena and I sat at a table, sparking the general discussion, and frequently Medgar sat with us. The tenor of the group was quite democratic.

But by this time there was already an indication of a vague factional division.

To many of us, especially the youth and those involved with them, it had been clear, from Monday on, that the power structure had no intention of negotiating in good faith. We were aware, of course, that in the South especially and certainly in Mississippi, political leaders often disguised their real intentions with a great deal of heated oratory and "hooraw," and that at the same time they were saying that they would never do something, they would actually be quietly doing it. We knew that if sufficient pressure was mobilized, especially in a direct-action sense, against Mayor Allen Thompson and the businessmen, he and they would ultimately be forced to work out constructively a positive settlement with the Jackson civil rights movement. But it was our opinion that the good-faith negotiations and their tangible and positive effects would materialize only when that grassroots pressure was brought. All week long the signs of resistance had been mounting: the mayor's several adamant refusals even to negotiate, let alone make substantial reforms; the willingness of business-men to join with the mayor; the governor's pledge of support to the Jackson power structure; the statement issued by the Women for Constitutional Government; and the various activities being set up by the Citizens Council. And Mississippi was not going to let Jackson crack without a struggle.

We were tired of waiting, and we wanted now to move forward in the direct-action phase. Medgar was also impatient.

Most of the adults, virtually all of whom were comparatively affluent and felt that they could identify with our group without fear of serious economic reprisal, disagreed with us, and felt that additional avenues, with respect to negotiation efforts, should be exhausted before any direct action began. Those who believed most strongly in this were the men coming out of the I. S. Sanders group, including I. S. Sanders himself, and many of the ministers. Gloster Current tended toward this view.

On Friday the division became apparent. I. S. Sanders issued a statement on behalf of his Citizens Committee for Human Rights, asking Mayor Thompson to "call together a committee composed of responsible citizens of both races to deal with our mutual problems." This was fine, but the Sanders statement went on to say that his organization was not "an extremist, protest, or legal action group," that it was "composed of some of the most level-headed and responsible citizens of the Negro community who are deeply concerned over the impending prospects of a repetition here of the tragedy in Birmingham . . . we feel that we would be derelict in our duties as responsible citizens were we to sit idly by until our city has become engulfed in disorder and possibly violence."

This statement, which marked a departure from the apparently militant position of the Sanders group as we had seen it at its initial meeting, was viewed by some of us, especially the younger people, as being something of a slap at the NAACP, and especially at the direct-action protest techniques that were closely identified with the youth.

But the Sanders statement, which was explained to us as being aimed toward publicly pressuring the mayor into negotiating with *bona fide* "responsible" members of the black community, rather than Uncle Toms, did not create any sort of serious division on the strategy committee, although many of us felt that it could not secure its goal. General unity and consensus were key aims. It was decided that the following Tuesday, May 21, we would hold a community mass meeting, open to the public, to choose by secret ballot members of a negotiating committee whose names we would then convey to the mayor. It was definitely felt that if the mayor then refused to negotiate in good faith or if he rejected any members of the duly elected negotiating committee, direct action would begin right away. A strong statement to repudiate again the mayor's announced wish to meet with his sort of "responsible" Negroes, and to lay the groundwork for our proposed negotiating committee, was issued: ". . . no meeting with representatives of the Negro community who are not democratically chosen or representative of a broad cross-section of opinion will be considered satisfactory to the Negro community."

We continued to spend as much time as possible making contacts in Jackson. The white sections of town through which we occasionally drove seemed very quiet indeed. Although I don't know what we expected to see that was unusual, it was not difficult to speculate that either the white community *really* didn't expect the black community to move forward or, if some whites did, they felt confident that the mayor, and all of the police power, and the Citizens Council would prevent anything noteworthy from occurring. In the black sections, though, where we were constantly talking with people, we found a tremendous amount of rising interest; and there was every reason, we felt, to expect that before too long adults would transcend their fear to a point where their direct involvement in the Jackson movement would be real. The young people, of course, were extremely restless, wondering when the campaign would begin in earnest, and we told them "soon, very soon."

Mercedes Wright, of Savannah, Georgia, adviser to the Georgia NAACP Youth Council, arrived in Jackson to assist us, and we were also soon joined by Willie Ludden. Both were eager to move.

There were additional signs of resistance from the segregationists over the weekend. We had made copies of the initial letter that on May 12 we had drawn up for the mayor and the business organizations and, to make an effort to better inform the white community of our case and of our position, had mailed capies to many of the white ministers in the Jackson area—along with a brief notation indicating, in case they couldn't guess, that the communication was an outgrowth of the May 12 resolution. However, this was immediately interpreted by some of the white clergy as a warning on our part that we were also going to integrate the churches. Dr. J. Clark Hensley, an official in the Hinds County Baptist Association, immediately notified the white Baptists that they had best "evolve a plan in the event that [blacks] want to integrate our churches." That had not, of course, been the purpose of sending the letter, but we had been considering doing just what Dr. Hensley so obviously feared we might.

More ominously, M. B. Pierce, chief of the Jackson Detective Bureau, stated that the police department was marshaling its forces, pointing out that it "recently completed an eight-week school in various police methods, including the control of riots and mass gatherings." Pierce hinted at the possibility that the Jackson police would "call on the Hinds County sheriff and the Mississippi Highway Patrol for assistance."

On Sunday afternoon, Sheriff J. R. Gilfoy of Hinds County briefed his thirty-odd deputies and constables on the matter of handling demonstrations, and pledged his "complete cooperation" to the Jackson Police Department.

Further, lest anyone in the white community of Jackson think of negotiation with the black community, Tom Ethridge, arch-segregationist writer for the *Clarion-Ledger,* warned:

> . . . Jackson has no "moderate" white faction in a position to claim legal authority for negotiating surrender. . . . Pressure and boycott is a game that can be played two ways. Business establishments yielding to agitator demands reportedly are experiencing slumps in white trade at Birmingham. In other words, while establishments so inclined are free to let agitators dictate their policies and practices, customers are also free to avoid places which knuckle under to the NAACP et al.

The Mississippi Council on Human Relations, organized the year before at Tougaloo, had never thrived, despite the hard work poured into it by a few dedicated persons like Dr. A. D. Beittel of Tougaloo and Mrs. Wallis Schutt of Jackson. On Monday, May 20, it convened at Tougaloo, with about fifty white and black persons in attendance. We had given Dr. A. D. Beittel copies of the May 12 letter, which he distributed at the meeting. Mrs. Schutt delivered an impassioned speech in which, as a white Mississippian, she said that the crisis approaching in Jackson was developing because of the long-time failure of the white community to cope realistically with the basic problems of Mississippi. I. S. Sanders asked the white people who were present—and very few were native Mississippians—to try to build meetings between members of his Citizens Committee and the white businessmen. Some of the white people present indicated that they had endeavored to talk with the mayor, but to no real avail—he was adamant. Several had discussed matters privately with several of the white businessmen, and apparently none of them was prepared to negotiate.

The Council on Human Relations did about the only thing within its power and passed a resolution calling on citizens of good will in Jackson to give blacks a "peaceful opportunity to seek for themselves the human rights recognized by our laws and taught in our churches and synagogues." The group asked that a "bi-racial committee with respected citizens acceptable to both racial groups" be set up to "work out satisfactory solutions to the difficult problems of racial adjustment without violence and bloodshed."

While the Mississippi Council on Human Relations was meeting, Mayor Thompson began a series of meetings with his entire police force to lay plans for the suppression of demonstrations. The Jackson Junior Chamber of Commerce approved a resolution supporting the mayor's position.

Medgar had succeeded, with the assistance of the Federal Communications Commission, in securing equal time on television to answer the speech given by Allen Thompson a week before. He went down Monday and his seventeen-minute speech was taped for TV. Later that evening, following a brief strategy session, several of us, including Medgar, brought Cokes and went to a little home adjacent to the Masonic Temple where a television set was available. There we sat, crowded into a small room, and listened to one of Mississippi's greater public addresses:

> I speak as a native Mississippian. I was educated in Mississippi schools, and served overseas in our nation's armed forces in the war against Hitlerism and Fascism. . . . Most southern white people, whether they are friendly or hostile, usually think of the NAACP as a "northern outside group." . . . At least one-half of the NAACP membership is in the South. There have been branches in Mississippi since 1918. The Jackson, Mississippi, branch was organized in 1926 —thirty-seven years ago. . . .
>
> Now the mayor says that if the so-called outside agitators would leave us alone everything would be all right. This has always been the position of those who would deny Negro citizens their constitutional rights. . . . Never in its history has the South as a region, without outside pressure, granted the Negro his citizenship rights. . . . It is also in the American tradition to demonstrate, to assemble peacefully and to petition the government for a redress of grievances. Such a petition may legitimately take the form of picketing, although in Jackson, Negroes are immediately arrested when they attempt to exercise this constitutional right. . . .
>
> We feel that Mayor Thompson will help Jackson if he will consult with a democratically selected bi-racial committee, some of whose members may be members of the NAACP. He would profit from the experience of other southern cities. . . .
>
> Tonight the Negro knows from his radio and television what happened today all over the world. He knows what black people are doing and he knows what white people are doing. . . . He knows about the new free nations in Africa and knows that a Congo

native can be a locomotive engineer, but in Jackson he cannot even drive a garbage truck.

. . . Then he looks about his home community and what does he see, to quote our Mayor, in this "progressive, beautiful, friendly, prosperous city with an exciting future"?

He sees a city where Negro citizens are refused admittance to the City Auditorium and the Coliseum; his children refused a ticket to a good movie in a downtown theater; his wife and children refused service at a lunch counter in a downtown store where they trade; students refused the use of the main public libraries, parks, playgrounds and other tax-supported recreational facilities. He sees Negro lawyers, physicians, dentists, teachers and other professionals prevented from attending meetings of professional organizations. He sees a city of over 150,000, of which 40% is Negro, in which there is not a single Negro policeman or policewoman, school crossing guard, fireman, clerk, stenographer or supervisor employed in any city department or the mayor's office . . . except those employed in segregated facilities. He sees local hospitals which segregate Negro patients and deny staff privileges to Negro family physicians. The mayor spoke of the twenty-four-hour police protection we have . . . there are questions in the minds of many Negroes whether we have twenty-four hours of protection, or twenty-four hours of harassment. . . .

What then does the Negro want? He wants to get rid of racial segregation in Mississippi life because he knows it has not been good for him nor for the State. He knows that segregation is unconstitutional and illegal. . . . The Negro citizen wants to register and vote without special handicaps imposed on him alone. . . . The Negro Mississippian wants more jobs above the menial level in stores where he spends his money. He believes that new industries that have come to Mississippi should employ him above the laboring category. He wants the public schools and colleges desegregated so that his children can receive the best education that Mississippi has to offer. He believes additional Negro students should be accepted at Old Miss and at other colleges. He feels strongly about these and other items although he may not say so publicly.

. . . Jackson can change if it wills to do so. If there should be resistance, how much better to have turbulence to effect improvement, rather than turbulence to maintain a stand-pat policy. We believe there are white Mississippians who want to go forward on the race question. Their religion tells them there is something wrong with the old system. Their sense of justice and fair play sends them the same message.

But whether Jackson and the State choose change or not, the years of change are upon us. In the racial picture things will never be as they once were. History has reached a turning point, here and over the world. Here in Jackson we can recognize the situation and make an honest effort to bring fresh ideas and new methods to bear, or we can have what Mayor Thompson called "turbulent times." If we choose this latter course, the turbulence will come, not because of so-called agitators or presence or absence of the NAACP, but because the time has come for a change and certain citizens refuse to accept the inevitable.

Negro citizens want to help all other good citizens bring about a meaningful improvement in an orderly fashion . . . the two races have lived here together. The Negro has been in America since 1619, a total of 344 years. He is not going anywhere else; this country is his home. He wants to do his part to help make his city, state and nation a better place for everyone regardless of color and race.

Let me appeal to the consciences of many silent, responsible citizens of the white community who know that a victory for democracy in Jackson will be a victory for democracy everywhere.

To anyone rational there could be no question regarding the sincerity of Medgar Evers, or the merit of his words. But the power structure of Jackson, and the system of Mississippi, were not rational on matters such as this. There were unquestionably those in the white community who subscribed to the essence of what Medgar had had to say, but they remained silent, choked by the same mantle of fear that so long had strangled their community and state.

To the *Jackson Daily News* the next day, the speech of Medgar Evers was something from which to assemble a few scattered, out-of-context quotations, under the headline "Mix Drive Talked Up."

Our first community mass meeting since the events of May 12 was scheduled for Tuesday evening, May 21, at the Pearl Street African Methodist Episcopal church, of which the Rev. G. R. Haughton was pastor. The affair was designed to select the negotiating committee, which would then be submitted to the mayor; to secure approval at the mass meeting of a number of specific demands that had crystallized; and to obtain the authorization of the meeting for a number of telegrams that we had drawn up and that we hoped to send to the mayor and a number of businesses and business organizations. We worked very hard— I, Medgar, Gloster Current, Mercedes Wright, and others.

We also knew that the Youth Council members and Tougaloo students and other young people saw this Pearl Street AME meeting as one of the last interludes before the beginning of direct action. There was no doubt in the minds of many of us that the mayor would reject the elected negotiating committee, and when that happened, there was only one road ahead.

The meeting was scheduled for 7:30 P.M. It was a hot, muggy

evening. Several of us were there well before seven, and even then the Jackson police were thick in front of and behind the church and in the dusty alley in back. Usually sitting in their cars, they also walked up and down the sidewalk. Their purpose was clear: to frighten people away.

For a time it looked as if they had succeeded. As with southern meetings, this one was late in getting started; even as 7:45 approached, only a handful of people had arrived. Some of the students and I had made up some picket signs with action-oriented messages, which we hung on the walls of the church. A few local newsmen arrived, happy at the relatively few people in attendance, and they joked about "finding a place to sit."

Then, just as we were beginning to panic, the church suddenly filled rapidly. People, most of whom we had never seen before, were coming from all over Jackson—some comparatively affluent, some poor, some old and some young. Abut 600 were present when we finally began at 8:30 P.M.

The Rev. Mr. Haughton presided. Bette Anne Poole, one of the December pickets, led off with some very intensive freedom singing. She was joined at once by all of the young people. Then the adults swung into it. Speeches began: Gloster Current promised the "full legal and financial resources" of the NAACP and hailed a Supreme Court decision of the day before ruling that sit-in demonstrations in public business places could not be interfered with by local officials. Sympathy boycotts and demonstrations, said he, might well be conducted by 500 or so NAACP branches against those chain stores represented in downtown Jackson.

Mercedes Wright told of the long struggle for freedom in Savannah and discussed a boycott of a year and a half that the black community of that city had carried through successfully.

I reviewed the history of the Jackson boycott movement, told the people that it was still continuing and that if the power structure refused to negotiate in good faith, "there would be no end to demonstrations . . . a course of action that has never before been attempted in the state of Mississippi or the city of Jackson." I read the resolution made a week before by the top officials of the NAACP that pledged its support to the North Jackson Youth Council and the whole Jackson movement.

Medgar made it clear that time was running out. "We're anxious to negotiate, but we aren't going to wait a week or two weeks for him [Thompson] to make up his mind."

Support was then promised from several quarters in the community. The Rev. E. A. Mays, president of the Interdenominational Ministerial Alliance, spoke for his group; and the Rev. L. L. Williams, pastor of the Virden Grove church in North Jackson, pledged the backing of the Baptist Ministers Union. I. S. Sanders gave assurance that his Citizens Committee was squarely behind the movement. Dean Charles Jones of Campbell College and Dr. A. D. Beittel of Tougaloo promised full cooperation from their institutions.

The specific demands that we had all drawn up were now presented to the people by the Rev. Mr. Haughton for approval or disapproval: the hiring of black police and crossing guards, initiation of fair employment practices, desegregation of public buildings and parks and schools, desegregation of restaurants and drugstore lunch counters, and a bi-racial committee. With much cheering, stamping of feet, and clapping, the demands were unanimously approved.

Nominations for members of the negotiating committee were called for. About two dozen nominations came from the floor. Ballots were passed out; people voted for the fourteen who they felt would best represent them, and the votes were counted by ballot counters who had been elected at the meeting.

The mass meeting approved our various telegrams. One went to Mayor Allen Thompson:

Negro citizens representing NAACP, Ministerial Association, Jackson Citizens Committee for Human Rights, students and others voted at meeting Tuesday, May 21, on persons considered best suited to represent Negro community in any meaningful negotiations for change in practices and treatment in downtown businesses. Monday's sweeping decision by Supreme Court gives additional support to our legal position and right to demonstrate peaceably and otherwise protest. We are fully prepared to do this, if necessary. Such a step, as you know from experiences of other communities, harms local business and would adversely affect city's image . . . urge you immediately consult with us about representative bi-racial committee to begin negotiations as in other progressive cities.

Another went to national chain-store officials:

For nearly six months Negro community in Jackson, Mississippi, engaged in campaign to effect better treatment of Negro shoppers. Also for jobs in outlets of your corporation. . . . Jackson NAACP and other groups planning protest demonstrations which can have adverse effect upon your business locally and nationally through sympathetic protests in other cities. . . . Respectfully urge you to authorize your local manager to . . . serve customers on equal basis and importune mayor to appoint representative committee to develop at once program leading to desegregation of your facilities.

A third went to nine Mississippi business organizations:

. . . NAACP and other groups in state are pressing for use of unsegregated public accommodations and for fair and equitable employment in places of business where they trade. . . . In view of economic loss to state resulting from these efforts, respectfully urge your association use its good offices to effect meaningful negotiation between business men and democratically selected Negro leaders to begin negotiations immediately toward changing undemocratic practices. . . .

The meeting concluded with more freedom songs. Then, with the exception of the local newsmen, who were no longer laughing and joking, all of us stood, locked arms, and sang "We Shall Overcome":

We shall overcome, we shall overcome,
We shall overcome . . . someday
Oh, oh deep in my heart, I do believe
We shall overcome . . . someday.

We are not afraid, we are not afraid,
We are not afraid . . . today
Oh, oh deep in my heart, I do believe
We shall overcome . . . someday.

The local newsmen were looking very uncomfortable as the meeting broke up, and people went outside, still humming the freedom songs, with many of them carrying boycott leaflets. The police were still out there, parked and watching, but the people were looking through them and beyond.

In the back of the church, the tellers had finished counting the names on the ballots. The mass meeting had selected seven ministers, one funeral director, a doctor, I. S. Sanders, two youth leaders—Bette Anne Poole and Johnny Frazier—me, and Medgar. The names were conveyed by telegram to the office of Allen Thompson.

By now, the area around the church was deserted, and even the police were leaving. Several of us talked briefly about the situation. Most of the ministers and those connected with the I. S. Sanders group expressed hope that the mayor and the businessmen would now negotiate. Gloster Current expressed great optimism. Medgar was uncertain. Ed King knew white Mississippi well—in many ways, better than any of us—and he doubted that either the mayor or the businessmen would back down from the adamant position they had taken. There was no question in my mind but that we would have to carry the campaign into the streets. The Youth Council members and the Tougaloo students certainly agreed. We could see direct action looming ahead.

Allen Thompson reacted the way most of us had expected. On Wednesday he rejected ten of the fourteen members elected by the mass meeting, accepting only I. S. Sanders, the Rev. S. Leon Whitney, the Rev. G. R. Haughton, and funeral director E. W. Banks. To these he then added eleven blacks whom he had picked, all of them considered very conservative. One was Percy Greene. Another was Jacob Reddix, president of Jackson State College. Sydney Tharp, the attorney who had written the mayor the letter of support, was included. Another was a minister whose Sunday radio program was supported by one of the stores we were boycotting. Still another was a man who, on the public payroll of the Sovereignty Commission, traveled around the North, talking about what a fine place Mississippi was for its black citizens. The others, most of whom were retired employees of the city and state, were certainly not considered to be persons who could or would express the grievances of the black community.

It looked as if the time to move forward had very definitely arrived. That feeling was strengthened when the Jackson Chamber of Commerce sent a telegram to the NAACP expressing its support of the mayor:

> Merchants have the freedom of choice as to employment and customers served. Our basic objectives are (1) a better economy, (2) a better community. In furthering these objectives we have increased employment opportunities for all Jackson citizens without discrimination as to race and creed. Your demand for negotiations, under threat of demonstrations and intimidations, to accelerate changes which can only come by mutual understanding and respect for rights of all people, is a case of attempting wrong means to accomplish your objective . . . economic pressure, civil disobedience, and mass hysteria will only delay the possibility of mutually satisfactory solutions to complex problems.

At the strategy committee meeting that night, several of us called for direct action to begin within the next day or so. There was intense discussion. Several ministers and a number of people active in the Citizens Committee felt that additional effort should be made in the direction of negotiation. The young people made it clear that they were tired of waiting. Medgar could see no alternative but to launch the action phase of the campaign. One minister came up with the surprising news that he had heard that a number of the more liberal white clergy might involve themselves openly in an effort to start negotiations. The meeting lasted for a long time, sometimes proceeding formally, sometimes extremely informal. Finally it was decided, again in the interests of unity and consensus, to wait a little longer, until, say, Friday or Saturday, and to send a strong telegram immediately to the business organizations flatly rejecting the committee whom the mayor had proposed:

> We hereby reject the proposal made on May 22 by Mayor Allen Thompson on the grounds that (1) the committee he proposes is not truly representative of the Jackson Negro community and (2) the type of committee he proposes virtually ignores those representatives of Jackson's Negro community democratically selected at the community meeting of May 21 in the Pearl Street AME Church and (3) the committee he proposes is not bi-racial in its composition. We now call upon the businessmen and the businesses involved to immediately negotiate in good faith with our democratically selected representatives.

If such good-faith negotiations do not occur we shall have no alternative but to commence intensive direct action quite shortly indeed.

The four men from our group whom the mayor had agreed to accept sent him telegrams announcing that they would not take part in his proposed meeting, because "the majority of the committee named was not democratically selected by the Negro community."

On Thursday, one of the mayor's own selections, a retired director of the black parks and recreational areas, indicated that she would meet with him. Apparently the rest of the mayor's own group were hesitant, perhaps because of the disapproval of the black community, to accept his offer. Nevertheless, on Thursday Thompson announced that he would hold his meeting the coming Monday, May 27, at 2 P.M. He further said that he would formally call for a Jackson-wide vote of confidence if demonstrations did occur and if he heard that anyone objected to his method of handling them. And he said that he expected demonstrations:

> The NAACP and its coordinated agitator groups will follow through on threats to demonstrate. We've known it for a long time. What we are going to decide is whether Jackson will be run by its duly elected officials or by the NAACP and other agitator organizations. . . . If we give in to their threats and demands, they will be running the city from now on. Racial demonstrations are going to lead to big trouble in some city. . . .

The mayor's position could scarcely be more clear. Several of us now began to travel through Jackson with great intensity, telling the young people especially that talk was over. We were thinking in terms of Friday or Saturday as the time for the real beginning. "Get ready," we told them.

That evening, when our strategists assembled, it became obvious that another delay was developing. For some time, Ed King had been quietly endeavoring to persuade a number of the more liberal white ministers in Jackson to join with the black clergy and, among other things, to take a *public* interracial stand on behalf of human rights. Earlier in the day, there had been some communication between a few of these white ministers and their black colleagues. The white clergy had declined to take a public stand at this point but, expressing shock and horror at the approaching crisis in Jackson, had finally indicated that they would use their influence to bring a larger number of white ministers into a constructive endeavor the next day, Friday. It was felt not only that this would involve a public interracial position but that a substantial number of the white clergymen could be persuaded immediately to seek to influence the mayor and the businessmen to meet the demands of the Jackson movement.

All of this was, for Mississippi, unusual indeed. But to many of us on the strategy committee, including Ed King, who knew his state well, direct action was still the only solution. In our minds, it was clear, and each day's developments confirmed it, that the power structure had no intention of negotiating in a positive fashion. By now, Friday as a beginning day for the action seemed out, owing to the interracial clergymen's affairs, and it looked as if all would begin Saturday.

By Friday morning, a few other of Mayor Thompson's selectees, such as Sydney Tharp, had agreed to meet with him at 2 P.M. Monday.

On Friday there was increased communication between the black clergy and a larger number of the more liberal white ministers, who in turn indicated great fear regarding the impending confrontation between the Jackson movement and the power structure of the city. Although they refused to take a public position on behalf of human rights—and certainly not a public *interracial* position—the white clergy said that they would contact Mayor Allen Thompson and attempt to persuade him to modify his stand, at least to the point that he would agree to accept, for the coming Monday meeting, most of those who had been elected by secret ballot at the May 21 mass meeting. Further, they said that they hoped to meet with the Jackson Chamber of Commerce and persuade the businessmen to take a more realistic position.

The white ministers expressed fervent optimism that something positive might yet be worked out without demonstrations, and they asked the black clergymen to withhold direct action in Jackson pending the outcome of these meetings. Most of the black ministers agreed to lend their efforts toward the postponement of the demonstrations and to consider meeting with Mayor Thompson on Monday, if he would modify his position concerning those elected at the May 21 mass meeting.

White clergymen went to the mayor. Blandly, he took the position that he had no intention of telling the businessmen how to conduct their affairs any more than he would tell the ministers how to run their churches, and expressed some disapproval of *their* attempting to advise *him*. But cagily, he stepped back a bit. Telegrams were sent out by the mayor to the four men from our side, elected at the May 21 meeting, whom he had accepted—as well as, apparently, to those in the group that he had selected who had not yet responded. The telegrams again asked for attendance at the Monday meeting, saying, "The purpose of the meeting is not to reach any agreement binding on the Negro community or city officials—but to explore ideas as citizens of Jackson that will be to the best interest of all citizens."

The mayor indicated that he would take additional representatives of the black community—clergymen from the Ministerial Alliance, for example—and that they could be among those elected by the May 21 mass meeting.

This whole turn of events provoked a great deal of informal discussion among many of us that evening. Again, as many times before, it seemed that this was simply delay and more delay, out of which nothing tangible would develop. It was clear that the pressures already generated had, breaking Mississippi precedent, led to historic bi-racial communication between the ministers, but it also seemed clear that direct action in the streets was the only real solution.

It was an extremely confused situation. A number of us, and certainly the young people, wanted direct action, fast. Medgar was edgy about the delay. On the other hand, rumors were afoot, as far as many of the ministers in the Jackson movement were concerned, that on Monday Allen Thompson would find a way to negotiate, make substantial reforms, and open the door to good-faith negotiations with the businessmen.

Although the division within the strategy committee was not irreparable, it was more distinct than it had ever been before. Finally, once again in the interests of unity and consensus, it was agreed to do what many of the ministers had apparently already agreed to do—postpone direct action pending the outcome of Monday's meeting with the mayor.

The ministers would go to Allen Thompson's meeting, but if his position appeared to be essentially negative, they would walk out. Direct action in Jackson would commence on Tuesday, May 28.

On Saturday, the four men from our side whom Allen Thompson had agreed earlier to accept—I. S. Sanders, funeral director E. W. Banks, the Rev. G. R. Haughton, and the Rev. S. L. Whitney—sent telegrams to the mayor indicating that they would meet on Monday. The Rev. L. L. Williams and the Rev. E. A. Mays, both in our group, also indicated to the mayor that they would attend the affair as representatives from the ministerial associations. Several other ministers in our group quietly indicated their intention of sitting in on the session. Ed King, white, but a minister, was to go along and see if he could attend. And by this time the mayor's own selectees had practically all indicated that they would be there.

It was, in its own way, a quiet weekend. The banner headlines and hysterical radio and television coverage that had accompanied matters up to this point subsided to some extent, and the *Jackson Daily News* said hopefully that there were "growing signs that NAACP leaders have been unable to rally sufficient support among the local Negroes to make threatened demonstrations effective." This was far from the case, of course, but all of us knew that such a charge was the price we had to pay for delay. Our enemies were quick to seize on anything that could be construed as lack of strength.

The *Jackson Daily News* still felt sufficiently aroused to levy an attack at "wild-eyed mobs" who "threaten again to try to grab control of municipal government in Jackson." And the Jackson power structure knew full well that an explosion of direct action could take place at any time. The police were conspicuous in and around the Masonic Temple, and there were now more downtown than ever before. A rumor was circulating that the mayor planned to imprison all arrested demonstrators at the State Fairgrounds. The telephones that we used were so heavily wiretapped that at times any communication seemed impossible. The feeling that a confrontation was shaping up was not limited to Jackson alone. Earlier in the week, one of the tiny handful of somewhat moderate state legislators, Joe Wroten, representative from Washington County, had called for the establishment of bi-racial committees throughout Mississippi. His advice had been scorned. However, his hometown of Greenville was, because of several rather cosmopolitan paternalistic white families, as well as a moderate newspaper editor, Hodding Carter, probably the most "relaxed" Mississippi community. It did move to set up bi-racial meetings between the black community and the power structure.

Over the weekend we once again traveled throughout the whole Jackson area, telling people that "the time is coming—look for action to begin next week." There were many, youth and adult, who by now did not appear to be *really* sure that any action would ever take place. We assured them that barring some sort of miraculous change of heart by the mayor and the white businessmen, Jackson would see a wave of direct action unlike anything that had ever occurred in the state of Mississippi.

On Sunday, May 26, commencement was held at Tougaloo. The day was extremely hot and the affair was held out on the lawn. Along with the heat, the shadow of what lay ahead hung over the whole proceeding; most of the speeches dealt, in a general fashion, with the struggle for full human rights. When it was over, I visited at length with a number of parents of students. They were anxious to know what was happening in Jackson, and I learned from them that black communities in some of the most remote areas of Mississippi were following with great interest the recent developments in the capital city. Some of the Tougaloo students were going home for the summer. Many others, however, were staying in the area for the beginning of the direct action. A large number had signed up for summer-school sessions, which were to begin in about two weeks, and many of them were prepared to participate actively in the Jackson movement.

The commencement exercises had been fine, but during much of the affair I had been thinking about our immediate problems. Later that evening I talked with many of the Tougaloo students and Youth Council members. We agreed that at this point, the key to the situation lay in getting the direct action actually under way on Tuesday. They agreed to drift down to the Masonic Temple the next day, Monday, in order to help generate an atmosphere of immediacy and militancy.

Late the next morning a number of us, including many college students, began to assemble casually in and around the Masonic Temple. Many of the high-school students were to join us later that afternoon when their classes were over. Medgar felt that it was time to move. We talked with one another and with the various adults who came in and out, stressing the necessity of action, and taking the attitude that unless the mayor and the businessmen genuinely reversed their position, Tuesday would have to be the day on which action began. National news media had been calling down from the North for the past several days, asking what was taking shape, and some of their advance scouts had even been through Jackson. On this day their calls seemed to increase, and they were told that a strong likelihood of direct action existed, commencing Tuesday.

In the late morning, about a dozen of the liberal white clergy met with the Jackson Chamber of Commerce. Nothing was determined, although apparently some of the businessmen and more of the ministers felt that the meeting between the black representatives from our movement, the mayor's selected blacks, and the mayor and the two city commissioners might well produce tangible results.

That meeting took place as scheduled at 2 P.M. in City Hall. Eleven black representatives from the Jackson movement were on hand. All were ministers except E. W. Banks and I. S. Sanders. Ed King attempted to attend the meeting, but the mayor balked at this bi-racial aspect and, according to the plan of the black clergy, Ed left quietly. Six of the mayor's own selectees were present. Immediately, Mayor Allen Thompson read a lengthy statement of his position, which soon after a brief introduction made it quite clear that his stand was as recalcitrant as ever: ". . . those who profit by discord, strife, and misunderstanding have attempted to picture my actions as arbitrary unwillingness to cooperate, disregard for feelings of certain individuals, and obstruction of the rights of Negro citizens." Seemingly unaware of the fact that he had, himself, assumed from the beginning the position of the symbol of the city's economic and political structure, he said, "I do not have the legal or moral right to bargain away rights of merchants and businessmen of either race."

Wrapping himself in such matters as his role in raising money to send the Jackson State College football team out of state for sports events and raising money for the proposed new black YWCA, he spoke glowingly of the black schools and other black facilities, which he termed "equal."

Again he attacked:

> The present agitation, on the part of paid agitators and organized pressure groups threatening economic boycotts, civil disobedience, mass marches designed to disrupt the normal business activities, and create mass hysteria, in order to force bargaining . . . can only

lead to distrust and ill-will. . . . I will not appoint a bi-racial committee.

There are two choices facing us as citizens of this city. We can place our duties as citizens above prejudice and loyalty to local or outside pressure groups and maintain a climate of mutual trust and respect [or] . . . follow the leadership of outside or paid local leaders of pressure groups . . . [this] will lead to more ill-will, and eventually to disorder and possible violence.

He said that "If the Negro citizens will reject the pressure policies and practices of racial agitation," the city might hire several black police. He talked of the new clubhouse and library that the city was promising to build in a black park, but said, "We cannot proceed, however, on the proposed $100,000 expenditure for a Negro swimming pool . . . as long as there is the threat of racial disturbance."

When Allen Thompson had finished, the Rev. E. A. Mays, spokesman for the Jackson movement group, told him, "I don't believe, from the speech you gave, that there is anything in it that will coincide with the things that we have in mind."

He and the others then arose to leave. The mayor asked to hear the list of movement demands again, and the Rev. Mr. Mays read them, one by one. The eleven representatives, joined by two of the mayor's own selectees, then walked out of the room.

The time for talking and discussion had now ended. All attempts at negotiation had failed. It was now time for us to carry through what day by day for over two weeks we had threatened: nonviolent direct action demonstrations in Jackson, Mississippi.

We discussed demonstration strategy far into that night. For some time many of the demonstrators had been lined up and fully committed. It was our feeling that the next day's demonstrations would include a sit-in and a picket attempt, both conducted on Capitol Street. The day after that, Wednesday, there would be more of this, and again on Thursday. This, we felt, would serve to crystallize the community mobilization on which we had been working so long. Then, on Friday, when the high schools ended their academic year, we would begin, with these stalwarts of the Youth Council and involving as many college students and adults as possible, the "intensive and massive" demonstrations—street marches. With enough of mass marches, day after day after day, and with as many of those mass-march participants as possible staying in jail for a time in order to bring focus on the situation from all parts of the nation, we felt that we could crack Jackson wide open, and set in motion a process to begin opening up to democracy the entire, sovereign State of Mississippi.

7

It was hot and muggy on Tuesday, May 28, when we gathered at the Masonic Temple in the middle of the morning.

Tougaloo students Annie Moody and Memphis Norman, and Pearlena Lewis of the Youth Council, were to sit in at the lunch counter at the Woolworth store. Shortly after that demonstration was scheduled to begin, five others were to picket in the downtown area—Ed King's wife, Jeannette, another Tougaloo faculty wife, two young ladies from Jackson who had attended Jackson State College, and the Rev. Eddie O'Neal, president of the Tougaloo student body. Ed King, who at that point was not known by the police, would be in the downtown area as a sort of spotter, as would be several Tougaloo students. The past practice of immediate arrests was expected.

The police were traveling continuously back and forth around the Masonic Temple. At about 10:30 A.M., a man took the three sit-ins and casually drove them around Jackson, with the understanding that he would leave them off near the downtown area in time for their demonstration, set for 11:15 sharp. He was to stay in the vicinity and report any developments to us. About fifteen minutes after he left, we took the other demonstrators and, with a wary eye open for police, who knew our cars, drove them to the downtown area. As we left, Medgar notified the news services. The group we took were carrying their picket signs in shopping bags. The white members of the demonstration, Jeannette King and the other faculty wife, were to go around a block from one direction; the black group would come around from the other direction. They would picket together at 11:30 A.M.

Police seemed to be everywhere in the downtown area.

When everyone had been deposited on the edge of the business section, we returned to the Masonic Temple to sketch out the mass meeting that would be held that night at the Pearl Street AME church, and to gather another group for a demonstration briefing. While we were talking, a call came from the man who had taken the sit-ins downtown. He was calling from a pay telephone a block from the Woolworth store, and he told us that the three sit-ins had entered the store right on time, and had immediately seated themselves at the "white" lunch counter. The waitresses then turned off the lights and closed the counter down. The three were still sitting there, and although the police were gathering out front, none had entered the building.

The man also told us that the pickets had demonstrated and had been immediately arrested.

The next time he called was at about 12:15. He was extremely shaken. A crowd of white teenagers and some adults had gone into the Woolworth store, he said, and after some preliminary cursing had begun to pour mustard and ketchup over the three sit-ins.

Then Memphis Norman had been pulled from his stool and brutally kicked unconscious. The police had then entered the store to arrest the man who had done this, and also arrested Memphis. He did not know whether Memphis was receiving medical care. The crowd was growing rapidly, he said, and there were a large number of police outside who were doing nothing to keep order within the store.

I started out of the NAACP offices. Mercedes Wright said she wanted to join me. Medgar came up and indicated that he was also going, but Mercedes and I persuaded him not to; he was indeed a marked man to hoodlums such as those downtown. As we were getting into my car, a Jackson State student, Walter Williams, arrived and joined us.

I drove fast and the three of us were silent as we moved in and out of traffic, keeping an eye open for the police. We parked several blocks from Capitol Street and decided that we would proceed separately to the Woolworth store. I walked on one side of the street, Mercedes on the other, and Walter Williams trailed me by about a hundred yards.

Often we had speculated on relationships between the Citizens Council and the Jackson police, on the one hand, and gangs of white hoodlums on the other. Now as we approached the Woolworth store, our suspicions were strongly reinforced.

There were at least 100 people gathered in front of it, and many were yelling. The police, including Captain J. L. Ray, were also standing in front of the store as a steady stream of white people poured inside. About half a block from the store, I put on my sunglasses since, although Ray didn't know either Mercedes or Walter Williams, he did know me, and I didn't care to be arrested until after I was inside. I eased by him with no difficulty and then, taking off the glasses, looked around.

It was an incredible mob scene. There were at least 300 white people inside, most of them screaming and yelling. The majority were young; some were well dressed and some were not. But also standing inside were many adults, including some extremely well-dressed men who were talking with those young hoodlums who were obviously playing leading roles in the mob. The sit-ins had been split up. Annie Moody was sitting at one end of the "white" counter with Joan Trumpauer, who had originally been in the downtown area as a spotter, and who had obviously joined the demonstration. Mustard and ketchup had been thrown all over them. Down at the other end of the white counter were Pearlena Lewis and Lois Chaffee of Tougaloo, who had been with Joan Trumpauer and had also joined the affair. Newsmen were taking pictures and several radio and TV correspondents were moving back and forth.

Ed King was moving around in the crowd, wearing his clerical collar and attempting to inject a note of sanity. He saw me and immediately came over. Mercedes Wright was now inside, and Walter Williams was just coming in the door. I said that I would join Annie Moody and Joan Trumpauer. Mercedes, whose complexion is so light that she could easily pass as "white," was to move in and out of the crowd and also attempt to make contact with the Justice Department. Ed King would continue to circulate through the mob, and would attempt to get in touch with Dr. A. D. Beittel and ask him to get Federal help. Walter Williams would join Pearlena Lewis and Lois Chaffee.

I moved through the milling crowd to one end of the counter, and Walter Williams moved to the other. As I got close to Annie and Joan, a white man, thinking that I was approaching to do the sit-ins harm, yelled, "Hit 'em, boy!"

I sat down on a stool. Looking down the counter, I could see Walter Williams make it through.

I barely had time to greet Annie and Joan when I heard people behind me asking, "Who is that s.o.b.?" Then I heard my name called. Next, a radio commentator who was apparently giving a blow-by-blow description to a Jackson network stepped over, asked my name, and I gave it to him. The name was called out some more; then the crowd pushed in behind us. I could hear terms such as "nigger lover" "communist," "red."

Trying to ignore the mob, I turned to Annie Moody and Joan Trumpauer, who appeared very glad to see me. Joan said that after Memphis had been kicked and arrested, a white youth had pulled her from the stool and dragged her to the door, but the police had stepped in and she had been able to return to the counter. Both felt that Memphis had been severely injured.

From the little that I could see by turning my head around very carefully, the crowd appeared to be much larger. The shouting, screaming, and cursing had reached a high pitch. Suddenly ketchup was poured all over us, then mustard. Someone, who had apparently picked a paint spray can off one of the shelves, sprayed paint over us. I could feel it on my back, and someone was telling someone else, "Paint the word nigger on him."

I thought, "We could get shot very easily just sitting here." I looked down the counter and saw a large group surrounding our associates.

It was all mass insanity, unlike anything I had ever experienced. It was chilling and unreal. The presence of newsmen calmly taking notes, of TV men shooting film, of radio announcers coolly reporting each incident, made the whole thing seem like a horrible nightmare. My blood was pumping fast and my skin crawled.

Someone struck me several hard blows on the side of my face. I almost passed out and had to grip the counter for support. My face was bleeding. Then I was struck on the back of the head and almost passed out again. I was dizzy and could hardly hear myself talking, but I asked Annie Moody what she thought of the final examination questions that I had asked in Introduction to Social Studies. She smiled and said that she felt they were much too tough. Joan began to talk about her final exams. More ketchup and mustard were poured over us. Then sugar was dumped in our hair. We talked on.

Down the counter, Walter Williams was knocked to the floor. He arose and took his seat again.

A hand with a water glass reached around, threw something liquid in my face. Then suddenly, my eyes were on fire, and I knew what had been mixed with the water: pepper. Now I could no longer see. Rubbing made everything much worse. My eyes felt as if they were being eaten out. We stopped talking, and Annie Moody found a handkerchief and handed it to me. I wiped tears and pepper from my eyes, and in a few minutes, although the gnawing feeling continued, I could see a little. Annie motioned down the counter and I looked in that direction.

A young black man of high-school age was walking through the mob and was joining the demonstration. Down at the other end of the counter, George Raymond, from New Orleans, a CORE worker who had just arrived in Jackson to work with Dave Dennis, was joining Pearlena, Lois, and Walter. Then I saw Dr. A. D. Beittel, who walked up behind us and asked how we were. I told him that somehow we seemed to be making it right along. A huge white man came up to the Tougaloo president and asked him who he was. Dr. Beittel looked at him, hard into the eyes, and the white man backed away. A. D. Beittel then sat down at the lunch counter.

There was a loud crashing sound in another section of the store, then a series of wild whoops and rebel yells. They were tearing up the store! And now a loudspeaker began to blare away. "This store is closed. Please leave the store. Please leave the store."

The mob began to thin. One of the newsmen came over to me. Through my half-closed eyes, I recognized him as Cliff Sessions of UPI, a native white Mississippian, who we considered a decent fellow. He was badly shaken and told me, as he reached the counter and gave me some paper napkins for my eyes, that this was the worst thing that he had ever seen. "These are your people, Cliff," I told him, "but not mine." He nodded sadly.

The store was now almost clear of the hoodlums. Ed King came over, followed by Mercedes Wright. We joined the other sit-in members and, with Dr. Beittel, walked to the door. A crowd of several hundred was gathered out front and the police were very thick. Dr. Beittel asked Captain Ray for police protection, and Ray said that he would provide a paddy wagon to take us wherever we wished to go. By now it was clear that we were not going to be arrested. I said that I didn't care to ride in the paddy wagon. Ed King left to get his car, and Mercedes went to get mine. While we were waiting, I said to Captain Ray, "Fine brand of Christianity you practice in Jackson."

He looked at me, but could not meet my eyes. "If you're going to do things like this," he said, "you've got to expect this."

A long black car, driven very slowly by a uniformed chauffeur, came up Capitol Street. When it drew abreast of us, it slowed almost to a stop and an elderly white lady, sitting alone in the back seat, looked out. She appeared struck by horror and her face was contorted, not with hatred but with deep shock. She saw us staring at her, and then she looked quickly away and the car continued past. Ed and Mercedes came with our cars. We climbed in and, under police guard, were escorted back to the Masonic Temple. As I got out I saw Jacob Reddix, president of Jackson State College, walking into a nearby insurance office. He too stared and appeared deeply shocked.

We stayed at the NAACP offices a short while. Medgar told us that he had learned that many FBI agents were in the Woolworth store during the demonstration, and he was appalled that they had not stepped in when it became clear that the police would not do so. Medgar also told us that shortly after Mercedes, I, and Walter Williams had left, he had turned on his radio, and had heard a Jackson radio station practically telling people to go downtown to the Woolworth store. We then left for the office of Dr. Britton, a black physician, where we were treated. A man took several of us to his home so that we might wash up and lent us some clean clothes.

I went back to Tougaloo. Eldri and I were, I think, more glad to see each other than we would have been after a year's separation. She had heard the reports on the radio and had begun cooking a large meal, not only to keep her mind occupied but in preparation for the large number of students who now began to arrive. Several had just heard a radio report to the effect that the dozen or so liberal white clergy had all signed a statement calling for communication between the races, then expressing their support of the mayor's ability to handle the situation. The students did not know whether the statement had been made before, during, or after the sit-in.

We ate fast. A neighbor who had a telephone came over and said that the college switchboard had referred a long-distance call of mine to their home. I went over. It was an old friend calling from Tacoma, Washington, and he had seen the whole thing on television. It was only then that I realized that the Woolworth sit-in had received national coverage. A few minutes later an acquaintance called from Arizona to say that he and others couldn't understand why we didn't draw guns on that mob and "shoot the hell out of some of them."

When we had finished eating, I took a group of students to the Pearl Street church, where the community mass meeting was scheduled. On the way out the Tougaloo gate, we saw a car approaching. It was the public relations director of the college and Memphis Norman. Memphis told us that he had been jailed, then taken to a hospital, and finally released on bond. He was not in good shape but said that he would join us.

We were, to say the least, very much interested in how the black community of Jackson was going to react to the mob violence; it was our feeling that the people would not back away. We were right. Despite the heavy numbers of police around the Pearl Street church, there were, half an hour before the meeting was due to begin, several hundred people in and around the building. There were more newsmen than I had ever seen before, many of whom were apparently from out of state, since they didn't talk like Mississippians and greeted us cordially as we entered the church. Once inside, I was beckoned immediately into the Rev. Mr. Haughton's study. Medgar, Gloster Current, Mercedes Wright, I. S. Sanders, about a dozen ministers, and several youth leaders were gathered there. Everyone was extremely excited.

Medgar brought me quickly up to date. The sit-in, he confirmed, and all of its violence had been publicized from one end of the country to the other. Late in the afternoon, the mayor and the city commissioners had suddenly indicated that they would be glad—very glad—to talk again with the ministers they had met the previous day. Several clergymen, including the Rev. Mr. Haughton and the Rev. Mr. Mays, and I. S. Sanders as well, then went to see Allen Thompson. Immediately it was clear that a change had occurred. Mayor Thompson had reiterated his promise to hire black policemen and school crossing guards. He said that he would take down all segregation signs, and would even try to persuade white-owned filling stations to end their segregated restroom system. He said that he would comply with various Federal court decisions and would allow blacks to use the previously all-white parks and libraries and other public facilities, and that he would provide protection for them while they did so. A black representative would be placed on the Jackson parks and recreation committee. School desegregation was, as a result of the NAACP lawsuit, in court and he expected the schools to soon desegregate. Commissioner D. L. Luckey had promised that blacks would be hired for worthwhile positions in city government and many of those already on the city's payroll would be upgraded. A bi-racial committee would not be officially set up right away, the city officials told the blacks, but might well be initiated in the near future; in any event, discussions between the mayor, representatives of the black community, and the city commissioners would definitely continue.

Small wonder, then, that the people in the Rev. Mr. Haughton's study were jubilant. By many standards, the reforms that Allen Thompson was prepared to make were not much, perhaps, but by the standards of Mississippi and its rigidly segregated capital city, this was a beginning.

I could not believe that it was true. But the mayor had obviously changed his position profoundly. The only explanation lay in the fact that the incredible mob violence during the sit-in, and the subsequent national publicity, had generated powerful forces—from both the outside world and from within Jackson. It seemed possible that somewhere a faction existed, perhaps among the businessmen, that was exerting a moderate influence.

It was now time for the meeting to begin. Since the ministers had somehow emerged as the negotiating committee, at least for the time being, it was decided that they would discuss their meeting with the mayor and the commissioners, to see what the people at the mass gathering felt about it.

It was a wonderful meeting! Almost a thousand people were packed into the church, and out front and standing on the lawn by the windows were many more. Newsmen lined the front rows. Freedom singing was going on full blast. All of us spoke, and those who had been involved in the sit-in received a huge standing ovation.

Then the Rev. Mr. Haughton and others discussed their meeting with the mayor. As they reached the point at which the mayor had indicated that substantial reforms would be made, the whole meeting grew suddenly hushed, the newsmen all jerked to attention, and several of them left to find a telephone.

When the ministers had finished, the mass meeting roared and stomped its approval.

We then indicated that the demonstrations would be "temporarily suspended" and that the next several days would see intensive testing, to determine whether or not the mayor's agreement was sound. "The doors are being opened to us," said Haughton. "Let us walk through them with dignity."

We made it very clear that the Jackson movement would stay intact regardless of what happened, since it might well be necessary to launch further demonstrations. And in any case, the boycott of the downtown area would continue in order to secure fair employment and fair consumer practices and to secure open restaurants and hotels. A prominent business lady in the black community, Mrs. Claire Collins Harvey, announced that she was organizing the Council of Women's Organizations, which would concentrate on the boycott. When the meeting was over, an out-of-state newsman came up to Medgar and me. Did we really think, he asked, that the mayor's agreement would stand up? We told him that we didn't know, that we were very surprised to learn of his new position, and that only time, the next few hours, would tell.

We did not have to wait even a few hours. Shortly after that, following a brief discussion of testing techniques for the next day, I went home with the students. Ed King's car came right behind mine, for our mutual safety, since the road to Tougaloo was dark and lonely. As I parked by our house, Eldri came outside. I asked her if she had heard what the mayor had done.

She said yes, and then asked me, "Have you heard what he just did?" Allen Thompson's statement had come over the radio just a few minutes before. He had denied emphatically that he had made any such concessions. Eldri had gone to another house and telephoned the Pearl Street church, but we had all left. She had then talked with the Rev. Mr. Haughton, who had just heard the new turn of events. The minister, she said, had seemed sick at heart. He had told her, "The mayor has lied to us before. We should have known better than to believe him."

There was no doubt but that Allen Thompson *had* agreed to the reforms. But the whole heritage of Mississippi, and the Citizens Council machine that was so enmeshed with the political-economic structure throughout the city and the state, had brought its full weight to bear; and the mayor had then moved back.

We telephoned people that night off and on until the early-morning hours: telling them to spread the word that the movement was going to move right ahead, with ever-growing intensity. We asked that, if possible, they come to the Masonic Temple in the morning. Those who had heard of the mayor's apparent reversal were bitterly angry. Several ministers said that they would take part in no more discussions with Allen Thompson. There were no signs of anyone giving up and losing heart.

Very late that night, hoodlums threw a molotov cocktail at Medgar's carport, next to his home. The fire was quickly extinguished with a garden hose. When called, the police eventually arrived and dismissed the incident as a "prank."

The position of the mayor was much featured by all of the Mississippi news media the next day. All he had agreed to do, he said, was hire several black police and school crossing guards, and now, "These two things will not be considered immediately." Thompson claimed that he had said that public facilities, such as parks and playgrounds and libraries, might accept a few blacks, but only because of recent Federal court decisions, and that if blacks used these facilities in large numbers, everything would be closed down. He had given in on nothing, said he, and a "city official" was quoted as saying, "Negroes are told of the alleged promises; they test them and find they are not true; and, feeling that the mayor has broken his promises to them, they are willing to participate in mass demonstrations."

Other cries were carried. The *Clarion-Ledger* in a front-page editorial, "Jackson Is Unique in Its Unity," said:

We are facing troublous times in Jackson. . . . Already the

first act of violence, regrettable and deplorable, has been committed against innocent pawns in the NAACP's unconscionable game of chess. . . . In cities where demonstrations have been successful, parts of the community split off to meet the demands of outside agitators.

Jackson is unique in its unity in this regard. The Chamber of Commerce, the business community generally, the women's groups, service clubs, civic leaders—are all openly and wholeheartedly backing the Mayor and Commissioners in plans to resist mass demonstrations. We will not be a divided city.

Jackson will be criticized unfairly for any act of violence. But these acts have been precipitated by the Kennedy administration and particularly the attorney general's office. If the national leadership met as diligently with Negroes in efforts to prevent further mass demonstrations, as they are in forcing white leaders to lie prostrate in front of this moving mass of hysteria, calm again would prevail. . . .

Tom Ethridge, the *Clarion-Ledger's* top segregationist writer, indicated that, indeed, all was not *quite* as unified as he would like to see it:

In other cities besides Birmingham, wealthy business "leaders" have been quite liberal toward NAACP demands via bi-racial negotiations. . . . As an alternative to losing profits, they find it quite easy to tell the middle or poorer class of white that he integrate a little bit, peacefully—for the sake of "business as usual."

By a coincidence, some of Jackson's most broad-minded people— where integration is concerned—live in "silk stocking" neighborhoods, eat high on the hog, band together in social exclusiveness and are isolated personally from harmful effects of race-mixing which they so tolerantly favor for others—as an alternative to any inconvenience for themselves. . . . A number of groups and organizations dedicated to Jackson's best interests have gone on record as backing Mayor Thompson's stated position. However, others have not done so and should come forward at once with public expressions of support for and confidence in our elected officials in this time of crisis.

Lines are being drawn and it is time for Jacksonians to stand up and be counted—either for or against keeping the peace, safeguarding personal freedom and protecting property rights.

The *Jackson Daily News,* in a front-page editorial, "How Incidents Are Manufactured," added its bit:

Are so-called racial demonstrations in Jackson designed to help Negroes or are they deliberately arranged as publicity stunts to arouse national hate passions in order to raise money from gullible contributors in the big population jungles of the North and East? . . .

NAACP stooges, usually college students or professors and ministers, arrive and go about their designated duties of provoking an incident, arousing passions and letting nature take its course. Adequate time will allow some untoward conduct, giving television and news cameramen time to develop their pictures for the late afternoon network news programs. This procedure will be repeated until somebody, white, Negro or "Red," will sponsor bloodshed and thus desired results are achieved by the propagandists. . . . Our fine law enforcement authorities are fully trained to cope with professional hate merchants.

In a statement which the *Jackson Daily News* carefully explained had been prepared *before* the Woolworth sit-in, R. B. Johnson, Jr., a tobacco distributor who was president of the Jackson Citizens Council, said:

Our law enforcement authorities know what to do and we are convinced that they are capable of doing their jobs. . . . We must refuse to cooperate with the agitators in their evil plans to create racial violence in Jackson. . . . As battle lines are drawn, we can be thankful that Jackson is organized to resist. We must remain cool, calm, and confident that we shall maintain our segregated way of life, which is in the best interest of all of our people . . . authorities have planned carefully, and will see to it that Negro and white agitators obey our laws. . . .

The *Wall Street Journal* on May 29 saw a bitter fight ahead in Jackson, Mississippi:

. . . it seems practically assured that Jackson is in for a siege similar to Birmingham's . . . the city already has laid elaborate plans to cope with demonstrators. Jackson's 600 policemen and firemen are on momentary call, plans have been made to deputize 1,000 whites as auxiliary police and the support of the state highway patrol has been enlisted. . . . Unlike Birmingham, where a group of moderate whites quietly negotiated with integrationists to head off further racial strife, most whites here heartily approve the city's stand. . . .

Whites are being urged to back the city's position by the Citizens Councils of America, a South-wide segregationist group headquartered in Jackson. The Jackson Citizens Council alone boasts 6,000 members, many of them business and civic leaders of the city. . . .

Mississippi State Senator Hugh Bailey, from Winona in Montgomery County, said that he would handle the legal defense of the white man who had been arrested on the minimal charge of assault for kicking

Memphis Norman—Benny Oliver, a former Jackson policeman. "I'll carry his case all the way to the Supreme Court, if necessary," said Senator Bailey.

On this day, Wednesday, the Student Nonviolent Coordinating Committee was holding a conference at Tougaloo, mostly concerning voter registration in the rural areas of the Delta. A bus full of SNCC workers and local people coming down to the conference was halted on the outskirts of Greenwood by the highway patrol; the bus was taken by the police; and the SNCC workers and others had to walk back into Greenwood—although eventually, they arrived at Tougaloo. It was clear that the Mississippi authorities feared that they were supporters of the Jackson effort who might join the demonstrations in the capital city.

There was no question but that in the hours since the Woolworth sit-in and the beginning of demonstrations in Jackson, hysteria and recalcitrance were mounting rapidly throughout the entire State of Mississippi.

The United Church of Christ, a sponsor of Tougaloo, issued a strong statement calling upon the Federal government to provide Federal marshals for the protection of blacks and their few non-black allies in Jackson. In Washington, D.C., Michigan Congressman Charles C. Diggs, himself a black who had on many occasions visited Mississippi, called on President Kennedy to send detachments of Federal troops to Mississippi. "Negroes and whites are on a collision course," he said, "and in the absence of Federal protection . . . I shudder to think what might be anticipated."

But whatever happened, we had our course of action laid out. There were many people, most of them young but several well along in years, gathered at the Masonic Temple by the middle of Wednesday morning. Some were to demonstrate within a few hours, and others would go out the next day. We began to usher groups into the auditorium of the Temple, where Dave Dennis and George Raymond conducted lectures on nonviolence—illustrating that in practice sessions with mock sit-ins and simulated violence. Then we took those who would be going out to demonstrate into another room, where we briefed them on strategy. Steve Rutledge, Tougaloo student and officer of the Youth Council, arrived from having made a survey of the downtown area, and reported that there were large groups of white hoodlums moving up and down Capitol Street as well as 200 to 250 police. Most blacks, of course, hadn't been shopping on Capitol Street for months, and now, Steve told us, there were virtually no black shoppers—and scarcely any white shoppers either. He said that the Woolworth store had closed its lunch counter and had taken the seats off, and that several other variety and drug stores had done the same thing. One drugstore, apparently, had not been going to close its lunch service, but when a large crowd of whites, obviously expecting a demonstration to take place, gathered in front of the business, it shut down also.

The police were very thick on the street in front of the Masonic Temple. We began to take the demonstrators downtown, going out a back door of the Temple and into the cars that had been quietly brought around behind. We left the groups off, as usual, at the edge of the business section. Shortly after noon, the first two contingents, eleven pickets including Mrs. Doris Allison of the Jackson adult NAACP, were arrested immediately when they attempted to demonstrate in front of the Woolworth store. A little later, four others were arrested in another picket effort. We sent five sit-ins into a restaurant owned by Aleck Primos, an official of the Jackson Citizens Council, and they were quickly arrested.

Several of the demonstrators, when arrested, sat down. Police brought black trustees from the city jail to carry them into the paddy wagon, and the *Jackson Daily News* derisively dubbed this technique "squatting":

> . . . some bucks squatted in the gutter. . . . We wonder what kind of education is being dished out at Tougaloo College. The latest status symbol for a Tougaloo graduate seems to wander about downtown, squat down on the sidewalk with the knees and legs in the gutter and await the paddy wagon to come and clean up the area.

By this time, all of the newspapers in the area were printing the names and addresses of those arrested, thus opening them up to economic and other reprisals.

With one exception there was not, in contrast to the previous day, any violence involved in these demonstrations. The exception was Ed King, who, becoming well known in his clerical collar, was struck by a white man while watching one group of demonstrators being arrested.

High excitement was sweeping the black community in Jackson. We traveled around the city later that afternoon and found everything in a great stir of anticipation. With those Youth Council members who had just got out of their high-school classes for the day, we continued strategy planning for the end of the week, when the high-school year would end. They envied those who were already demonstrating and looked forward to their own active participation enthusiastically. The next day, Thursday, they planned to do some freedom singing at their high schools over the noon hour. And, on Friday, just as soon as school was over, we would be commencing the really powerful medicine: the mass-march demonstrations. *And we would keep those mass demonstrations going.* As they had indicated so many times in the past, the youth agreed to remain in jail as long as possible, to inspire those on the "outside" to lend all possible support to the Jackson movement.

The violence of the Woolworth sit-in, the mayor's reversal, and the beginning of direct action in Jackson all had served to unify the various components of the strategy committee. But about this time, vague rifts once again began to appear. Several of us, including Medgar, felt that eventually we would have to involve large numbers of adults in the demonstrations, and although some were already participating, many more would be inclined to overcome fear and join in actively, we felt, if the ministers would themselves demonstrate and go to jail. There were several clergymen who agreed. But there were others who did not, and because of this, those who were willing decided to wait. Then there were several clergy, and other adults as well, who appeared to be against the idea of high-school students participating in demonstrations, and even more felt that if the youth did go to jail, they should be got out immediately. But the youth themselves had no intention of not participating actively in the demonstrations, and were quite firm in their wish to stay in jail for a time. Those of us involved with the young people supported them strongly.

There were even more people at the church that night. All of us spoke, condemned the mayor's turnabout, and pledged a major campaign in Jackson. We had just learned that Roy Wilkins would be coming to Jackson on Friday and sometime during the weekend would lead a demonstration. Some of the Youth Council members reported that after school they had gone to the "white" library—where the Tougaloo students had been arrested two years before—and had spent three hours in there reading.

Newsmen were present in even greater numbers. The freedom singing went on and on and on, so intensely that one almost expected the church walls to fly off in four directions.

It was another great meeting. There was no question; the black people of Jackson were coming into the mainstream of the movement, more and more of them each day.

Tougaloo College had been receiving many threats that our home would be bombed and shot into and set on fire. After the mass meeting, very late that night, I went to Medgar's house to borrow one of his many firearms. I had just stopped at a traffic light down on Lynch Street when a car full of white teenagers pulled up. There was a tense moment, but they didn't know me, just yelled happily, "You know what we're doing?"

"And what are you doing?" I asked them.

"Out knocking niggers," yelled one. "Nigger-knocking!" The light changed and they drove off. I looked for their license number, but they had thoughtfully removed it. I continued on to Medgar's house and borrowed his old 44/40 Winchester and some cartridges. The first big-game rifle that I had ever owned, in Arizona, had been a 44/40 and I liked the idea of having one around.

On Thursday morning we again gathered at the Masonic Temple. Again we held the classes on nonviolence, and with those who would participate in the day's demonstrations, we worked out the direct action plans. The police were much in evidence out front, and just before 11 A.M. we slipped out the back door, into the waiting cars, and took our contingents to the edge of the downtown area. One of the women who were involved was a middle-aged registered nurse who had simply walked into the Masonic Temple and announced her intention of going to jail. She was quite excited, and as she got out of my car, her pocketbook on her arm, she said as her eyes shone, "This is the *biggest* thing that I've ever done."

The downtown area was even more heavily policed than the day before, and the hoodlum elements were much in evidence. Some of the demonstrators picketed; others sat in at the Primos restaurant. All were immediately arrested. There was no violence.

But there was violence, shortly after the downtown arrests had occurred, when some of the students at Lanier High School went out on the lawn during the noon hour and began to sing freedom songs. They were immediately joined by other students, and soon several hundred were singing. At first, the police just drove by the school, back and forth; then, when police cars with dogs in them began to go by, the students began to yell. Dozens of police arrived on the scene and, clubbing several, began to force the Lanier students into the high-school building.

We were at the NAACP offices when we heard the news from Lanier. Immediately Ed King and I left for the school, carrying with us a minister who had children enrolled there. As we approached it was clear that the police had cordoned off the entire neighborhood; groups of them were posted at every road leading to the school. Quickly we found a little road that had no guards posted, drove as far as we could, and walked the rest of the way. The building was surrounded by police, who recognized Ed and me and refused to let us through, although they did let the minister in when he explained that he was a parent. Another minister, the Rev. Lee Clark, came out of the immediate area of the school and joined us. He said that several parents had earlier been beaten by the police and arrested as they attempted to get into the school, and that one lady had been struck all over her body with blackjacks when she tried to rescue her three children. We talked briefly and decided that the time had now come for the ministers, and others, including ourselves, to stage a demonstration downtown in protest of police brutality. By this time, the Lanier situation was quiet and the school had closed down for the day.

We headed back to the Masonic Temple. There we learned that the students at Brinkley High had sung their freedom songs over the noon hour, but that although the police had come, there had been no incidents. Medgar called the Justice Department and protested the clubbing of the parents and students at Lanier, agreeing with us that a ministers' demonstration downtown was necessary. Mercedes Wright was furious at the conduct of the police, and she felt that a protest involving clergymen was needed. We had decided that the Federal building—the post office— would probably be the best place, since it was centrally located, and if the demonstration were held on Federal property, there was a thin chance that we would not be arrested. We began to make telephone calls to various ministers, informing them, in the event they hadn't heard, about the Lanier situation, and asking them to join us at 4 P.M. at the post office for a demonstration made up primarily of clergy. We received positive responses and several indicated that they would call their colleagues. I made up a large sign on cardboard saying, "We Pray for Our Children in Jackson."

There was no question, however, but that "our children" were handling matters well. The Lanier and Brinkley students had sung their freedom songs, and next day students from those schools as well as from Jim Hill High School and the colleges would be meeting, as we had planned, at the Farish Street Baptist Church for the first of the big demonstrations. Cleveland Donald, Jr., and the other Youth Council members involved with the high school had done their jobs well. The network of student contacts that had been built up by the Youth Council for the past year was very definitely going to be making a powerful contribution to the Jackson movement.

Many statements, indicating both hysteria and recalcitrance, were now coming over the radio and appearing in the newspapers. Meeting Thursday, Allen Thompson told city officials and others that Jackson could handle "10,000 demonstrators." Stating what we had already heard, via rumor, he said that the Mississippi State Fairgrounds was being readied for use, and that the fairgrounds was being ringed by a hog-wire fence. And, said he, "if we need more space, I'm sure the governor will allow us to use the state penitentiary." He condemned Tougaloo College as a "cancer of this racial mess . . . filled with race agitators," and charged that there were rumors that the Federal government was readying troops for use in Jackson.

"This mess will pass," said the mayor, "and we will be just like we were before it started—unless we give in to the demands and threats of these radicals."

He also announced that the public swimming pools in Jackson "won't be open just yet because of minor water troubles."

Ed King went quickly out to Tougaloo to pick up another faculty member, Bill Hutchinson, who wanted to demonstrate, as well as anyone else who would join us. Several others, including Mercedes Wright, the Rev. Charles Jones of Campbell College, and Steve Rutledge, went with me downtown to the Federal building, which is on Capitol Street. We parked several blocks away and, scattering out along the sidewalk, headed toward our destination. I carried the cardboard sign in a paper bag. The Shriners were holding a convention and we saw many men wearing red fezzes. We reached the Federal building without incident and went inside the post office to wait for the ministers and any others who might come.

Our group was, of course, interracial, and many post office patrons saw us. Someone must have carried the word, because shortly hoodlum types—some of whom we recognized as having been in the Woolworth store—were also drifting into the building. We stood at one end; they stood at the other end. Suddenly police were assembling outside and, significantly enough, were wearing blue riot helmets. Several more of our people trickled quietly into the post office. But except for the Rev. Charles Jones and the Rev. Lee Clark, and of course Ed King, who had gone to Tougaloo and was expected at any moment, none were ministers.

More hoodlums came into the post office and stood looking at us. More police with riot helmets were assembling outside. Again certain suspicions seemed confirmed concerning relationships between the Citizens Council, the police, and white hoodlums.

More Tougaloo people entered the post office and joined us, including the Rev. Eddie O'Neal, president of the student body. Ed King was parking his car outside, they told us, and would be with us in a moment. The crowd of hoodlums had grown to about seventy-five. They continued to look at us. Eddie O'Neal and I stood talking, no more than a dozen feet from the first line of hoodlums, and we talked about the hot weather.

All during this, people had come into the post office, got their mail quickly, and left. We could hear the postal employees working in the mailroom. Upstairs were Federal offices—the FBI, the U.S. marshals, the Federal District Court. Life continued in the Federal building in Jackson, Mississippi, as it always did, except for more than a dozen civil rights demonstrators, a large crowd of hoodlums, and about 100 police outside. Ed came in. We waited a few more minutes for the ministers, but it was clear they were not coming. I had laid the cardboard sign on a table by us, and suddenly an elderly white lady who had her mail and had taken it to the table, saw the sign—and ripped it to shreds.

With scarcely any clergymen, we went outside for the ministers' demonstration. The crowd of hoodlums followed us and stood in the doorway. The police waited for us at the bottom of the steps. We knelt on the steps, Eddie O'Neal attempted to lead us in prayer. J. L. Ray moved in. We were arrested for "breach of the peace" and thrown into the paddy wagon. Ed King was carried to the wagon, still praying. As we were being driven off, we sang "We Shall Overcome," and life went on in the Federal building of Jackson, Mississippi.

We were taken to the city jail and booked. There was not sufficient bail bond available at the time to get all of us out; more money was expected from New York City in the morning. Two could get out, and Ed King was one of them. His reason was good: on Friday, the white

Mississippi Methodist Conference, with which Ed was affiliated, would hold its annual meeting in Jackson; since the Citizens Council adherents wanted Ed ousted, the conference would be conducting what amounted to a "trial" of Ed concerning his civil rights activities. He was going to be spending Thursday evening seeing those friends whom he did have in the conference.

As usual, we were segregated on a black/non-black basis in jail. Bill Hutchinson, Steve Rutledge, and I shared a cell together. We could not talk about the campaign, however, because the cells were undoubtedly "bugged."

Shortly before noon the next day, we got out, except for Joan Trumpauer, who, because of technicalities relating to her prior conviction as a Freedom Rider, had to remain until Jack Young could file certain legal papers to free her. I went to the Masonic Temple, where I learned the obvious: the ministers had decided not to demonstrate at the Federal building and go to jail. Everything was set for the mass march of students, who would assemble at Farish Street Baptist as soon as the schools adjourned early in the afternoon. Medgar had sent a telegram to the Justice Department protesting the arrests on Federal property, but there had been no real response to that, nor to the earlier protests concerning the police brutality at Lanier. Roy Wilkins would arrive quite late that afternoon. Radio and other news-media reports indicated that the Jackson Police Department not only had brought in its huge auxiliary but was also deputizing other volunteers. The whole sheriff's department was now being readied for use during the demonstrations. Colonel T. B. Birdsong, Mississippi's safety commissioner, had ordered 100 highway patrolmen into Jackson. The mayor was taking the position, which the city had always taken as far as civil rights activities were concerned, that no parade or marching permits would be issued to anyone.

And the weather was getting very hot.

A friend had taken my car to Tougaloo the night before, after we had been arrested, and I now took a black cab to the college to pick up the car and see Eldri.

Tougaloo was excited about everything, and in a good way. Not only, of course, had those students who had remained after commencement been involved in the Jackson movement, but the SNCC conference that had just been held on campus, although dealing primarily with voter registration in the Delta, had had a very stimulating effect on everyone. Something had happened at our home, also. Guy Carawan and his wife, both well-known folk singers, had been through for the SNCC affair and had visited Eldri. Maria had watched the little Carawan boy walking, and she too had begun to walk. Eldri indicated that there had been an increase in the number of threats coming into the college concerning us, but that the people on campus were keeping a close watch on things. I ate lunch quickly and went back into Jackson.

The Farish Street Baptist Church was filling early. Young people were assembling, and a number of adults were on hand. Outside, the police were already becoming very numerous.

A number of students from Brinkley High came into the church. They told us that other Brinkley students, walking the long trek from their school to Farish Street, had been followed by police and many had been arrested and, presumably, taken to the State Fairgrounds. Students from Lanier and Jim Hill arrived. A number of college youth were also present. Before long, there were almost 600 students gathered at Farish Street Baptist. Everyone was talking at once, everyone was excited, everyone was enthusiastic.

Outside, hundreds of police were assembled all around the church.

The strategy upon which we decided was that the students, two and three abreast, would walk from the church, down the sidewalk, toward Capitol Street—which was many blocks away. They would carry American flags and would sing songs. Willie Ludden would lead the march. When arrested, as many as possible would remain in jail.

The Rev. S. Leon Whitney, pastor of Farish Street Baptist, collected from the students anything that the police might, when they searched the demonstrators, construe as being "deadly weapons," such as pocket knives. The collection plates used during the church services were soon filled. Then we mounted the platform and addressed the students—Gloster Current, I, Medgar, and others—but the best talks were given by the student leaders themselves. These young people had supported the Youth Council movement for many long, lean months. This was their day, and their talks were short and to the point: "Let's march!"

So, two and three abreast, carrying American flags and singing freedom songs, they marched out of the church, turned right on the sidewalk toward Capitol Street, and slowly walked toward what awaited them. And a great deal was waiting.

The whole area was surrounded by police in riot helmets, but down a block in the direction of Capitol Street were hundreds and hundreds of law officers. They stretched from the buildings on one side of the street straight across to the buildings on the other side, rank after rank after rank of them. Their blue helmets, their clubs, their guns glinted in the hot sunlight. Behind this solid wall were large numbers of state highway patrolmen, recognizable in their brown helmets, and behind them were sheriff's deputies. And behind all of this were city garbage trucks.

Newsmen were being kept back by the police.

Straight into all of this marched the students, singing and with their flags held high. When they reached the first rank of police, the officers yelled, "Run! Run!"

Some students in panic broke ranks and ran, chased by lawmen who fired shots above their heads. But the others marched straight into the wall of police, had their flags torn from their hands and thrown into the dirt of Farish Street. Some were clubbed, such as Willie Ludden, who was surrounded by police and knocked to the ground.

The students were hustled and shoved through the ranks of police, back into the groups of highway patrolmen, then to the sheriff's deputies, and finally were thrown into the garbage trucks.

Many Jackson black people had withdrawn into houses and buildings when the police arrived in the area and began setting up their human barricade, but some were standing and watching. Several were also clubbed.

With cold-blooded, mechanical efficiency, the demonstration was "handled"—each step obviously well planned and each step executed with ruthless precision made all the more vicious by the utter calm with which it was carried out. Medgar and I watched it together, on the sidewalk, and saw almost everything that happened.

The grim lines in his face seemed more deeply cut than ever. "Just like Nazi Germany," he said.

Several representatives from the U.S. Department of Justice quietly observed the proceedings.

The whole affair was over in a matter of minutes. The fleet of garbage trucks moved off to the State Fairgrounds, and we heard freedom singing coming from the back of every one. Almost 500 had been arrested in Jackson that afternoon.

A woman standing on the sidewalk picked up one of the fallen American flags. She was crying softly.

On the way back to the Masonic Temple we drove through the downtown area. Confederate flags seemed to be flying everywhere. Police were everywhere. Hoodlums were everywhere.

The situation was in high gear at the Masonic Temple. Roy Wilkins was expected shortly. Prior to the mass meeting that was to be held in the building's auditorium that evening, he was scheduled to hold a press conference. We were elated that the Jackson movement was rolling fast ahead. It was our job, all of us, to keep it moving with the greatest intensity. Everyone expected Roy Wilkins to announce that he would lead a mass demonstration the following day. Several of us, especially those who had witnessed the brutal suppression of the Farish Street march, decided to ask several of the ministers if on Sunday they could lead all or part of their congregations out of their church doors, marching toward the downtown area. It would be very difficult for the law officers, no matter how many there were, to arrest that many people.

Ed King came in, tired and angry. He had come away from the Methodist Conference in time to see part of the Farish Street situation. By a vote of 87 to 85 he had been expelled from the conference. Many people whom he had known for years had turned away from him. While there, someone had let the air out of his tires.

A number of the ministers came into the NAACP offices. Virtually none had seen the Farish Street demonstration, and they wanted firsthand details. They were shocked and angry. Then I asked several what they thought of their leading their congregations from the churches on Sunday. The ministers were uncertain, wanted to think it over.

Some clergymen felt that the students should be got out of the fairgrounds camp as quickly as possible. In the discussion several of us gave reasons for the students' staying in for a time, pointing out that the young people themselves wanted it.

Roy Wilkins arrived from New York City. He was a man for whom we had much respect and we were glad to see him. Several other NAACP staff people were arriving from New York also, most of them involved in public relations. Several, we learned, were going to be around for a number of days. Also, some of the top NAACP lawyers would soon be coming to Jackson.

By this time, many people were coming into the NAACP offices to meet Roy Wilkinss and to talk about the Jackson campaign. All seemed to have the same feeling that we had—a very good and strongly optimistic feeling. It had been a long, tough haul, and much more lay ahead, but matters seemed to be clicking right along. With the exception of several ministers, the talk was tough and militant.

Then somehow it became clear that Roy Wilkins was uneasy, quite restrained. Someone had told us once that this was his manner; but in an office full of vibrant people in the middle of a campaign that only hours before had witnessed the great courage of hundreds of Mississippi students, it seemed strange. Something wasn't clicking.

Roy Wilkins and Medgar discussed the matter of a telegram to President Kennedy regarding the Farish Street arrests, and especially the brutality and the concentration-camp aspects of the fairgrounds enclosure. Medgar felt that it was time to ask for Federal troops. Roy Wilkins did not; nor did he feel that a Federal presence of that sort should be requested. It was ultimately decided to ask for U.S. marshals.

Roy Wilkins's press conference took place at the back of the Masonic Temple auditorium. Many newsmen were present. Everyone felt that at this point Roy Wilkins would commit the NAACP to a continuation of the intensive campaign, and that he would announce that he would lead a mass march.

Roy Wilkins, as was his manner, talked slowly and calmly. He condemned the nature of Mississippi, Jackson in particular. He pledged that the NAACP would continue the campaign in Jackson. He indicated that he might demonstrate in the city, but he gave no indication of what sort of demonstration it would be. Nothing was said about any mass demonstrations.

I now began to feel uneasy. The press conference concluded and the mass meeting was scheduled to begin in just a few minutes. Some people were already arriving. Roy Wilkins and several other NAACP staff people went upstairs to the offices.

Several people standing around had been quite active in the Jackson movement. Carefully, and without indicating my own uneasiness, I asked what they thought about the press conference. After momentary hesitation, they said that they expected Roy Wilkins to "lay it on the line" during his speech. I said nothing.

Well over 1,500 people attended the mass meeting. A number of the SNCC workers had come all the way from the Delta, and I saw James Forman, executive director of SNCC, who had been spending some time up in the cotton country. But most of the people who came were from Jackson, and for the first time, a great many were people from the lowest economic brackets. A tense air of anticipation hung over the hot auditorium.

Those of us on the strategy committee sat on the platform. As Roy Wilkins began his address, not only did everything become hushed, but we could see the people become almost taut with expectation.

Roy Wilkins was not an orator but his voice was strong. Again, he condemned Mississippi and Jackson:

> The oppression of Negroes here is an American phase of Hitlerism. Mississippi officials regard Negro citizens of this state as animals, not as human beings. . . . This city has added another touch to the Nazi spirit with the setting-up of hog-wire concentration camps. . . . There remains the establishment of the oven to complete the picture of Nazi terror.

This was what needed to be said. But there was no talk of any mass demonstrations.

The demands of the Jackson movement were discussed, and Roy Wilkins again pledged that the NAACP would continue to back the campaign in Mississippi's capital.

But there was no talk of mass demonstrations.

While the meeting was in progress, into the auditorium came Willie Ludden, limping from his injury, accompanied by several of the students who had only a few hours before been arrested. We gave them all a thundering ovation. Willie Ludden came to the platform and spoke briefly, and his words were strong and good.

But it was clear that something was indeed strange if the students so soon were coming out of jail.

The mass meeting concluded. The people seemed extremely restless as they left, and it was obvious that there had been a letdown. Ed King and I talked with several of the youth leaders who had not been in the

Farish Street march and who had heard both the press conference and the speech. They were disappointed. My feeling of unease was now very strong.

Many more students who had been on the Farish Street march had arrived from jail. We asked what sort of place was the fairgrounds. They said that it was rough; the police shoved some of the students around, spat in the water buckets, threw food on the ground. But that was not why they had gotten out, they told us. There had been a few, of course, who had wanted out, and there were some others who had needed medical help. But the local NAACP lawyers had arrived and had said that they were taking students out of jail. The police apparently wanted everyone out also, and some parents arrived.

There had been a great deal of confusion among the students in the fairgrounds stockade, and it had taken awhile for them to figure out what was happening. By that time, many were already out of jail, but there were still a number who refused to come out.

I went upstairs to the NAACP offices. Someone I didn't know was at a telephone, with a list of parents who had children at the fairgrounds. I didn't see Roy Wilkins.

A little later when I saw Medgar, I casually asked him, "I thought those students who wanted to stay in were going to be allowed to do so. What's up?"

He looked very tired. "There were other opinions, I guess," he answered.

As I walked out of the NAACP offices, I saw Jim Forman of SNCC in the corridor. He wanted to know how things were going. Suddenly, I felt very tired.

I told Jim Forman that I thought everything was all right.

He looked at me closely. Then in a bluntly friendly voice, he asked, "NAACP going to cut off the bail bond from under you?"

His question startled me. Then I told him, "No. I don't think so." And I didn't think so.

Downstairs, many students were standing in the hallway. I did not know what Roy Wilkins's plans were, but I knew what we had to do. I told the students to spread the word that there would be some action next day, and to come to the Masonic Temple in the morning.

8

It was hot the next morning, Saturday, June 1, and despite the prevalence of police parked in front of the Masonic Temple, a good many people, including more adults than we had had before, were filtering into the Masonic Temple, where we ushered them into the auditorium for the classes in nonviolence that Dave Dennis and George Raymond had been conducting.

Several SNCC people, down from the Delta, were around the area. One was Jesse Harris, who was himself a native of Jackson and had been involved in civil rights matters in the city. More young people had been released from the fairgrounds camp. Those under eighteen had had to sign pledges, given them by the city authorities, promising to take part in no further demonstrations. Some, however, were still in, and were refusing to come out.

The NAACP offices were frenetic and the new staff people, down from the national office, were busy preparing public relations material under the direction of Jesse DeVore, who had just arrived from New York City. Although we had people who were downstairs and ready, Roy Wilkins was definitely not planning to lead a mass demonstration. But he was planning to get arrested, and a picket demonstration—of Roy Wilkins, Medgar, and a local woman, Mrs. Helen Wilcher—was planned. We made up the picket signs, and in the early afternoon I took them down to the junction of Farish and Capitol streets, about half a block below the Woolworth store. I let them off and, carrying the picket signs in paper bags, they quickly walked up to the Woolworth store and picketed—Roy Wilkins wearing a "Don't Buy on Capitol Street" placard. They were immediately arrested and taken to jail. A Justice Department lawyer, Thelton Henderson, who was himself black, observed it all and was nearly arrested along with the three. There was no violence.

I headed back to the Masonic Temple. While I had been taking the three pickets down, a number of public statements had been issued via all of the local mass media. Governor Ross Barnett, with reference to the Farish Street mass march, had just praised Mayor Thompson, the city police and auxiliary, the sheriff's department, and the state highway patrol, and "others too numerous to mention . . . for the splendid manner in which you are handling your difficult tasks." Barnett, saying that he had been approached by the city's legal representatives on the matter, pledged that the resources of Parchman penitentiary were available for "approximately 300 of the agitators and hoodlums."

Lieutenant Governor Paul B. Johnson, himself a candidate for governor in the August primary, praised Jackson for "preserving the peace and keeping order" and in maintaining "devotion to southern principles and traditions."

At almost the same time that Roy Wilkins, Medgar, and Mrs. Wilcher had been arrested, Mayor Thompson himself was issuing a statement denying any police brutality concerning either the Farish Street arrests or the treatment at the fairgrounds stockade. He said that Jackson was prepared to "handle 100,000 agitators if pressure groups want to send them down here." The mayor said that he might well hold a special bond election that would include from "$500,000 to one million dollars for construction of jail facilities to handle just such an emergency." To some newsmen he said, "If you come back two years from now, you will find things just about as they are now." With reference to the 1961 Freedom Rider arrests, he continued, "I told you that two years ago and it has proved to be true."

The *Jackson Daily News,* apparently quite proud of the fairgrounds concentration camp, was running a little front-page scorecard called "Agitation Box Score," which kept a record of how many demonstrators had been arrested, and on what charges, how many were still in jail, and how many were out on bond. By this time the newspapers had given up listing the names and addresses of those arrested, obviously because there were so many people involved.

There was still much rushing around at the NAACP offices. A public relations staff employee told me that as soon as Roy Wilkins had been arrested, more than 500 NAACP branches had sent telegrams of protest to President Kennedy. Then a call came to Gloster Current from Jack Young. Roy Wilkins, Medgar, and Mrs. Wilcher had been charged not with the usual "obstructing the sidewalk" but with "restraint of trade." The reason, apparently, had been the sign "Don't Buy on Capitol Street." In any event, bond had been set at $1,000 each.

Gloster Current appeared disturbed at the bail-bond figure.

Downstairs, we now moved to organize the people who had been assembling since late morning and who were willing to participate in a demonstration. There were about 200. Many of the students who had been arrested the day before were uncertain about their status, which had apparently not been clarified by the lawyers, and the anti-demonstration pledge card complicated matters even more. Several, however, decided to accompany this demonstration and thus return to jail. In addition, a larger number of adults than before were participating in this march. The ministers, however, were not around, and very few had been seen that day.

It was now well into the afternoon. The police were still prevalent around the Masonic Temple but appeared to be thinning, perhaps because the expected Roy Wilkins arrest had occurred. We moved out of the auditorium into the corridor and began to line the marchers up, two and three abreast, facing the front door. Some had various picket signs and several were carrying small American flags. They were just getting ready to march out the door when Roy Wilkins and Medgar came into the building.

We greeted them warmly and Medgar gave a quick recital of their adventures: the bail bonds had been posted immediately and they had not been placed in jail cells.

Roy Wilkins said nothing for a few moments; he simply looked at the marchers. Then he said, "No more marches. Not today, anyway, and probably not for a while."

I asked him what he meant. He reiterated what he had said.

The marchers stood there looking at us.

"These people are all ready to go," I told him. "We've got to keep this thing going. We've got to have this march—and other mass marches."

Medgar suggested that we go upstairs. We did, accompanied by Ed King and several others. There was a great deal of tension as we continued the discussion. Once again, Roy Wilkins made it clear that he felt that there should not be a march.

Gloster Current took the position that perhaps the marchers could just sing freedom songs in the Masonic Temple.

I looked at Medgar. He was saying nothing, and again it seemed to me that he looked very tired.

"We've come a long way on this," I said. "But we have a long way to go. It's imperative that we keep this thing moving with the greatest possible intensity." A strange feeling had come over me, and it seemed as if we were all suspended in the middle of another dimension where things happened that never should. Matters weren't clicking into place; they were beginning to jam up.

Ed King was talking, supporting the idea of marching that afternoon— and again and again.

"It took us a long time," I said, more to Roy Wilkins than to anyone else, "to get support from the national office of the NAACP. It's taken a long time to build this movement. If we don't have this march, and many more mass marches, we're never going to crack Jackson open—or Mississippi."

Roy Wilkins was thoughtful for a few moments and looked out the window. No one said anything. Finally he spoke.

"Well," he said, "go ahead and have it."

We arose. Someone asked that we take all the signs from the demonstrators that called for a boycott, so that there wouldn't be any more

$1,000 bail bonds. Roy Wilkins, Medgar, and other NAACP staff went into the offices. We went downstairs.

Many of the demonstrators, apparently feeling that the march had been called off, had already left, but we sent people after them and were able to get several back. There were now about 100 in the line. We took all the boycott signs. The marchers agreed to stay in jail.

Several people came in and said that nearly all of the police had departed.

The marchers went out the front door of the Masonic Temple, some singing freedom songs. We followed them. As planned, they turned left on the sidewalk, down Lynch Street, in the direction of the far-off downtown area.

In contrast to the day before on Farish Street, many people were now coming out of their houses to watch the march go by, and some were following along behind.

A police car came by very fast and the driver was talking on his radio. It was clear that the law officers had been caught off guard.

The march was moving very fast now, and Ed King and I, along with a growing number of people, hurried along behind it. A white man came up behind us, a Justice Department lawyer.

The march had now gone two blocks and many carloads of blue-helmeted police were coming up Lynch Street at great speed. The marchers turned left, into a group of houses and down a little dirt road. The whole neighborhood was turning out to watch, and many joined the large group of people who were following the demonstration.

The police had now surrounded an area about a block wide. We could hear sirens everywhere. A contingent of police led by a man in plainclothes suddenly came into view and tried to block the march.

But the demonstrators bypassed them and with their flags held high and now, almost frantically singing freedom songs, dodged back and forth, a long weaving line, trying to evade the Jackson police.

Then police carrying guns and clubs poured into the area. The bystanders, who outnumbered the marchers, were ordered back. Two large garbage trucks arrived on the scene. One by one, the marchers were placed in them. Suddenly, Ed and I saw a policeman club a young man named James Jones. The Justice Department man was a few feet away, and we immediately told him.

He looked in that direction. Jones was now being carried to a squad car and was thrown into a back seat.

"I'm sure they didn't hit him," said the Justice Department man. He seemed to be peering through his glasses, which he then took off and wiped. "They wouldn't club him after they had arrested him," he went on. "I imagine that the fellow just sat down."

The large number of people who had watched silently were now beginning to drift away, and the police were slowly withdrawing. The garbage trucks, followed by several squad cars, passed us. Freedom singing was ringing out loud and clear from the back of the trucks, but no noise came from the squad car carrying James Jones.

Several of the people recognized us and came over. A number of them had seen James Jones struck, and two or three said that they thought someone else had also been hit.

The Justice Department lawyer had left.

The people were angry. "We're just not going to let this stop us at all," said an elderly woman. "Not at all." She said that she had been talking with several of her friends, and *they* had been talking, and they all felt that everyone ought to get ready to go to jail.

The other people agreed. Several small children asked me when the next march would be. I told them that I hoped that it would be very soon.

We went back to the Masonic Temple. There was great activity in the NAACP offices where the public relations people, under Jesse DeVore, had put together a large number of mimeographed statements, obviously intended for newsmen, on the history of the Jackson situation. The feeling of unease that had been building in me from the night before and had picked up sharply at the meeting with Roy Wilkins was suddenly heightened when I realized that several NAACP staff people were talking a great deal about a voter-registration campaign and the boycott—but nothing about mass demonstrations.

Since people were pouring in and out of the offices, it was very difficult to talk. Roy Wilkins was leaving Jackson for New York City. I reported the incidents of police brutality that had occurred during the march. Several of the ministers came into the offices and we brought them up to date on the afternoon's demonstration. Then, to the surprise of Ed King and myself and several others who had heard nothing about it, we learned that there had been another meeting with Mayor Thompson that afternoon. The mayor, once again, had extended the offer of several black police and school crossing guards—apparently not impressing anyone. I raised again the possibility of several of the ministers leading all or part of their congregations out of their churches Sunday toward the downtown area, even turning back when the police came, but at least marching. The idea did not seem well received, although two or three of the ministers indicated that they felt that such a plan had merit and would consider it. But none made any specific commitments.

By this time, Medgar had gone somewhere. It was the supper hour and other people were leaving. Several of us, much disturbed by the apparent drift of things, went back to Tougaloo. A number of students rode with me, and they wanted to know what was going to happen. I told them I wasn't sure, but that we would keep the Jackson movement going, just as intensely as we could. "And we'll win," I assured them. "We will win."

Later that evening I went back into Jackson and stopped at the NAACP offices. Medgar was not there, nor was Willie Ludden or Mercedes Wright. Gloster Current was in and out, and Jesse DeVore and several of his people were working late.

Steve Rutledge came into the offices shortly after I arrived. We talked with several of the NAACP staff people. They mentioned that Dick Gregory, the comedian, would arrive in Jackson to speak Monday night for the Jackson movement.

I said that was fine, but what we were going to have to have would be the mass marches—many of them indeed, again and again. Steve Rutledge agreed.

One of the NAACP staff persons from New York City said something about "entrenching the boycott," and "stimulating voter-registration efforts."

I explained that voter registration in Mississippi was a long, slow process, even in a larger city like Jackson. And I pointed out that the boycott in downtown Jackson had been going on for a long, long time. I said again that we needed mass marches, day after day after day.

There was a long pause. Someone began to talk about the big mass meeting to be held at the Masonic Temple the next day, Sunday evening, not a civil rights meeting. James Meredith, soon to graduate from the University of Mississippi, had recently initiated a scholarship fund for black youth, and the Sunday affair was to be under the auspices of that group.

Again I said that we were still going to have to have the mass marches.

Someone shrugged. There was another long pause. Everything was casual, everything informal. But threaded all through the atmosphere was a quiet kind of tension.

I tried again. There are many other people, I said, who feel the same as I do: that we've got to have those mass demonstrations in order to win in Jackson.

"Maybe so," someone said. Everything was still casual, informal.

I said that I thought this was going to have to be worked out in a strategy committee meeting, just as soon as possible. I turned to go, along with Steve, who wanted a ride back to the college. He had several of the mimeographed sheets in his hand, the ones that the NAACP public relations staff had been working on all day.

I picked up several of the sheets and looked them over. One was a copy of Medgar's speech; another was a sort of incident-by-incident account concerning Jackson, from 1961 onward. I scanned it, noting that the Tougaloo library sit-in of two years before was listed. Then I looked again. There was no mention of the Jackson boycott, no mention of the earlier picketing arrests, no mention whatever of the boycott from December straight on through.

The history of the Jackson movement began, it appeared, when the national office of the NAACP initiated a campaign in mid-May.

Amazed, I turned to Jesse DeVore. "There has been a long background to this," I said. "The boycott that began in December, mass distribution of leaflets, picketing arrests. Business has been choked off down there for months."

He shrugged. I pressed him, pointing out that he and other people in the national office of the NAACP had known this.

He shook his head. "I don't know anything about it," he told me. He went back to his desk.

Steve Rutledge and I went downstairs. The whole conversation had made me angry. The Masonic Temple was almost deserted. Several police cars were parked on the other side of the street, and halfway across the street to my car, we saw one of the cars used by Jackson police detectives pull out from a parking space. We climbed into my car and started off, and the detectives swung in behind to follow us. Steve and I drove several blocks through Jackson in the direction of Tougaloo. The detectives were making no pretense as to their mission, and just for the devil of it, I decided to lead them around in a few circles. We now changed course and began to drive aimlessly. There were many things on our minds.

Steve and I began to talk. There was, we agreed, no question but that the campaign in Jackson was being slowed down, even though none of the NAACP staff people, including Roy Wilkins and Gloster Current, were coming right out and saying so. Something was in the wind, but it was hard to pin down. In any event, there was no question in our minds— certainly not after the mass-march controversy with Roy Wilkins— that the brakes were being applied.

We didn't know why. Steve thought that perhaps the three $1,000 bail bonds might be the reason, but both of us knew that those three bonds were something of a fluke, a little something that the authorities levied especially in honor of Roy Wilkins's arrest. Money, we knew, should be no problem. The NAACP had a large bail fund and it was right at this time conducting a large fund appeal on the basis of what was happening in Jackson.

The detectives were still following us.

Federal pressure, I wondered. We knew the Federal government was endeavoring to keep everything cooled down. But the NAACP was committed to Jackson. It had pledged its full support.

Both of us wondered about the ministers. Virtually none had participated in any demonstrations, or even observed the direct action. Nor were they showing any signs of joining demonstrations.

How did the omission of any mention of the boycott from the NAACP fact sheet on Jackson fit into the situation?

The detectives were right behind us. As I lit a cigarette, I looked at my watch. Almost half an hour had passed since we had started driving. We decided to head toward the city limits, feeling that the detectives, whose jurisdiction was limited only to Jackson, would give up at that point.

Steve wondered about Medgar and the other field-oriented NAACP people. We knew that most, and certainly Medgar Evers, stood behind an intensive campaign. But their position as staff employees was tough, especially in a situation such as this one.

Nothing seemed clear as we talked, except that a vague but still definite effort was being made to slow matters down, and regardless of motivation, this was extraordinarily poor from a tactical standpoint— certainly at this crucial time.

We were now driving beyond the Jackson city limits, heading west on a paved country road. The detectives were almost riding my bumper. We drove on for about a mile. I didn't know this area too well, and neither did Steve; and the night suddenly looked very dark and very lonely. I looked again in the mirror and saw that a third car was now behind the detectives.

This was too much. I pulled over to the side of the road and stopped. The detectives stopped. The third car, which we saw was a regular Jackson police vehicle, passed us, and stopped just ahead of the point where we were parked. Suddenly I was bitterly angry.

Telling Steve to stay in the car, I got out and walked to a point about ten feet from the detectives.

"It's a hell of a nice night for a ride, isn't it?" I asked.

The voice that came out of their car sounded almost shaken. "You bet it is, Cap," it said. "Mighty nice night."

I turned away, got back into my car, and backed it around in the road. With the detectives still following us and with the police car right behind them, we drove back into Jackson. After two or three more miles, both cars passed us.

On the way to Tougaloo, I stopped and bought a copy of the Sunday paper, which always came out on Saturday night. Ross Barnett's offer had given the headline: "Parchman Facilities Offered by Governor." We read through another article, essentially a summary of Saturday's events. Two-thirds of the way through, however, a paragraph caught my eye. It dealt briefly with the afternoon meeting with the mayor:

Thompson met for over an hour with 12 Negro leaders, including ministers. . . . He said the hiring of Negro policemen would start as soon as the leaders met with their people and told them to stop taking part in mass demonstrations. "I don't mean the little things,"

he said; "we're going to have that as long as outside pressure groups
are working on some of the people."

Neither of us felt that the ministers involved had in any way concluded
any agreement with Mayor Allen Thompson. But the mayor's quotation on
mass demonstrations proved one thing—he knew what could wreck
segregation.

Late that evening I talked at length with Ed King and with those
student leaders who were not in jail. They agreed fully that the internal
situation in the Jackson movement, especially with respect to tactical
approaches, had taken a strange and negative turn. We adjourned for the
evening agreeing that we would do everything we could do to keep the
mass movement intact and proceeding in such a way that Jackson would
crack wide open.

The next morning, Sunday, was hotter than the previous morning.
Ed King had a chapel service to give at Tougaloo, but Steve Rutledge
and I drove into Jackson to the Masonic Temple. No police were in
evidence, and all seemed much too quiet as we parked and walked to the
door. It was locked. I peered into the building but could see no signs of
life. Up on the second floor, the blinds were all drawn tightly at the
windows of the NAACP offices. The car of no one I knew was parked
in the area. Several high-school students came up. They said that they
had been around at least an hour, but no one had come to open the
building. A good many other people had come, the students said, but had
gone away after waiting awhile. They wanted to know when there
would be another mass march. I told them, carefully, that I didn't know,
but hoped it would be quite soon. Steve and I went across the street
and into a little café. There were more young people there, some of them
connected with the Youth Council. They too wanted to know when there
would be some more action. We had breakfast.

A little later, we saw Mercedes Wright. All of us thought very highly
of her. There was no point in hedging on the matter, and I asked her
outright what she thought was happening to the Jackson movement,
especially massive demonstrations. Mercedes felt that there was nothing
fundamentally wrong. She recognized, as did most of us, that it was
regrettable that the majority of the ministers seemed unwilling to
demonstrate.

She knew that any break in the momentum of the movement would
not be desirable. It was her impression that demonstrations would
definitely continue and there would undoubtedly be more massive action
before long.

I said that I hoped we had mass demonstrations as quickly as possible.

Steve and I drove around some more. It was clear that nothing
was happening and that, as far as Sunday was concerned, nothing was

going to happen. People were still getting out of the fairgrounds stockade, but many of the more active youth members were still in there. Most of the other people involved in the Jackson movement were either in church or sleeping late. We drove back to Tougaloo.

There had been some excitement on campus shortly before we arrived. Just after chapel service, a strange white man had driven onto the college grounds. Ed King and several others had stopped him and had asked his business. He had gotten out of his car, wearing a revolver, and had refused to tell them who he was. He then left but not before they jotted down his license number. The Tougaloo people wanted to know what was occurring in Jackson and I told them—nothing.

Ed wanted to pick up a friend at the airport, so later he and I drove into Jackson. As we approached the airport, we could see police everywhere, and we remembered that James Meredith was arriving at about this time. All cars going into the airport were stopped by the police, probably under Federal pressure, in an effort to prevent hoodlums from entering. After a cursory check, all of the cars ahead of us were allowed to enter the area.

We stopped at the group of police. All of them recognized us, and the man in charge made it clear that we would not be allowed to drive into the airport. We asked him for a reason. He told us to move on, right away—to clear out of the area. We told him that we had a friend who was arriving in a few minutes on a flight, and that we had to pick him up. We were told to move away or we would be arrested immediately.

We pulled away and decided to go to the Masonic Temple. The police official ordered a car, in which there were two plainclothes detectives, to follow us. It looked like the one that had trailed Steve and me the night before. We drove with the detectives no more than a few feet behind us. We slowed down, and they slowed. We speeded up; so did they. For almost half an hour we traveled through one residential neighborhood after another, and once we even came to a dead end. We turned around, the detectives turned around, and off all went again. Finally we drove down to Lynch Street. Police were out in large numbers again, since James Meredith was going to be holding a press conference concerning his scholarship fund in one of the offices in the Masonic Temple. We parked and the detectives parked right behind us. We got out, but they remained in their car. I took their license number, and Ed and I went into one of the little cafés and called the FBI, reporting that we had been turned away from a public airport, and then followed by police. The FBI agent was polite but felt that the matter was out of his jurisdiction.

We walked half a block to the Masonic Temple and went upstairs. The NAACP office was open, but we did not know anyone inside. Someone suggested that everyone else was probably at the Meredith press conference. We went to the car. The detectives were gone. The police were gone from the airport, and we picked up Ed's friend who, having called Tougaloo and been told that we were coming, was wondering what had happened. We drove back to the college. The weather seemed hotter than I had ever known it.

We did not go to the mass meeting held under the auspices of the Meredith scholarship fund and devoted to that cause. I knew that that affair would adjourn at about 10 P.M., and that a number of people, including Medgar and Gloster Current, would be in the building. About 9:30 several of us, including Ed King and Steve Rutledge, drove into Jackson. Cars were parked for blocks on Lynch Street, and it was clear that the Meredith meeting enjoyed a large turnout. We finally found a parking space by Jackson State College and walked down to the Masonic Temple, past a number of police cars parked on Lynch Street, and into the building—through almost two dozen police posted by the door.

The Meredith meeting was still going on. Several people, mostly the New York public relations staff, were in the NAACP offices. We sat down to wait for the end of the meeting, and soon could hear it breaking up. A man came into the office who, although a businessman identified with the Citizens Committee of I. S. Sanders, was quite militant and frequently attended our planning sessions. He told us that he thought the Meredith meeting had been a good one, but that there were faster ways to freedom than classroom education. We told him of our experiences with the police at the airport, and talked briefly. He excused himself to go downstairs, saying that he would see us in a few minutes at the strategy committee meeting.

I asked him, "What strategy committee meeting?"

He told us that several of the NAACP staff people downstairs at the mass meeting had announced that there would be a special strategy committee meeting in the conference room adjoining the NAACP offices following the Meredith affair. He seemed surprised that no one had told us, in view of the fact that I was the co-chairman of the committee.

We were also surprised, although perhaps this was merely a mix-up in communication. People were now coming upstairs. We walked into the corridor in front of the conference room. Gloster Current came by us. He seemed momentarily surprised to see us there and mentioned that he had looked for us at the Meredith meeting. He walked into the NAACP offices. I looked around for Pearlena Lewis, the other co-chairman of the strategy committee, but could not see her. We went into the conference room. Something was clearly going on.

It was filling up rapidly. About a dozen there were the ministers involved with the Jackson movement. But I was surprised to see a number of other clergy who had never really been involved in civil rights matters. I could see no youth representatives except Steve Rutledge, who, with Ed King, seemed bewildered. If this was a strategy meeting, I was one of the two chairmen, and I walked up to the front table and stood there. Whatever was going on, it was certainly time to discuss the whole mass march situation, and I began to think of various ways in which it could be presented. I began to feel distinctly on edge. Something *was* going on. Then Medgar came into the room, and waved at me, and I greeted him. I looked out of the window, down onto the street. People were going home from the meeting and even some of the police were driving away.

I turned around. Gloster Current, coming into the room, walked up to the front. When he was two or three feet away from me, he said, "I've got a few things to say."

I nodded. For a moment I felt that something serious must have developed, something that he felt was extremely important.

I sat down, still thinking of ways to deal with the need for mass demonstrations. When Gloster Current began to talk, I gave him my full attention.

Before he had gone half a dozen sentences, what was happening was very apparent. The director of branches of NAACP, speaking a little faster than usual, informed us all that the Jackson movement was entering a new phase. A community-wide effort to really tighten the economic boycott of the downtown area would be involved, as well as voter-registration activity. Because of the broad nature of the Jackson movement, he said, it would be necessary to alter the structure of the strategy committee. It was felt that as many ministers as possible should be members of the committee, as well as those persons involved with the I. S. Sanders Citizens Committee and, of course, the youth and their advisers.

With such an enlargement in the structure of the strategy committee, he continued, it would be necessary, in order to provide all possible representation, for the chairmanship to be rotated.

I felt momentary shock when this had begun, but once over that I realized that a great many things of the past several days, and for a good while before that, were now in full perspective. And I felt angry, bitterly angry.

Someone was making the motion that someone else, a minister, function as the chairman of this meeting. The minister went up to the table.

There was more talking from the front of the room. Demonstrations, generally smaller ones, would *certainly* be involved, we were told. It was hoped that the young people and their advisers who had undergone beatings and jail would continue their good work. They were very much needed. The talk continued. There would be other approaches, we learned. The NAACP legal staff, from New York City, was planning to initiate shortly a series of court actions that were expected to have a positive effect.

The whole thing was now crystal-clear, including the new direction that the Jackson movement would be taking. I could, if I so wished, stand up and begin extremely heated, logical talk, but that would only create in the eyes of many the impression that I was simply power-hungry. For who could quarrel with the concept, a very democratic one, of rotating chairmen? And who could quarrel with the idea of increased community representation. No one in the room, either the original Jackson movement ministers or the newcomers, would appreciate the suggestsion that, even though virtually none of them had participated in demonstrations or had even observed them, they were somewhat less than militant.

In any case, to what avail? I looked around the room. These were well-dressed, affluent men and a few women. They were not the poverty-stricken people, living in the endless lines of shacks in the slum ghettos of Jackson who were still immobilized by fear of swift and certain economic reprisals if they became too close to the Jackson movement, but who were nevertheless making a powerful effort to overcome that fear—at least to the point of observing the demonstrations and attending the mass meetings. And they were doing this, gradually transcending their fear, because they knew what the Jackson movement meant to them and to their children.

To the people in this room, the Jackson movement also meant much, but their concept of full success would obviously fall short of the view held by the poverty-stricken.

Nor were the people in this room the youth who, already haunted by the knowledge of years stunted by segregation and only too aware of the deprivation incurred by poor schooling, were now desperately eager to secure as fast as possible their fair and full share of the world.

The meeting was moving along slowly. Much of the talking involved various affirmations from people, especially from the newcomers, concerning their support of the Jackson movement.

Then I could hear that it was being decided that membership on the strategy committee would not be expanded much beyond its present scope; and every effort would be made, in the interest of saving time, to conduct the meetings in a formal fashion. Now it was clear that the day of consensus agreements had ended.

I looked around the room again. One or two NAACP staff people looked at me, then quickly looked away.

It was obvious that whoever controlled the financial resources of the Jackson movement in the end controlled its basic drift.

Several of the youth leaders had entered and seemed confused by what was going on. Ed King looked at me and shook his head slowly, sadly.

Then the meeting was over. Everyone was going home. Several people greeted me, obviously unaware of what had occurred. The youth leaders came up to me with questions. They had a right to know what was going on, and I told them about it. We agreed to discuss it at length the next day. Ed appeared to be talking it over with the man who earlier in the evening had told us about the meeting.

Medgar came up slowly. We greeted one another cordially. There was a question in his eyes, and he asked it, "You'll be down in the morning, won't you? Down here as usual?"

I nodded. "You bet," I said. "You know I'm with it."

Those of us who were returning to the college went downstairs and out of the building. Almost all the cars had gone. The police were gone. We walked slowly up the street to the car. None of us said much on the way back to Tougaloo.

9

IT WAS VERY HOT the next morning, and the police, as usual, were parked in front of the Masonic Temple. But those were the sole continuing signs of the old era.

Evidences of the shift in orientation of the Jackson movement were only too apparent. For one thing, the NAACP offices did not open until quite late in the morning. Although many young people, and even more adults than on previous days, came to the Masonic Temple that morning, thinking that another mass demonstration would be held, they were told by the NAACP staff people that, while there would of course be some small demonstrations, the mass marches were being held up, as it was put, "for a time." Several of the youth leaders who had observed something of the situation the night before lined up several dozen students, secured a truck for transportation, and prepared to hold a demonstration. But they were stopped from doing so by NAACP staff who, again, took the vague position that the larger demonstrations were not going to be conducted at present. To me, it seemed increasingly clear that the era of mass demonstrations was over.

Those who came in the late morning to participate in a mass march were keenly disappointed, and most soon drifted away from the building. The youth leaders, whose abortive attempt had been blocked by the NAACP, were quite bitter. Even the NAACP staff people, the younger ones, such as Mercedes Wright and Willie Ludden, seemed very uncertain about what was developing. Medgar appeared very tired but in public expressed optimism about the continuing momentum of the Jackson movement. Reports filtered in to us indicating that several of the ministers were now telling people about a "cooling-off period." It was difficult to determine whether this was a glimpse of official NAACP policy or a matter of their own wishes. Dave Dennis, who was still conducting classes in nonviolence, was not at all enthusiastic about the new turn of events. George Raymond, his CORE co-worker, went to Canton to help lay groundwork for a voter-registration campaign.

Dick Gregory, the civil-rights-oriented comedian who was in Jackson briefly, had been scheduled to address a mass rally Monday night but was forced to return to his home in Chicago because of the death of his baby son. We had felt that he might be persuaded to play a role in helping "spark" things.

Most of the out-of-state newsmen were leaving Jackson. The SNCC people who had been around the city for the past several days were now drifting up to the Delta.

While we were preparing to take half a dozen pickets down to Capitol Street, it became clear indeed that another problem was lifting its head: Bette Anne Poole, one of the original Capitol Street pickets in December and long a mainstay of the Jackson boycott, had joined the staff of CORE. She was making picket signs and had put "CORE" on a picket sign as well as "NAACP." Several NAACP staff people raised strong objections. I became rather angry at them. Finally it was resolved by Bette, who on her own volition removed "CORE" from the signs.

We took the pickets downtown and they were quickly arrested.

By this time, court trials were being held each day. Many of us were busy going back and forth from the city court, since the NAACP did not approve of the Kunstler technique of attempting to move cases into the Federal courts. The man who operated the parking lot near the city building always gave us a long, hate-filled stare as we arrived and departed. Frequently, there would be as many as thirty blue-helmeted police on the steps of the building, sometimes as many as twenty inside. On a number of occasions as we waited outside the courtroom for a session to begin, the police would walk back and forth around us, muttering a continuous refrain of "niggers, white niggers, commies, jew bastards." In the courtroom we refused to segregate ourselves and got away with it. A recent U.S. Supreme Court decision had ended courtroom segregation but until now Jackson had not observed the ruling.

The trials themselves were monotonous, with everyone thoroughly bored—defendants and friends, court officials, prosecutors, lawyers, and even the police. Jack Young, the NAACP attorney, and his law partner Carsie Hall gave the best defense that they could under the circumstances, and the judge on occasion even pretended to be pondering the merits of the defense; but the guilty verdicts were a foregone conclusion. The cases would then be appealed. Often hoodlums would be sitting in the back of the courtroom and as we left would grin and laugh at us.

By now, most of the demonstrators arrested on Friday and Saturday were gone from the fairgrounds stockade, although a total of about ninety, mostly young, people refused to leave.

On Monday afternoon we were shown a copy of the day's edition of the *Wall Street Journal,* which, obviously impressed with the arrest of Roy Wilkins on Saturday, felt that the NAACP was indeed committed to Jackson:

> The racial unrest that shook this troubled city over the weekend has irrevocably committed both the segregationists and the integra-tionists to a showdown struggle here that neither side can afford to lose.

This development overshadows the actual events—the mass demonstrations and the swift, efficient arrest of hundreds of Negro activists who participated in them. Consider just one of the weekend's happenings: The demonstrating by Roy Wilkins, the top national leader of the National Association for the Advancement of Colored People, and his almost instantaneous arrest.

The personal involvement of Mr. Wilkins, head of an organization that has up to now put its emphasis on legal remedies, puts the NAACP in a position where it can ill afford to lose in Jackson. Mr. Wilkins himself concedes as much: "We're committed here and we expect to win—even if this thing may not be as carefully planned as Omaha Beach. We knew what the odds were when we got involved."

But a little later in the afternoon, someone brought me a copy of the *Jackson Daily News,* and there, unfortunately, the appraisal of the local situation seemed more accurate. The headline read, "Mayor Asks Applications from Negroes—Strife Over." The gist of the article was that Mayor Allen Thompson had, around noon, "in a hastily assembled" news conference, stated publicly that the civil rights campaign in Jackson was "all over." He told the newsmen that "things in this city are in such wonderful shape" and indicated that he was now willing to take applications for black police and school crossing guards.

The article went on to say that a "move to seek a court directive barring mass picketing, sit-ins, parading, and damage to private businesses is expected against NAACP leaders and various NAACP sponsored groups." In other words, the power structure was hinting about securing an injunction against us.

I went back to the first part of the article, the portion where according to Allen Thompson things were "all over." My initial reaction, riding on a wave of bitterness, was that a deal had been concluded somewhere quite recently. But I rejected that. The mayor was no fool. His police, parked in front of the Masonic Temple, had obviously reported that no particular activity was under way at the building.

In another news item on the page—"Thompson Eyes Race for Governor"—Allen Thompson once again indicated that he might be available for the August gubernatorial primary. There was little doubt but that this traditional ambition of his was closely involved with his wish to secure credit for the successful suppression of what had been the most vigorous mass civil rights movement in the history of Mississippi.

Carrying the copy of the *Jackson Daily News,* I went up to the NAACP offices. Medgar was talking with some out-of-state newsmen who were getting ready to leave Jackson. He told them that they should stick around, that the Jackson movement was still going full steam ahead, that it was by no means over. They listened politely, said good-by to us, and left, asking that they be informed if "something really breaks." It seemed apparent that they did not expect much more to occur.

Medgar had seen the *Jackson Daily News* and it angered him. His reaction, it was clear, was to strike back—hard. But later we had an intense discussion involving many members of the strategy committee and the NAACP staff. As an active member of the committee, if no longer chairman, I raised again the necessity of mass demonstrations as soon as possible, and I pointed to the mayor's statement of the afternoon. Everyone had read it. I raised the mayor's statement of the previous Saturday, when he had said that he was not worried about "the little things": the smaller demonstrations. I was supported by other members of our direct-action group: the youth leaders, Ed King and Dave Dennis. But we made no progress. No one liked the mayor's statements, and no one was happy about the fact that the power structure felt that matters were easing. But the official position of the NAACP—no mass demonstrations, certainly not at this time—was again made very clear. The large number of ministers supported this position.

There were those who said that the very fact that the segregationists were considering securing an injunction against us indicated the vitality of the movement. But several of us replied that, as in the case of Birmingham, no civil rights movement stopped simply because segregationists obtained a court order from a segregationist court. If the city officials were considering an injunction now, we said, it was only because they knew that the Jackson movement was losing its momentum. The power structure could then claim that the injunction, or even the threat of it, played a major role in stopping us. Once we began to lose the initiative, we pointed out, Allen C. Thompson would take it.

Finally, it was decided to make a strong public statement, taking sharp issue with the mayor. This was done, and the demands of the Jackson movement were reiterated; indeed, the terminology "daily demonstrations" was included.

It was clear that an element of real bitterness had entered the strategy committee discussions. The divisions were no longer vague: a few of us on the committee, oriented toward massive demonstrations, on one hand; and on the other, the national office of the NAACP and, as nearly as we could tell, virtually all of the ministers and several other adults involved with them. Those NAACP staff persons whom we knew to sympathize with our position said little in these discussions.

It was also clear that morale was slipping badly at the grassroots. There were not nearly as many people at the Monday night meeting as at many of the previous gatherings, a situation not due entirely to the necessary departure of Dick Gregory. The people who came to the Monday-night meeting seemed quiet, much too quiet.

From the standpoint of the number of those arrested, matters improved somewhat on Tuesday. Twenty-eight young people, in a total of five picket demonstrations and a sit-in, were arrested in the downtown area, and four adults were seized by police in another demonstration. One of the four was Mrs. Barbara Masser, who at her home in Massachusetts a week before had seen the Woolworth sit-in on television and had boarded a bus for Mississippi. She and three other women held a "mothers' demonstration" at the City Hall, in which they held placards saying, "When Children Suffer, Americans Suffer." There was no violence in connection with any of the arrests.

Despite these Tuesday demonstrations, another disturbing trend was apparent. That morning there had been a substantial decline in the number of people in the Masonic Temple for the classes in nonviolence and the usual discussion of the day's affairs. The news, from what we could gather, was spreading around the grassroots that the active phase of the campaign was over.

There was evidence that the Jackson movement was of interest to other civil rights organizations. An out-of-state man who held a prominent post in CORE came into Jackson unofficially to observe the situation. Like us, he felt that it was extremely unwise, from a tactical standpoint, to end the mass demonstrations, and he expressed the hope that large-scale direct action would be resumed. But he felt it was unlikely that CORE could participate, anymore than, say, Dave Dennis, George Raymond, and Bette Anne Poole. We learned from him a little more about the delicacy of inter-organizational relationships between the civil rights groups, including the fact that the NAACP Legal Defense and Educational Fund frequently furnished much legal aid for the non-NAACP organizations. It was felt, and we of course knew it to be the case, that the NAACP would resent any large-scale involvement in Jackson by other civil rights organizations.

Much the same thing was indicated by a representative of SCLC who, at this time, came to Mississippi for an unofficial survey of the Jackson situation. He too was very much disturbed by the termination of the massive demonstrations and hoped that they would be resumed. But he was not at all certain that SCLC would be able to be of any assistance in Jackson.

Later that day, there was more intensive discussion on mass demonstrations. By now, even more bitterness was being generated within the strategy committee. Interestingly, concern was expressed by several of the ministers regarding the shortage of adults involved in the demonstrations of Monday and Tuesday. We immediately told them that the end of the massive demonstrations was being viewed as the end of the active phase of the Jackson movement; consequently, people were withdrawing their interest, and fear and fear-based apathy were again becoming paramount.

One of the youth leaders pointed out to the ministers that if the clergy would demonstrate and go to jail, undoubtedly other adults would do so. To this, there was silence.

On Wednesday morning, even hotter than the previous days, the police in front of the Masonic Temple appeared to have definitely diminished in number. Downtown, there were now very few police in comparison to those of even a few days before. Even the hoodlum element on Capitol Street seemed to have waned greatly in number. Very few potential demonstrators came to the Masonic Temple to attend the nonviolence classes. Nine young people in two demonstrations were arrested in downtown Jackson during the afternoon. These students were neither picketing nor sitting in. Their "demonstrations" consisted of walking up and down Capitol Street, carrying small American flags and wearing T-shirts with "NAACP" on the back—innovations on which several NAACP staff had insisted, since, as we were told, these tactics might avoid arrests.

Late in the afternoon, the *Jackson Daily News* came out with two separate stories. One was headlined "No Participants: Statistics Indicate Negro Move Failing." The other said, "Negroes Desperate for Support."

The Citizens Council issued a statement opposing even the hiring of black police.

About the only optimistic thing was, simply, that a number of the young people still stoutly remained in the fairgrounds stockade.

That night, following a mass meeting in which it was clear that attendance was very definitely waning, and with fewer police than ever out front, we had the most bitter strategy session in the history of the movement.

A number of us called for the immediate resumption of massive demonstrations, and again, we were told by several NAACP staff people that these would not take place at this time. I asked Gloster Current if he were planning, ever, to approve the initiation of mass direct action, and I said that it looked to me as if there were no plans for such action ever again in Jackson. I said that we all knew that the Jackson movement was dying.

New York staff said that in the whole history of the NAACP in Mississippi, the black people of the state had not given enough money in memberships and contributions to pay for even a few days' involvement in Jackson. They felt that the Jackson movement was doing well.

Several of the ministers supported the NAACP position. But there were a number who were unusually silent. One clergyman said that the Jackson movement was not doing well and that there was no point in pretending otherwise. He went on to say that the reasons for the lack of Mississippi black financial support of the NAACP stemmed from rank poverty and many other factors too well known by everyone present to even recite.

The NAACP staff people were silent.

It was a tense and angry meeting that solved really nothing. To several of us, it seemed evident that there was a thin possibility that some of the ministers might be changing.

Summer-school classes were just beginning at Tougaloo, leading the *Jackson Daily News* to run an editorial attack on the college that condemned it as an institution "affectionately known as Cancer College," where "a new course is being installed . . . called Rapid Hate."

I was teaching a little social science each morning, and since this took place quite early, I had no difficulty in arriving at the Masonic Temple each day before things there began to function. On Thursday, June 6, I stepped out of my classroom and, on the way home to get my car, was stopped by a student who told me that he had heard that a number of sheriff's deputies were on campus, looking for me. This came as no surprise, and when I arrived home I told Eldri to call Jack Young if I was arrested. Then I walked over to Ed King's house, which was nearby, and told him what the student had said.

We looked outside and, indeed, a Madison County sheriff's car full of deputies was parking by my house. I walked over toward it, and Ed came also.

The deputies obviously recognized both of us. They climbed out of their car. One, smiling unpleasantly, asked in an obviously formal fashion who we were. When we told him, he presented us each with a sheaf of papers. The deputies then returned to their car and left.

Each of us had been served with an injunction, issued by the Hinds County chancery court and prepared by a number of attorneys, including Tom Watkins. It was entitled *City of Jackson vs. John R. Salter, Jr. et al.* And the *"et al."* haphazardly included Dick Gregory, who was in Chicago, Ed King, Dr. A. D. Beittel, J. W. Jones—a SNCC worker who had gone back to the Delta—the Rev. Charles Jones of Campbell College, Gloster Current, Mercedes Wright, Medgar, Willie Ludden, Dave Dennis, two youth leaders—Bette Anne Poole and Johnny Frazier—who had been among those elected to the negotiating committee more than two weeks before, the NAACP, CORE, and the trustees of Tougaloo College. And then, apparently to wrap all of this up, the terminology "their agents, members, employees, attorneys, successors, and all other persons in active concert with them" was duly attached.

The injunction itself left us all with little more than the right to breathe:

> . . . you are hereby commanded and temporarily enjoined, until further order of this Court, from engaging in, sponsoring, inciting or encouraging mass street parades or mass processions, or like demonstrations without a permit, unlawful blocking of the public streets or sidewalks, trespassing on private property after being warned

to leave the premises by the owners or person in possession of said private property, congregating on the streets or public places as mobs, and unlawfully picketing business establishments or public buildings in the City of Jackson, Hinds County, Mississippi, and from performing acts calculated to cause breaches of the peace in the City of Jackson, Hinds County, Mississippi,

and from conspiring to engage in unlawful street parades, unlawful processions, unlawful demonstrations, unlawful boycotts, unlawful trespasses, and unlawful picketing,

and from doing any acts designed to consummate conspiracies to engage in said unlawful acts of parading, demonstrating, boycotting, trespassing and picketing or other unlawful acts and from engaging in acts and conduct customarily known as "kneel-in's" in churches in violation of the wishes and desires of said churches.

You will refrain from doing any of the foregoing acts until the further order of this Court, upon penalty of contempt.

The order was to remain in effect pending a hearing in the Hinds County chancery court.

Attached to all of this was a summons into the chancery court for a hearing, and the hearing was set for the first Monday in September, *three months away.*

There was no question but that the injunction had to be defied; it was just one more reason for demonstrating massively in Jackson. We left for the Masonic Temple.

The police were even more diminished along Lynch Street and the weather was hotter. Very few people had shown up to demonstrate, and those who had shown up had been told by the NAACP that all action was being held up until a decision was made concerning the injunction. Once again everything was frenetic in the NAACP offices. Added to everyone else who was usually there were several NAACP lawyers who had come to Jackson a day or so before to file several pieces of litigation. Medgar, Gloster Current, and several others had already been served with the injunction, and as we talked, other persons came in who had either been served or who expected to be at any time. Dick Gregory, who would arrive in Jackson the next day, was expected to receive his copy of the injunction as soon as he stepped off the plane.

The NAACP legal staff had scheduled a press conference for Thursday noon, at which legal-action plans were to be announced. The press affair was now postponed for a day, and we went into the conference room to discuss the injunction.

There was not as much debate on the matter as I had expected. Once again, I called for the immediate resumption of massive direct action, to defy the injunction and to crack Jackson. Though it became clear once more that this sort of action was not to take place, everyone, after considerable discussion, agreed that the injunction had to be defied. Several ministers, entering the room and having heard the news, agreed that it could not stand unchallenged from the standpoint of demonstrations, but it was apparent that they meant the smaller type of demonstration.

The NAACP attorneys took the position that the injunction was illegal, although they felt that any demonstrations should wait until the next day, when various legal papers challenging the city's action would be filed. The attorneys indicated that they would move immediately to prepare that particular matter, and that they already had a lawsuit in preparation that asked for an end to police arrests of peaceful civil rights demonstrators, and one that attacked the segregated nature of several of Jackson's major restaurants. They planned to work all afternoon and evening preparing these, and wanted all of us to come down to Jack Young's law offices to give affidavits and pertinent information.

This was good news, certainly, but we knew that it would be a long, long time before the litigation traveled through Mississippi's courts, whether the state judiciary or the state-dominated Federal Courts.

An NAACP statement was issued on the city's injunction:

Jackson officials once again demonstrated their unique capacity for speaking from two sides of their mouths today by seeking to enjoin NAACP-sparked demonstrations and selective buying activities currently being executed to expose Jackson's rough and rigid racial abuses . . . our movement is sharp, vital, and inclusive.

It was a good statement for the public.

Just before we left for the lawyers' offices, several young men came in who had on their own volition attempted to use the publicly owned municipal golf course, which was "white." Golf-course officials had refused to let two of them play, claiming that golf shoes were needed. Two others, however, had golf shoes and surprisingly had been allowed to play. But the officials removed all of the tables and chairs from the clubhouse so that the men could not sit down. And white men let the air out of their tires while the police watched.

We spent most of that afternoon with the attorneys. The legal action was prepared. Much later I picked up a copy of the *Jackson Daily News*, whose headline not unexpectedly read "Demonstrators Told to Cease." The news story was long and involved; one would have thought that Jackson, Mississippi, had just won a major court victory. One portion of the news story was interesting: in submitting reasons for the injunction, the city had discussed the long Jackson boycott movement, beginning back in December. It appeared that Tom Watkins, at least, remembered how it all began.

Friday morning seemed much hotter than anything before, and the temperature was expected to go over 100 degrees. There were only a very few police in front of the Masonic Temple. The injunction had stirred interest, and there were more young people and adults trickling into the nonviolence classes than had been the case for several days, but most drifted quietly away when they learned that there were no massive demonstrations scheduled. In the NAACP offices, most of the talk now involved the legal action phases of the situation, and the attorneys were beginning the long, frustrating journey into the various state and Federal courts.

There was also a feeling of optimism, which several of us did not share, regarding the desegregation of the golf course the previous day. With the exception of Medgar, NAACP officials appeared to feel that this indicated a significant behind-the-scenes retreat on the part of the power structure. But we could see no indication of any great victory. In the end, it fell under various high Federal court desegregation rulings and, like the library, was of no great pertinence to the immediate needs of the many thousands of black people in Jackson. The withdrawal of the seats in the clubhouse and the deflation of tires made the whole thing minimal. Then, to cap it all, several students came in to tell us that a little while before about thirty-five black youngsters, having heard that the golf course was open, had wandered over to a "white" park and attempted to play softball. Police had arrived and ordered the children to move on, and the youngsters withdrew to a nearby black neighborhood. Then the police arrested twenty-one of the children, charging that they were blocking a street.

New York staff felt that if fewer children had tried to use the park, the arrests would not have taken place, and that such "testing" should not be in large numbers. Several of us, of course, disagreed, and the whole argument of massive action again rose to the surface with all of its bitterness.

A little later, the golf course once again refused to admit blacks. Only the library, which no one was really interested in as an issue, remained open.

We took twenty-six young people downtown that day, and there was brief picketing, with several also carrying American flags. All were quickly arrested. The police were for the most part gone from the downtown area, and although the boycott was holding up well, most of the white shoppers, absent from Capitol Street since the Woolworth sit-in, now seemed to have returned.

By this time almost everyone had come out of the fairgrounds stockade.

The Jackson newspapers and other mass media were talking mostly about the legal maneuvers of the NAACP, and giving everyone the impression that the Jackson movement was just about over.

There was no question in my mind, or that of Ed King, Dave Dennis, and the youth leaders, that the Jackson movement was almost dead. The grim picture was very much in focus, not only to ourselves but to a great many people at the grassroots. The NAACP staff people were either cheerful advocates of a roseate view or, like Medgar, increasingly silent. There were a few representatives of other civil rights groups traveling in and out of Jackson—such as John O'Neal of SNCC and Jerome Smith of CORE—and they, aware of what was developing, agreed that there was no hope unless the massive demonstrations were immediately resumed.

A number of NAACP staff persons and several of the ministers were beginning to step up the campaign against "other organizations"; this had been initially indicated by the dispute over "CORE" on Bette Anne Poole's picket sign the preceding Monday. Even Dave Dennis was being viewed, especially by some of the New York NAACP staff, with ill-concealed hostility. The few remaining SNCC people now returned to the Delta. With the exception of Dave Dennis, who stayed with us, other CORE people moved on to Canton to help George Raymond, who had gone there several days before.

The NAACP continued to take the position that everything was moving along very well. There were more embittered debates within the strategy circle over massive demonstrations.

That night almost 2,000 people came to the Masonic Temple, where the noted singer and celebrity Lena Horne gave a performance for the Jackson movement, as did Dick Gregory, who had come to Jackson to demonstrate and was on the program. Each was excellent and each, on the civil rights matter, was genuinely militant. But to those of us who knew what was occurring, and to an obviously increasing number of local people, it all had a hollow ring.

All of us, the whole strategy committee, were sitting up on the platform during the mass meeting. Sitting in front of me, a little down to one side, were several NAACP staff people. A nine-year-old boy who was brought to the platform, had his arm twisted earlier in the day by a policeman who sought to make the boy say "sir." The boy took the microphone, recited what had happened to him, and then shouted, "We've got to march!"

The audience stirred. Very delicately, an NAACP staff man led the boy away from the microphone.

I went back to Tougaloo that night to an empty house. Threats had been pouring into the college regarding what was going to be done to our home; Eldri had begun putting Maria over at Ed King's house each night. Then we decided that both Eldri and Maria should leave Jackson for a time. Eldri had been reluctant to go, but we pressed the issue since, although it was clear that the Jackson movement was dying, we knew that retaliation was even more likely to occur. The night riders would become more certain of themselves.

Some of these hoodlums were already sure of themselves. Frequently now, we would see carloads of white youths on the roads around Tougaloo, especially those roads between the college and Jackson. Several shots had been fired onto the campus from cars passing swiftly at night. A few days earlier in the week, someone—we suspected a white cabdriver—had loosened the lug nuts on the front wheels of my car while it was parked briefly in the city.

Eldri had left Friday afternoon for Minnesota by airplane. She traveled under her maiden name, since we knew she might be arrested by Jackson authorities just for the sake of harassment if they knew she was leaving, and since we suspected that the police kept close liaison with the airport ticket offices. Since my car would be immediately recognized, another faculty member drove her to the air terminal. She cried as she left, and even Maria, scarcely more than a year old, seemed unusually solemn. Now, back to an empty house and aware that the Jackson movement was nearly dead, I wondered if we had not made a mistake by sending Eldri and Maria to Minnesota.

That night shotgun blasts were fired into a grocery store owned by one of the ministers.

Saturday was an extremely hot day. Only a handful of police were in the area of the Masonic Temple. There was scarcely a pretense of civil rights activity—since, as we were told, some financial adjustments were being made concerning bail-bond resources and arrests at this point had been deemed undesirable. It was almost a moot question, because very few people came into the Masonic Temple. Some of the ministers seemed very much concerned, almost afraid, because of the shotgun blasts that had been fired into their colleague's grocery the night before.

Dick Gregory was very much concerned about the lack of momentum in the Jackson movement and issued a strong statement to newsmen explaining why he was returning to Chicago: "The NAACP decided to go into the courts—and I'm no attorney. I came down here to be with that little man in the street; and I was willing to go to jail for ten years, if necessary, to get this problem straight."

The strategy discussions became even more acrimonious.

A number of the out-of-town NAACP staff people indicated to us that they were leaving Jackson "for a time." Others said that they were departing the first of the week but would "be back." Medgar was tired and extremely discouraged.

The *Jackson Daily News* devoted much of its front page to a feature story discussing the fact that the Women for Constitutional Government had during the previous two weeks been feeding the large numbers of police and other lawmen on duty in Jackson. Its editorial was devoted to the fact that the *Worker,* a Communist organ in New York City, had condemned Jackson for its suppression of civil rights demonstrations. Said the *Jackson Daily News,* "the NAACP is walking hand in hand with the Communists in connection with the current ruckus."

"What current ruckus?" we asked ourselves.

On Sunday, June 9, almost by habit we gathered at the NAACP offices. About two dozen young people, mostly students, had volunteered to visit white Jackson churches in an effort to attend church services. But not unexpectedly, it was made clear that they were not to get arrested. Subsequently, several gained entrance to a Roman Catholic church which had always been open to all. About seventeen other students, however, were turned away from half a dozen Protestant churches, including First Baptist, where Governor Ross Barnett functioned as a Sunday-school teacher. It appeared that nearly all white clergymen and laymen were in support of the exclusion of blacks, but at least two ministers were not. The two clergymen at Galloway Memorial Methodist announced their resignations only minutes after several students had been turned away by church laymen. One, the Rev. Jerry Furr, the assistant pastor, had earlier in the year joined the twenty-seven other Methodist ministers in signing the statement calling for an end to racial discrimination in Mississippi. The senior minister at Galloway, Dr. W. B. Selah, who had been at the church for nineteen years, had issued his own statement along these lines. Now both were resigning.

"I know in conscience," said Dr. Selah, "there can be no color bar in a Christian church, so I will ask the bishop for another appointment."

The Rev. Jerry Furr said, "I could not willingly serve a church that turns any people away."

At the offices in the Masonic Temple, we quarreled on the matter of massive demonstrations; by now there were disputes concerning *any* demonstrations. We were told that heavy emphasis would be placed on a voter-registration campaign.

It was even hotter on Monday, and one had to look hard to see even one police car along Lynch Street. A few people came into the Masonic Temple, asking if there would be any demonstrations that day, and were told by an NAACP staff man to check back later. They did not return.

The NAACP attorneys were in court, pressing the various pieces of litigation, and were already encountering a multitude of obstacles. At one hearing in the Federal District Court, Mayor Allen Thompson explained that in Jackson there had always been "voluntary separation of the races" and that, in the suppression of civil rights demonstrations, "no more effort than was necessary" was used by law-enforcement officials.

We had another confrontation, tough and intense and angry, on the matter of strategy. Again, I called for massive demonstrations immediately —as did the other direct actionists.

Now we were told that not only would there *definitely* be no more massive demonstrations in Jackson but that even the smaller ones were now going to be tapered off—a process which had, of course, already occurred.

Several of the ministers stirred uneasily at this, and one or two indicated that church members had talked with them and had taken the position that things were slowing down too much.

One of the young people pointed out that the ministers, with only an exception or two, had still not demonstrated and gone to jail. And someone pointed out that Gloster Current had not been arrested.

Then, quite aware that there had been no indication that SCLC would do so, I very slowly and deliberately raised the possibility that perhaps the time had come to tender an invitation to SCLC, asking it to enter the Jackson situation to assist in the campaign—if it could still be called a campaign. Others in the direct action group immediately supported the idea.

The lines drew tight and sharp. The NAACP staff people, except for Medgar, who said nothing, condemned the idea with the most heated vigor. The Jackson ministers, either by their silence or through their words, supported the NAACP position; but it seemed clear that in several cases they supported it reluctantly. The debate went on and on and on. We were reminded how much more the NAACP had done for Mississippi than Mississippi blacks had done for the NAACP. We called for mass demonstrations—indeed, any demonstrations—and we talked of SCLC. All of this got nowhere; it was clear that the status quo would remain.

Late Monday night someone showed me a copy of a Sunday edition of the *Washington Post*. A headline pinned the situation accurately enough: "Jackson NAACP Drive Appears to Be at a Standstill."

Very late Monday night, we began to consider various approaches to securing assistance from SCLC.

The heat pressed down on Tuesday, June 11. Only a police car or two occasionally cruised past the Masonic Temple. And only very few police were stationed in downtown Jackson. Significantly, we saw no police anywhere who were wearing the blue riot helmets. Everything was very quiet in Jackson, Mississippi.

With the exception of Medgar, who, although tired and withdrawn, was still as cordial as ever, those NAACP staff still around were cold and hostile; it was apparent that the talk about SCLC had brought about the final severance of relationships that had actually been breaking for days.

About ten youngsters showed up at the Masonic Temple. Finally it was agreed that we could take them down to Capitol Street and they could wear the NAACP T-shirts, but to avoid arrests they were to carry no signs and carry no flags.

Steve Rutledge and I took a group of the youngsters in my car. As we were climbing in, Jackson police drove past. They saw us, slowed until I was headed in the direction of downtown, then began to follow. With nothing better to do, and with the youngsters still in my car, we led the police around Jackson for a time, then drove out to Tougaloo. The police stopped near the city limits, but when we drove back into the city, they were waiting. We returned to Tougaloo and tried another road into Jackson. By this time the police had apparently decided that something was up and had all of the roads posted. With an entourage of Jackson police cars behind us, we drove into Jackson again, then finally downtown. I let the youngsters off, and they walked up and down Capitol Street wearing their NAACP T-shirts. Neither they nor several others who went down later in the afternoon were arrested.

Steve and I drove around Jackson, trailed now by the detectives who had on other occasions specialized in following my car. Finally, on Farish Street, I pulled over and parked, and they pulled in behind me and stopped. I got out and went over to their car, asking just why they seemed so intent on following us. Steve got out. When I approached their car door, which the driver had quietly opened, he suddenly gave it a terrific push. It struck me, almost knocking me down. Both detectives then got out, and one drew his revolver. I asked them their names and their police rank, and after much condemnation of me, they gave the information. With them following, we went to the home of the Rev. Tom Johnson, who was still connected with the advisory committee to the U.S. Commission on Civil Rights and reported the incident. Tom called the police department, and as we all knew would be the case, there was no concern expressed from that quarter. By this time, though, the detectives had driven off.

Steve and I returned to the Masonic Temple. Medgar was standing in the auditorium of the almost deserted building. We told him what had happened and learned that a short while before he had almost been swiped by a police car, which had deliberately swerved to hit him while he was crossing Lynch Street. The Jackson police had been following him around also. He was very tired and worn, with sharper lines in his face than before, and he seemed quietly sad. We talked for a time, not about the Jackson movement. Then I went back to Tougaloo.

Civil rights demonstrations were taking place all over the nation these days, except for Mississippi, and earlier that afternoon two black students had been quietly enrolled in the University of Alabama, despite Governor George Wallace's stand-in at the door. Early in the evening, President John F. Kennedy went on national television to issue his plea for Federal civil rights legislation:

The fires of frustration and discord are burning in every city, North and South. Where legal remedies are not at hand, redress is sought in the streets in demonstrations, parades, and protests, which create tension—and threaten lives. We face, therefore, a moral crisis as a country and a people. It cannot be met by repressive police action.

It cannot be quieted by token moves or talk. It is time to act in the Congress, in your state and local legislative body, and, above all, in all of our daily lives. . . .

These were good words indeed. But we knew, all of us who heard him in Mississippi, just how white Mississippi acted and would continue to act, in the state legislature and in daily life.

The mass meeting that night was held in a small church, and even so, it was not full. The trend of the past few days was again quite clear: people were fast dropping away.

Another trend was now very clear: most of the meeting was devoted to a discussion of voter registration. The NAACP's chief voter-registration man for the lower south, W. C. Patton, was at the meeting, having just arrived in Mississippi, we now learned, to organize a voter-registration campaign in Jackson. With him as a visiting speaker was an NAACP official from Memphis, Tennessee, who told us that blacks in Memphis had found that voter registration was the "key to integration." But as almost everyone at the meeting knew, there was, in most of Tennessee and especially in its larger cities, such as Memphis, virtually no obstacles at all to black voter registration, and certainly no barriers compared to the situation in Mississippi, including Jackson.

The new trend of civil rights effort in Jackson was being laid down.

An effort was made by NAACP staff people at this meeting to sell the NAACP T-shirts.

And Medgar looked very tired.

When the meeting was over, Ed King took me to a filling station on Lynch Street where I was having my car serviced. The events of the afternoon, being followed continuously by the police, had led me to feel that all possible effort should be initiated to forestall any breakdown of the car. Then we returned to Tougaloo, our cars almost bumper to bumper. Carloads of white youths were frequently seen now around Tougaloo and on the roads leading to the school.

Back at Tougaloo, we talked briefly at Ed King's home. It was obvious that the action phase of the Jackson movement was now, with the entrance of the voter-registration campaign, officially over. There was no question in our minds but that the time had come to utilize every means at our disposal to bring SCLC into Jackson. We felt that a formal petition, addressed to Dr. Martin Luther King, requesting SCLC involvement, and signed by all of us who wanted a rebirth of the Jackson movement, would be a beginning. The young people were definitely in accord with this, and we felt that certainly a number of adults must also feel the same way. There was even a likelihood that several of the ministers, after they realized that the Jackson movement was now dead, might well attach their names to such a petition.

It was very late at night. I started to go to my home. Ed reminded me to keep out of the lighted areas of the now still campus.

At home, everything was silent, and I turned off the light and climbed into bed and lay there thinking for several moments. Ed's warning bothered me, as did the events involving the detectives that afternoon and Medgar's experience with the swerving police car. I knew, too, that frequently following a strong civil rights speech by the President or his brother, the Attorney General, strange, angry things happened in Mississippi. I turned on the light, got out of bed, and brought the 44/40 that Medgar had lent me out from the corner of the bedroom. I laid it on the floor beside the bed. Then I went to sleep.

I had slept probably only ten minutes or so when I was awakened by someone at the front door. Reaching for the rifle, I asked who it was.

The voice came again, and I recognized it. It was George Owens, business manager of the college. I went to the door and opened it. He stood there and I could see his face only dimly. A call had just come for me, he said, but realizing that it was late at night, he had asked for the message. He hesitated, then went on, forcing his words: "Medgar Evers has been shot. He is probably dead."

10

GEORGE OWENS AND I looked at each other in the dark Mississippi night. Everything in my mind seemed to come to a stop and it felt, there for a brief moment, that out and beyond from where we stood stretched nothing at all—that everything was a dream. I looked around. There was a little mist rising from the ground. The stars seemed cold. Dogs were barking in the distance. I looked at George Owens again and asked him to repeat what he had said.

He told me all that he knew. Medgar had been shot in front of his home moments after he had gotten out of his car. He was badly wounded and the man who had tried to call me, whoever he was, knew only that Medgar was not expected to live.

I went immediately to George Owens's house and called Houston Wells, Medgar's next-door neighbor. Houston Wells told me that Medgar was dead, that he had died just a few minutes before at a hospital. About 12:30 A.M., Wells had heard a shot fired and had then heard Myrlie Evers scream. He went outside with his revolver and saw Medgar lying a few feet from his car in a pool of blood. Wells fired a shot into the air and called for help. Neighbors came immediately, and a few moments later the Jackson police arrived. Under police escort, Houston Wells had taken Medgar to the University Hospital. The only words that Medgar had spoken had been garbled and incoherent, something concerning "turn me loose."

After thirty-seven years of life, Medgar Evers had been struck down by that ultimate manifestation of the ancient hatreds of Mississippi— the claw on the trigger in the night. When I finished talking with Houston Wells it was almost 2 A.M. My mind felt strangely clear. I said good night to George Owens and wandered out under the trees on the lonely Tougaloo campus.

There was no question about what now had to be done. If every good and every valid reason had already existed for the development of massive demonstrations in Mississippi's capital, there was now another. And on the whole Jackson movement a price tag had this night been placed, a price so high that nothing the movement secured could quite match what had been done. But we would come as high as we could in trying—and we would *try!*

185

Now we had to move! And move into the streets!

Ed King's house was dark. I banged on the door, receiving the same careful query that I had given George Owens. I told Ed and Jeannette what had happened, and neither of them, as I suddenly realized had been the case with my reaction, was surprised. But they too were stunned, and they felt a certain anguish that I did not: Mississippi was their state.

Jeannette King began to make some coffee. Ed and I talked. He agreed that there was only one direction now for the Jackson movement—full ahead. There was no question for any of us but that the black people of Jackson, given any encouragement at all, would join a massive movement. In fact, Jackson movement or not, it was our feeling that the people, one way or the other, would seek an outlet for protest, regardless of how anyone felt about it: our direct action portion of the strategy committee, the ministers, the national office of the NAACP, or the power structures of Jackson and the sovereign state of Mississippi.

I went over to the Tougaloo men's dormitory and began awakening students, telling them what had happened. They knew what needed to be done, and telephone calls began to go out to youth leaders in Jackson.

Dawn began to break over Mississippi. Ed and I and some students went to the home of Dr. A. D. Beittel. He too had heard what had occurred. We talked for a time; then Dr. Beittel called people in the U.S. Commission on Civil Rights in Washington. After he had spoken awhile he gave me the telephone. The man with whom I found myself talking was Norman Kurland, whom I had met months before while surveying poverty on the Delta. He was crying. I said that troops and marshals were needed in Jackson immediately. He agreed and said that he would convey this word to those in charge of such matters, but that, much as these were needed, they would probably not be sent.

When we left Dr. Beittel's house it was well past dawn. It was a beautiful day in Mississippi in the cool of the early morning and with a deep blue sky. I hated it, the superficial beauty of Mississippi.

I did not bother to cancel my early-morning summer-session class. No one would expect me there, and I did not expect the students to attend. We spread the word to as many students as we could find to get themselves ready and come into Jackson. Then Colia Liddell—now Mrs. Bernard Lafayette—arrived at Tougaloo, and it was good and almost symbolic to see the student who, almost two years before, had asked me to speak at the meeting on the ICC ruling and to become adviser to the Youth Council. She and her husband, both with SNCC, had been doing the tough, basic organizing work in Selma, Dallas County, Alabama. In Jackson for a visit, Colia now began assisting in the rallying of the Tougaloo students.

With Colia and others now busy on the Tougaloo campus, Ed and I and several students drove into Jackson. As we passed through the white sections, I again felt hatred toward Mississippi. In the black sections, as we drove down Rose Street and into Lynch Street, there were far more people than usual, standing and talking on the sidewalks and gathered on their porches. Once again, the Jackson police, in their blue riot helmets, were thick in the area of the Masonic Temple. We parked and walked up the sidewalk to the building. The police looked at us and we looked at them. Then they looked away.

The Masonic Temple was filling rapidly, and many people were standing in the corridors. Although most of the NAACP staff people had left Jackson a day or so before, the NAACP offices were again frenetic, filled mostly with local Jackson people. Gloster Current had gone out of the office. Pearlena Lewis and I talked. She too was not surprised but was still stunned. We learned that the ministers had called a clergymen's meeting at the Pearl Street AME church, and Ed King, as a clergyman, decided that he would attend, since it obviously would be a significant meeting. The telephone rang and I took the call. Someone laughed harshly, then hung up. W. C. Patton, the NAACP's voter-registration man, came into the office. Still interested in mobilizing people for a city-wide voter-registration campaign, he said little when we told him that there would be other developments. A radio was on and statements were being issued by many people from many places on the killing of Medgar Evers. We listened, but only for a few minutes, because now there were many things to do.

The White House said that President Kennedy was "appalled by the barbarity of this act." The full resources of the FBI were pledged by the U.S. Department of Justice toward apprehending the murderer. From New York, Roy Wilkins said that Medgar's murder "demonstrates anew the blind and murderous hatred which obsesses too many Mississippians," and acting for the NAACP, he posted a $10,000 reward for the killer. In Jackson, Gloster Current condemned the slaying as a "cowardly ambush murder . . . should awaken all Americans to the plight of Negroes in Mississippi."

Martin Luther King, in condemning the killing, said that it should build increased determination to "break down the segregation and discrimination barriers."

And there were other statements:

Ross Barnett, Governor of Mississippi, thought that the killing was a "dastardly act." Allen Thompson, who we now learned had been out of the city for two days vacationing in Florida, returned immediately to Jackson, saying that he was "dreadfully shocked, humiliated, and sick at heart." The president of the Jackson Chamber of Commerce said that someone "has applied the law of the jungle." Bidwell Adam, Citizens Council advocate and chairman of the Mississippi Democratic party, called Medgar's murder a "diabolical act" and said that the killer "has sprayed oil upon a fast consuming fire already out of control and [has] increased trouble throughout the land." White Mississippi officials were themselves posting rewards for the apprehension of the killer.

They were afraid.

But if they were afraid—the Barnetts, the Thompsons, and all the others—the black community of Jackson was bitterly angry. In one way or another, the people had been stirring for a long time, and in a more basic sense, all through the blood-dimmed and painfilled history of Mississippi, anger had been building for generations at the grassroots. For a month, since the NAACP board meeting on May 12, the issue of *freedom* had been out in the open as it never had before. The campaign to secure that freedom had gone on, sometimes militantly, but mostly, through no fault of the people, it had lagged badly and the frustration had increased. But even as the Jackson movement had waned almost into nothing, the death of Medgar Evers was becoming its resurrection.

I could see this in the eyes of the people, youth and adult, who were gathering in the downstairs corridor of the Masonic Temple. They were ready to move and there was nothing that anyone could do to stop what was now going to occur. We began to get the people together for the first of what we intended as a continuous series of massive demonstrations. Dave Dennis arrived, and a rapidly growing number of youth leaders, and Willie Ludden. We all talked a great deal about nonviolence.

Ed King entered the building with some good news. He had gone to the ministers' meeting at Pearl Street AME, and right away it had become clear that in the early morning hours after they had learned the news, many of the Jackson ministers had decided to demonstrate and go to jail. The few who had always been ready to do so but who had been held back by the others had now been joined by some of the more cautious clergy; and, said Ed, fourteen of them had got up at the close of the meeting and walked in a group right down Pearl Street toward the faraway downtown area. He said that the police had come even before the ministers had walked two blocks, that the clergymen had been immediately arrested and carried off to jail. Their final decision, their demonstration, and their arrests had all occurred within a brief time.

We now had the mass march ready to go out onto Lynch Street. There were more than two hundred people in it, half of whom were Tougaloo students and Jackson youth, and half of whom were adults. Most would remain in the fairgrounds stockade. Outside, the police were much thicker than anyone had ever seen them. People were gathering on the sidewalks and lawns along Lynch Street.

Just before we gave the word for the march to leave the Masonic Temple, Ed King prayed—a prayer for Mississippi, a prayer that the death of Medgar Evers would never be in vain.

Then we opened the doors. In ranks of two and three and singing freedom songs, the mass march moved out onto the sidewalk, turned left down Lynch Street in the general direction of the downtown area.

Immediately a number of Jackson police cars rushed down from the upper part of Lynch Street where they had been assembled. Other police cars, parked across from the Masonic Temple, turned out and headed down the street. All of the police cars passed the marchers, who were still on the sidewalk, and parked about three blocks below the point that the demonstrators now were. In the area where the police cars were now assembling were almost a hundred and fifty other blue-helmeted Jackson police, and scores of brown-helmeted Mississippi state highway patrolmen.

The marchers moved out into the street and walked, still singing, straight toward the assembled ranks of the lawmen. By now, hundreds of black people were gathering on the sidewalks. As the march approached the men who held the guns and clubs, a great hush fell over all of Lynch Street.

The march stopped a few feet from the blue-helmeted and brown-helmeted ranks. For a moment there was silence. Then the lawmen spread out so as to partially surround the long line of demonstrators. Then the police began to push and shove and club the people toward the garbage trucks that had just arrived and parked.

And a great roar now went up from the hundreds and hundreds of people watching, and the roar became the chant of *"Freedom! Freedom! We want Freedom!"*

Their faces twisted in rage, the lawmen, raising their clubs, forced at least fifty of the demonstrators from the long demonstration line into the watching, chanting crowds of people. Then the police turned back to the now reduced line of marchers and began to push them again toward the garbage trucks.

And the hundreds and hundreds of watching people again roared, *"Freedom! Freedom!"*

Then the Jackson police in their blue helmets and the Mississippi state police in their brown helmets surged, with clubs and guns in their hands, toward the great numbers of watching and chanting people. And in a great wave the people moved back and then, in another great wave, rolled forward again toward the police.

And the police moved back in retreat.

Now freedom songs were spreading all over the whole Lynch Street area as the last of the marchers who had not been forced out of the demonstration were shoved into the garbage trucks and, still singing, were carried off to the stockade at the fairgrounds.

Observers from the U.S. Department of Justice silently watched.

The lawmen were not yet quite through. Almost 150 people had been arrested, but hundreds and hundreds of others were still singing and chanting on the sidewalks and lawns and porches. Now the Mississippi state troopers assembled in military formation and, carrying shotguns and rifles, marched up Lynch Street. The Jackson police also grouped into military formation and, carrying guns and clubs, did the same thing.

The large throngs of people were silent and sullen, hatred written in every face. Back and forth along Lynch Street marched the police. But the people stood and looked at them.

When the official in charge of the Jackson city police saw Ed King and I standing there, he ordered his ranks to turn so that they faced us. Then he ordered them to halt. They stared at us and we stared at them. Then they marched back down the street.

When all of the police had left, we returned to the Masonic Temple. There, those of us oriented toward direct action discussed strategy very informally and very much to the point. There was no time to be lost: We had had two demonstrations, the ministers' affair and the mass march, and we needed more, much more. We decided that a mass march should be held that night, from the Pearl Street AME church, where the mass meeting of the evening was scheduled; that there should be mass marches the next day, possibly the next night, the next day—and if necessary, onward and onward. Major national focus was now upon Mississippi, Jackson in particular, and for all of the reasons that we had raised for so many days before, this was now the time to crack Jackson and to begin cracking Mississippi. The memory of Medgar Evers made this imperative.

We knew that in a very few days the funeral of Medgar would be held. We knew that, especially on that day, and assuming that his family agreed, there absolutely had to be a tremendous demonstration.

Gloster Current was now back in the NAACP offices, shaken by Medgar's death. Ruby Hurley, from the southeast regional office of the NAACP, had just arrived from Atlanta and was in a state of profound sorrow. Other NAACP staff people were beginning to arrive from out of state. There seemed to be no question in anyone's mind but that massive demonstrations were now necessary and quite desirable. For the first time in many days there seemed to be a feeling of unity among us.

The youth leaders began to spread out into the community to make certain that attendance would be heavy at the mass meeting at the Pearl Street AME church, out of which we would develop the night march. I went back to Tougaloo to get every possible student. By now it was deep into the afternoon and very hot.

Colia Liddell Lafayette and the student leaders had been busy on the Tougaloo campus. Some of the students were already, of course, in the fairgrounds stockade as a result of the morning demonstration, and there were many others prepared to join them as speedily as possible. Late that afternoon, I made a number of telephone calls into Jackson, asking for automobiles for those students who would be coming to the mass meeting and then would participate in the night demonstration. As the students gathered at my house, their enthusiasm was tremendous. When the cars arrived from Jackson, the students climbed in singing. Ed King took a load and I took a load, and in a sort of caravan, we headed into Jackson.

By the time we reached the Masonic Temple area, a good forty minutes or so remained until the meeting. Police again seemed to be everywhere. We left the Tougaloo students off at several Lynch Street cafés, and they agreed to come to the church shortly before the meeting began so that we might work out final strategy details for the night march. Then several of us went into the NAACP offices to see how matters were progressing.

Ruby Hurley and a minister were sitting at Medgar's desk, planning the details of the funeral that was going to be held on Saturday to encourage the greatest possible attendance. I indicated that we had a substantial number of Tougaloo students who would join the scheduled night demonstration.

Then I learned that the night march had been canceled shortly before, and that word to this effect was already being circulated.

It was a shock. Calmly, but with tension rising within me, I asked why. People were coming in and out of the NAACP offices; the atmosphere was hectic; it was difficult to talk. But the matter was extremely important, and I tried to find out precisely what was involved. First, I gathered that a number of the older NAACP staff were against the idea of a night march because they felt it was too dangerous. I learned also that the charges against those ministers who had demonstrated had been dropped by the city and that they had shortly before been released from jail. They too had objected to a night march on the grounds of the danger it involved. There were aspects of all of this that could be argued, including the matter of danger and, indeed, a discussion was beginning. Then another reason was given: there was a strong possibility that Myrlie Evers would address the mass meeting that night, and there was no point in upsetting her even further by a mass march that would follow her talk.

We were told that there was no question whatever that mass demonstrations during the daytime would be quite all right.

There were still many things about cancellation of the night march that disturbed me very much. I could tell that Ed King and several others were also quite concerned. Then several of the ministers who had been in jail came in and greeted us very warmly. Their attitude was clearly militant, and feeling that the Evers family would consent, they seemed to agree with those of us who felt that there should be a massive demonstration on the day of the funeral.

It was now time for the mass meeting, and we walked over to the Pearl Street AME church. The prevalence of Jackson police in front of the building, and behind it, and in an alley that ran on one side of it, had in no way deterred people from attending. The church was packed tight, wall to wall, and there were many outside at the windows. I told the Tougaloo student leaders that the night march had been canceled. Although disappointed, they agreed to come the next morning. A number of the Youth Council leaders, who had heard only a little while before that the demonstration had been called off, were quite critical of the development, but they agreed to mobilize people for the next day. The Rev. G. R. Haughton, pastor of the Pearl Street church, agreed to let us use the building for demonstration purposes.

The meeting itself was very moving. Most of the speeches were militant—far more so, it seemed to me, than at any earlier time. There was sorrow in the speeches and sorrow on the faces of the many hundreds who listened. There was anger in the faces of the people in the rows of pews, and there was anger in the speeches.

"Somewhere in the dark a sniper waited to play his part as the coward," said the Rev. S. Leon Whitney. "But bullets do not destroy ideas . . . and the best idea is freedom!" People responded with a huge roar of approval.

As I sat on the platform with the other members of the strategy committee and looked out at the vibrant people of Jackson, it seemed clear that nothing—nothing at all—could now stop the Jackson movement.

Then, along toward the end of the meeting, Myrlie Evers came slowly out of a door in the rear of the church and onto the speakers' platform. Clad in mourning clothes, with a tight face and tears streaming from her eyes, she spoke briefly to the hushed audience:

I come here with a broken heart, but I come because it is my duty. No one knows how my husband gave his life to this cause. He lived with this twenty-four hours a day. . . . It was my husband's wish that this movement would be one of the most successful in the nation and world. . . . I hope by his death that all will be able to draw some of his strength, courage and determination to finish this fight. My purpose here is to ask a favor of you. I do not want his death to be in vain. That would be as big a blow as his death itself. I ask you for united action in this effort in memory of my husband. . . . Nothing can bring Medgar back, but the cause can live on.

The church was filled with sobbing, and somewhere a small child cried out as Myrlie Evers withdrew.

It was announced that those interested in demonstrating would meet in the morning.

Even the newsmen, with the exception of the local reporters, joined in the singing of "We Shall Overcome."

As the meeting broke up that evening there seemed to be no question but that the Jackson movement was now rolling along with the greatest intensity. Quickly we talked with as many local people as we could, developing the idea of a huge, massive demonstration to take place probably right after the funeral on Saturday. The feeling of the people, regardless of economic position, seemed to be unanimous. The general situation, especially the great forward thrust of the people at the grassroots, bursting through the rigid walls of fear, had put even the most conservative in a position where they now had to go along with the massive action that lay immediately ahead.

Despite the apparent general agreement on large-scale direct action, especially where it had not been shared, several of us were quietly wary. The events of the preceding two weeks, as well as the situation involving the night march, had been of such a nature that we could take nothing for granted. Late that night, after I had returned to Tougaloo, I telephoned Bill Kunstler in New York City. He had been involved in the Jackson movement from its inception, and he knew the lay of the land. I brought him up to date on various developments, and he indicated that he was already planning to come to Jackson to observe the situation. Since Jackson had obviously become the scene of the nation's major integration campaign, there might well be a possibility, he said, that the Southern Christian Leadership Conference would offer its services to the general effort.

Very late that night, panicky Jackson police, possibly fearing an abortive demonstration, although none was being set up, moved several police cars onto the campus of Jackson State College. Many of the students had witnessed the brutal suppression of the demonstration on Lynch Street at mid-morning, and several began to throw bottles at the police cars. When more police arrived, the students withdrew. The police then left the area without making any arrests.

Thursday morning was extremely hot even before the sun had been up more than a very few hours. We assembled the Tougaloo students and brought them to the Pearl Street AME church. Police were again everywhere—all along Lynch Street, in front of the Masonic Temple, and in front of the Pearl Street church, where youth and adults were gathering. It was obvious that the lawmen did not know from what point the expected direct action would begin.

The NAACP staff were all over at the Masonic Temple. A few ministers dropped by the Pearl Street church to wish us well.

As we surveyed our forces, it seemed quite clear that we could indeed have two very adequate mass demonstrations during the day— one in the late morning and another in the afternoon. Proceeding on that basis, we first began to hold a general session in which Dave Dennis especially spoke on the necessity of nonviolence, since we were all only too aware of the rising hatreds that were sweeping the black community. At noon the first mass march was ready to go, about a hundred persons. Some carried American flags. Ed King gave a brief prayer; we opened the doors of the church; and the demonstrators, singing freedom songs, filed outside.

Marion Gillon, the Tougaloo student who was from Birmingham and who had been, weeks before, very excited about the developments in Alabama, walked past me, giving me a determined smile.

By the time the march was going out of the church, two or three hundred people had gathered outside of the building to observe, and there were perhaps two dozen newsmen. The police, having by this time decided that the Pearl Street church was the beginning point, were all over the area, but most of them were parked and assembled to the right of the church, since that was the quickest way to the downtown area.

Knowing that the majority of lawmen were down there, we had laid out another route. As the marchers went out into Pearl Street, they turned left and moved half a block to the Rose Street intersection. Thrown off balance, dozens of police cars turned and went around the block in an effort to confront the demonstration as quickly as possible. The mass march turned right at Rose Street, and marched down the middle of the street. We followed quickly, as did the several hundred people and the newsmen. At one point we overtook a white man who, with a camera in his hand and with what appeared to be a hearing aid in his ear, was walking slowly. The "hearing aid," we had learned earlier, was really a very minute radio apparatus, and the man, we realized, was one of the many FBI agents now in Jackson. Now the first contingent of Jackson police moved out into Rose Street to face the marchers. They were led, as usual, by J. L. Ray, who had very recently been promoted from captain to deputy chief. Other police arrived, until their forces numbered well over 100 men. About 150 of the people, including several of us, moved in very close to the scene to observe, and about twenty of us posted ourselves on a front porch very close to Rose Street. There were at least 300 other people watching from a short distance away. The hot breeze blew dust back and forth through the streets and yards. The faces of the police, as they began to tear the American flags from the hands of those who carried them, were filled with raw hatred. And there was hatred in the eyes of the people who watched this. Then the lawmen began to herd the marchers to the garbage trucks, which had arrived.

Then, as had been the case the day before, the people began to chant, "Freedom! Freedom! We want Freedom!" And the chant was carried over the whole neighborhood by hundreds and hundreds of people.

The police finished loading the marchers into the trucks. The 100 arrested demonstrators were joining all of us in chanting, "Freedom! Freedom!" Very deliberately, J. L. Ray ordered his men to clear away the people who were watching; and the police, many dozens of them, began to push everyone back.

Now the chant of "Freedom! Freedom!" had become a continuous roar.

J. L. Ray saw us standing on the porch, chanting. Within a moment, fifteen to twenty police with drawn clubs moved right up to the porch and stood there looking up at us. In another moment they were on the porch, clubs raised.

I heard one of them shout, "Here he is! Here he is!" Then there were police all around me. Several grabbed me and pushed me off the porch. I kept my balance and was still standing when I hit the ground. Then several police shoved me, and I felt a series of blows on my head and back. The next thing I knew, several minutes later, I was flat on the ground, and a lawman was standing over me with a partly drawn revolver and a club in his hand.

I could hear a woman screaming over and over again. Police dogs were barking somewhere. There was blood all over my head and shirt. J. L. Ray was standing nearby and ordered the police to take me to a paddy wagon. I was told that I had been arrested for disturbing the peace and resisting arrest. Newsmen were everywhere, taking pictures.

I was thrown into the paddy wagon. Then Steve Rutledge, who had also been arrested but not beaten, was pushed in with me. A young boy was thrown in next. Steve told me that I had been struck a number of times and knocked unconscious, and the police had gone after the occupants of the house. The boy with us had protested that it was his house, and the police had arrested him. His sister had not been arrested, but had been severely choked by a nightstick drawn tightly against her throat. Another boy, who had been standing behind a police car, had his leg broken when the officer put the car into reverse; and that boy too had been arrested. Steve said that he had seen Lois Chaffee of Tougaloo taken into custody.

We now noticed that the door of the paddy wagon was slightly ajar, but of course we made no move to escape, since we had no wish to oblige the police by giving them an opportunity to shoot us. The boy with us, however, was beginning to panic and suddenly said that he was going to leave. He started for the partly opened door, but we prevented him, pointing out what would occur. As we looked through the door, we could see that everyone was beginning to disperse. Then the door was locked; the paddy wagon engine started; and making the ride just as rough as he could by "two-wheeling" around the turns, the driver took us to the fairgrounds stockade.

At the fairgrounds we remained in the paddy wagon, with its doors shut tightly, for almost half an hour. It was very hot inside. Because of that and because of my head wounds, I began to faint—for the first time in my life. Finally the door was opened and we were ordered outside. A man in plainclothes helped me down.

Quietly, he said to me, "I'm sorry, professor."

I said nothing and stood there. He told me to go over to a squad car to be taken to the hospital. I asked if the other injured people were going to receive medical care and he said that they would.

I walked over to the squad car. The garbage trucks were still parked and full of marchers. Beyond them, I could see faces looking at me from windows of the buildings, the mass marchers from the day before.

Suddenly from the garbage trucks again came the chant, "Freedom! Freedom!" I answered them, "Freedom!" From inside the buildings the chant began, "Freedom! Freedom! We want Freedom!" I waved, and answering calls came from the garbage trucks and from those at the windows.

The Jackson police stood there, watching and listening. They seemed almost bewildered. Then two of them hustled me into a squad car and we left for the hospital.

The officer driving was short and fat. He immediately went into name calling, "Communist, nigger-lover, half-breed bastard." I ignored him and looked out the window.

The officer riding in the back seat, where I was, asked if it wasn't true that I was being paid considerable money to do what I had been doing. I told him that I was receiving no money from anyone.

At the University Hospital I was taken into a room for X rays. Then we had to wait almost an hour before the doctor could work on me. I saw several of the others who had been injured, accompanied by their respective police guards.

While we waited, the short officer stood and glared at me, then asked, "Is it true that you speak Russian?" I told him no.

The other policeman wanted to know if it was true that I was from Arizona.

I told him that I was from Arizona and that it was a great state. He was silent for a long time, then asked, "You ever do any hunting out there in Arizona?"

I told him that I had done a great deal of hunting in Arizona, and that between the time I was thirteen and my eighteenth birthday, I had owned a total of sixty-seven different firearms, usually half a dozen at a time, then trading them for others. I told him some of the different big-game rifles that I had had, mentioned a bear that I'd shot, several deer, wild turkeys, and other game animals.

He listened, fascinated. The short officer was also listening closely. Then I asked them about deer hunting in Mississippi.

They told me. While we waited for the doctor, we talked about big-game hunting. From time to time other people in the hospital looked at us curiously.

Then I was given seven or eight stitches by the doctor; my head was bandaged; and we went outside to the squad car—then to the city jail. On the way, the discussion concerning big-game hunting continued. As we approached the jail, the officer in the back seat asked me, suddenly: "Do you all think you're going to win here in Jackson?"

"Oh, yes," I told him. "We're going to win. And when we do, it's going to be a better city for everyone—and a better state, too."

The short officer who was driving said, "We're not going to let you win."

I asked him why not.

He was speaking fast now. "Because we're not going to have *any* changes, that's why. No changes at all." The officer in the back seat was silent.

"Why aren't you going to have any changes?" I asked the short officer.

But now he too was silent.

At the jail we parked and got out. A large number of well-dressed white women, obviously the Women for Constitutional Government who were feeding the police, swarmed around us. "It's him," yelled one of them. "Professor Salter!" One of the women seemed to be taking pictures. I felt like some sort of a strange creature, and the two policemen, apparently embarrassed, brusquely asked the women to clear the way. We went up to the office, where I was booked. Neither I nor the police officers who had accompanied me to the hospital said anything more to one another.

Steve Rutledge was in the cell in which I was placed. They had brought him up from the fairgrounds shortly before, and right across the corridor, Lois Chaffee looked at us from behind bars. Those of us who were non-black, it seemed, had been placed in the city jail, rather than allow the fairgrounds stockade to be desegregated.

I was thinking of the afternoon mass march that had been scheduled. Both Steve and I agreed that it had probably taken place by this time.

Several hours later, we were taken from our cells. Attorneys Bob

Carter and Frank Reeves, both from the NAACP national office, were there to start securing our release. They said that they had just arrived in Jackson and were still at the airport when Bill Kunstler had arrived. Ed King was there to pick up Bill, and had told him what had happened. Ed and Bill had checked with the jail, but I had not yet arrived, and they were told that I was at the hospital. Bill Kunstler had gone to the hospital, but I had just left there for the jail. Finally, Ed and Bill had told the NAACP attorneys that they would meet me either at Tougaloo or at the mass meeting scheduled later in the evening.

I asked the NAACP attorneys if the second mass march, the one scheduled for the afternoon, had taken place. They said that as far as they knew there had only been one demonstration, the one in which I and the others had been beaten.

We were out on bond shortly and, passing through the downtown area again full of police and hoodlums, went immediately to the Farish Street law offices of Jack Young and his colleague, Carsie Hall. A man from the U.S. Department of Justice awaited us, and we gave him the details of the day's brutality. He told us that cameramen from every major television network—ABC, CBS, NBC—had long film sequences of my beating, as well as some of the other events, and that it was likely that the Jackson police involved could be identified from these films. If so, he went on, Federal prosecutions might take place. He also told us that brutality at the fairgrounds had increased, that demonstrators were being placed in "sweat boxes."

I asked again about the mass march scheduled for later in the afternoon. Again, no one seemed to know about any of that, except for the fact that there had been only one demonstration. Someone had heard, though, that the ministers had gone to see Mayor Allen Thompson, but the result was not known.

By this time it was early evening. The mass meeting was due to start shortly and was, I knew, scheduled for the Blair Street AME church, some distance away. Steve and I were on foot, since my car was still at Pearl Street. I was groggy and light-headed, but we went into a little café and had something to eat. At the café I picked up a copy of the *Jackson Daily News,* which had a long front-page story discussing the civil rights activities in the city, and also indicating that the police and the FBI were apparently close to capturing Medgar's killer: a rifle had been found, with a fingerprint, and the bullet had been located. In the same issue was an editorial which, under the title "Violence Is No Answer," spent most of its space attacking "outside agitators" and "nomads who sow violence."

The *Jackson Daily News* was no longer keeping its little arrest scoreboard.

We took a black cab to the Blair Street church. Cars were parked for blocks and police were driving back and forth in front of the building. The meeting had obviously begun, and we could hear someone inside giving a speech. Several people standing by the door greeted us very warmly as we went inside. The church was packed with at least as many as had been at Pearl Street the night before. The ministers, Gloster Current, and others were sitting on the platform. Ed King was standing by a door leading into the pastor's office. I could not see Bill Kunstler.

Steve sat down in a pew and I went up toward the platform to see Ed. Midway, I was spotted by the people who immediately interrupted the speech being given to rise to their feet and cheer wildly. It was a tremendous welcome. Up on the platform, the ministers greeted me cordially; Gloster Current shook hands; and the speech continued. Ed King and I went off to one side to talk.

A great deal indeed was happening. Following the mass march, Ed said, the several hundred people who had watched it being suppressed and watched the beatings had become extremely angry. He and several other ministers had brought the people back to the vicinity of the Pearl Street church. There, some of the ministers, but not Ed, had taken the position that any further demonstrations that day would only incite violence. While all of this was going on, Ed continued, Gloster Current and Ruby Hurley began issuing statements from the NAACP offices that there would be no more demonstrations that day. The people had then gone home; but the next day, Friday, was to see at least one mass march. He told me that the ministers had gone to see the mayor, but the results had been unsatisfactory and several clergymen were going to report to the people on what had happened.

I asked about Bill Kunstler. He was in the minister's study, Ed told me, making a long-distance telephone call. Bill had come prepared, he went on, to announce that the SCLC legal defense arm, the Gandhi Society, was setting up a special fund called the Medgar Evers Memorial Bail Bond Fund. SCLC, apparently, was becoming quite interested in assisting the effort in Jackson.

Ed went on to say that there might be some question, because of the inter-organizational situation, as to whether Bill would even be allowed to address the mass meeting.

The SCLC interest was very good news! I said that I could get Bill Kunstler on the program. When I spoke to the mass meeting, as I knew I would, I would finish the talk by introducing Bill as the next speaker.

But Ed King had not yet finished his report. Medgar's funeral, as we had learned the day before, was going to be held Saturday at 11 A.M. It would be in the Masonic Temple. But there were rumors afoot, Ed continued, that the national office of the NAACP was backing rapidly away from any mass demonstrations growing out of the funeral.

This was indeed negative! Certainly, after everything else that had happened, it required no profoundly intuitive qualities to sum up everything and comprehend what was again happening.

I looked from the platform at the people in the pews. There were hundreds and hundreds of them, some affluent, most quite poor, some young, some old. They were people who were hot and sweating—and they were vigorous and angry. They were people who were pushing forward, pushing up, and they were people who supported the idea of massive demonstrations. They were not going to let the Jackson movement die.

It was clear to me that we had some other things favoring continuation of the mass-demonstration approach. An intense national focus was on Jackson, and on the NAACP, and it would not be able to function as it had several days before, especially not with the possibility of SCLC involvement.

The people at the grassroots were the real mainspring of the Jackson movement, and they were the reason, I told myself again, that it would not die.

Bill Kunstler came out of the pastor's study. He greeted me enthusiastically, but his news was negative. NAACP officials in New York City had heard of the possibility of an SCLC bail-bond fund named after Medgar and had protested this strongly to the SCLC leaders. Therefore, no such fund was going to be initiated. But, Bill felt, SCLC was still interested in assisting in Jackson. I told him that I would see that he got on the mass meeting's program.

Reports were given of the meeting that had been held with Mayor Allen Thompson that afternoon. A delegation of twelve, mostly ministers, had gone to see him and at the outset had protested the police brutality, which the mayor had not been much interested in discussing, although he said that he would "investigate."

The delegation had gone on to attempt to discuss the demands of the Jackson movement. Allen Thompson had been adamant and rigid. He would not, he said, set up a bi-racial committee, and he blamed the civil rights activities for the fact that he had had to close the city's swimming pools. The only points in the list of demands that he would even consider were the hiring of black police and school crossing guards; but the city was still looking, as he put it, "for the proper type of Negro." The delegation from the Jackson movement had warned the mayor that the black community was ready to erupt and that, in anger and fear, people were buying guns. But neither this nor the threat of demonstrations had impressed Mayor Thompson.

He told the delegation, "You're smart. Your people will listen to you. You can plead with them. I'm not threatening you, but we've got the guns; we've got the force. . . . We are going to see that these demonstrations don't get anywhere."

The delegation from the Jackson movement had then left.

It had been, then, an embittered meeting. One thing was clear as the ministers now recited it to the hundreds of people at the Blair Street church: the people were responding with anger. And as the anger came up from the people, the ministers who were talking, tired and drawn as they might be, were also becoming very angry.

It was hot in the church and I was sweating heavily, feeling again very groggy and faint. Someone motioned to me, saying that it was time for me to say a few words. There was another wild cheering session as I arose. Although very tired, my head felt clear as I spoke.

I said essentially what I had been saying, and what a number of us had been saying, for a long, long time. We needed massive demonstrations, into the streets and into the jails, and that was the only way that we could crack Jackson, Mississippi. "We must continue and intensify our mass marches until the evil system of racism falls," I told the meeting.

There was a great roar of approval.

"But we must do it nonviolently," I said. "I know how you feel about club-toting, gun-toting goons," I continued. "That does not mean that we must love the Jackson cops. I would sooner love a desert sidewinder rattlesnake."

There was another great burst of approval. Then I said that we had a "good friend" with us who would like to have a few words, and I turned the rostrum over to Bill Kunstler.

Bill talked very briefly and to the point. He introduced himself and his organizational affiliation, and then said that the Rev. Martin Luther King "wanted me to pass along the word that he is ready to do what he can to help the people of Jackson."

The thundering applause went on for a long time.

When Bill Kunstler had finished, the meeting continued. Medgar's funeral was discussed at length, but nothing was said about a demonstration. We were quite certain that there would be many demonstrations, mass demonstrations, including one on the day of the funeral. I had pushed, as intensely as possible, the necessity of massive action, and Bill Kunstler had discussed the Southern Christian Leadership Conference and Martin Luther King, and the people of Jackson had given their overwhelming approval.

The church seemed even hotter, and after a time I went outside. Someone told me that white youths with rifles had been seen in and around the church shortly before. We stayed out of the lighted areas.

When the meeting was over, people poured out of the church, and many were singing freedom songs. Several of us, including Youth Council leaders and Tougaloo students, reminded people to be sure to come to the Pearl Street AME church next day for a demonstration; and we also talked about a demonstration on the day of the funeral. The people expressed their support and several warned me to be careful, said they were sure there would be more killings.

But they were not afraid.

Several of us stepped across the street to a private home to see the national news on television. The family that had invited us made us comfortable and fixed some lemonade. While we waited for the TV news, Bill told me that when he went to the hospital to see if he could find me, he had asked a police officer where I was. The officer told him, "In jail— but we hope to see him somewhere else."

Bill had also talked with Eldri, who had heard about the Rose Street beatings and had called down from Minneapolis to find out how I was and how things were going. She, and Maria as well, had evaded Minneapolis newspaper reporters all day, since Eldri had no wish to go through a painful interview.

The national news came on, and much of it concerned Jackson. There was a long film sequence which showed the Jackson police moving up to the porch on Rose Street where I was standing. Just as it reached the point where the clubs were swinging, the Jackson station cut off the national TV film. The Jackson announcer's face appeared, and he said, "At that point Professor Salter stumbled and fell." Then the national TV film was turned on again.

Then, after picking up my car, and with Ed King driving right behind us, we went back to Tougaloo. A number of the active student leaders came over. We talked. There was no question in any of our minds but that—perhaps because of fear, financial conservatism, possibly even Federal pressure, or other reasons—the Jackson movement was again beginning to face an internal crisis regarding the question of continuing the massive demonstrations. We had had many days of this situation prior to the murder of Medgar, and now, even after that tragedy, marches were being canceled and postponed. The position of the youth, the people in general, and quite likely by now at least several of the ministers was very militant.

There was no question but that the Jackson movement had to go forward until at least its stated demands were secured. The key to that was intensive and large-scale direct action. One of these mass demonstrations had to be on the day of the funeral of Medgar Evers.

The Rev. Eddie O'Neal, president of the Tougaloo student body and a strong believer in mass direct action, knew many of the Jackson clergy, and had frequently endeavored to spark a more militant approach among them. There was one younger minister in particular, comparatively new in Jackson but prominent, whom Eddie O'Neal knew well, whom we knew, and who was definitely oriented toward a direct-action approach. After discussing the matter for a time, we decided to set up a telephone "conference call" between this Jackson minister, me, and Dr. Martin Luther King. We telephoned the clergyman in Jackson and he was definitely in accord. Some time elapsed while the operators set up the call. Then we were ready to go.

As it turned out, there were four of us on the call, since one of Dr. King's top aides was also involved. As all of us knew, the talking had to be done with the greatest possible care, since there was little doubt but that there were many ears on the wires.

The Southern Christian Leadership Conference was, of course, quite aware of what had occurred in Jackson, and it was not necessary for either the Jackson minister or me to discuss the basic causes of our difficulty, although these were implied; but it was necessary for us to stress the urgency of "involvement by certain other organizations." This we did at some length, very carefully.

The men on the other end were warm and friendly and understood immediately. A commitment, of course, we were told, could not be made right at this point. Certainly, however, the Jackson movement must receive all possible support. They would be in Jackson for the funeral, they said, and we could discuss the matter at that time. It was agreed that Bill Kunstler, I, and Ed King would meet the SCLC people at the airport on Saturday. The Jackson minister wanted to discuss the whole Jackson movement with several of us on Friday afternoon. It seemed that things were beginning to work out.

Friday was another day of searing heat. The police were again out in large numbers. As I walked into the Pearl Street church, someone showed me several of the day's out-of-state newspapers; and national focus was on Jackson. The *New York Times* had a front-page story, with pictures, concerning the Thursday beatings on Rose Street. The *New York Herald Tribune* was running an article entitled "Fires of Hate in Jackson."

Gloster Current had been quoted in the *Washington Post* as saying, "Salter is a special target" of the police, and that they "dislike him intensely and apparently would like to do away with him."

I talked with the youth leaders. The news they had was both good and bad. The bad part of it involved the fact that several of the NAACP staff, none of whom were at the Pearl Street church, had begun circulating word that anyone arrested on this day would not be able to be released from jail in time to attend the funeral on Saturday. Some of the ministers were also saying that. The purpose of all of this was quite clear to everyone, and one of the youth leaders reminded us that, two weeks or so before, people had been arrested at the Farish Street march, and the NAACP had moved to get them out within hours. Funerals, important anywhere, are of particular importance in the South, and certainly this funeral was a key event. There was no question but that this development was going seriously to impede our effort to build a mass march for Friday; and as the youth leaders reported, many people, including many of the young people, had indicated that they were going to hold back at this point on going to jail. Many of the people who were coming to the Pearl Street church were coming only to hear about new developments.

The good news, though, was indeed good. The word was really sweeping through Jackson to the effect that Saturday would see a huge, massive demonstration—bigger than anything that had yet occurred. A great many people apparently were talking about it, although the NAACP was leaning in the other direction.

About 100 people were gathered at the Pearl Street church— whether or not they intended ultimately to demonstrate on Friday. We took them to an upstairs room and Dave Dennis began to give his regular lecture on nonviolence. While he talked, I looked outside. Many police and newsmen were gathering, and it was clear that they expected something to occur. I talked to the people that we had assembled, making a strong plea for a mass march to occur within the day. I was beckoned to the door by someone who told me that FBI agents were at the church to see me. Dave Dennis took the meeting again. It developed that the agents wanted a statement from me concerning the brutality of the preceding day. They set up a tape recorder in the pastor's office and I began to give them the statement. I was about halfway through when Dave Dennis came to the door.

He and I went out into the main part of the church. Dave was crying from sheer frustration. Only a few, he said, were willing to march today. The statements by the NAACP staff had convinced most of the people that to be arrested meant foregoing the funeral of Medgar Evers. Virtually all of the people, he continued, were convinced that there would be a large-scale demonstration on Saturday. We talked the situation over quickly. Thirty-seven were willing to demonstrate. To send out a few people on a march would be a sign of weakness, but it would not be quite as negative if they participated in other types of demonstrations. We decided to send them downtown, where at least the Jackson boycott could be entrenched another notch. Dave was still crying as he went back upstairs, and I was angry. I finished the statement to the FBI men, who indicated that there was a strong possibility that Federal charges would be brought against the police who had clubbed me and the others.

By this time the meeting upstairs had adjourned. The thirty-seven were ready to go downtown. Someone remembered that it was Flag Day, so some American flags were brought in quickly. No pasteboard was available for picket signs, so we took a heavy marking pencil and wrote integration slogans on T-shirts. We then began to take the demonstrators downtown, with the police following right behind. As soon as a group left the car, the police moved in fast to make arrests, and many of the demonstrators were roughed up. A bit later, I was in the Pearl Street church talking to a black attorney from the Justice Department who was very bitter at the lack of constructive Federal involvement in Jackson. Bill Kunstler arrived, and since several more of the thirty-seven were due to go downtown, Bill said that he would take them. He borrowed my car, and when he returned he reported that the police had used clubs on the group he had carried. The Justice Department attorney recorded the information, quietly swearing.

Within an hour all thirty-seven had demonstrated and had been arrested.

Bill Kunstler, Eddie O'Neal, and Ed King had been spending the morning driving around Jackson. They too had picked up from the grassroots the groundswell of feeling concerning a massive demonstration the next day tied in with the funeral. But there was still considerable question in our minds regarding the role of the NAACP, most of whose staff in Jackson were apparently currently off somewhere in meetings that no one knew much about. There was no doubt in our minds that there would be a huge demonstration on Saturday. We returned quickly to Tougaloo, talked with some student leaders, then went into Jackson again to see the minister with whom we had spoken earlier on the matter of SCLC.

On the way in, we picked up a copy of the *Jackson Daily News*. The main headline read, "Top Court Upholds Demonstration Ban," and there we learned that the NAACP effort to get the U.S. Supreme Court to set aside our injunction had failed. The high court, which had not ruled one way or the other on the legality of the injunction, had taken the position that the NAACP had to proceed through lower courts before it could present its case to the Supreme Court. Mayor Thompson was quoted as saying that this was "wonderful news." As far as we were concerned, the injunction was patently illegal and we had no intention of abiding by it.

Another news story, reporting the ministers' meeting with the mayor, was headlined "Mayor Says Threats Won't Deter Law Enforcement."

The minister whom we had come to see greeted us cordially, and the discussion was candid. His first news dealt with the fact that because of the national focus on Jackson, and especially because of the mood of the people, it looked as if the NAACP was going to have to participate in some sort of massive protest march. Further, he told us, most of the ministers supported this position. We talked about the ministers.

They were good people, he said, and all of us agreed. But, he continued, they were very tired and of course completely unused to intensive direct-action campaigns, and some were definitely afraid. In addition, he told us (and we knew this too), the ministers had been subjected to continuous pressure from most of the NAACP staff, especially those from the national office, always toward restricting the scope of demonstrations and, as he put it, "keeping things under control."

But the murder of Medgar had changed this somewhat. While some of the ministers were still in the conservative group, others were now definitely pushing toward more intensive action. Further, it was his feeling that if we could talk with Dr. Martin Luther King the next day, as we planned, and then could see that Dr. King had an opportunity to speak with several of the other ministers, a formal invitation asking SCLC to enter Jackson, even signed by a majority of those clergy on the strategy committee, just might be secured. He wasn't certain of course, and he reminded us that his position, as a younger clergyman who had not been in Jackson long, was not especially influential. But he felt that there was a possibility that things would work out. We agreed to meet at the mass meeting in the evening, after which, we knew, there would be a strategy-committee gathering.

The mass meeting, held at the Pearl Street church, was again surrounded by police and was again huge. Many prominent persons from the North attended, and it was announced that many others—Ralph Bunche, high union officials, key religious figures—would arrive next day for the funeral. Many of the SNCC workers were again down from the Delta. Many of those arrested during the mass marches of Wednesday and Thursday had been bailed out of the fairgrounds stockade, to attend the funeral. The speeches went on and on, and the church became very hot. I wandered outside, where a large number of adults and young people were standing. Many were people whom I knew, but many I had never seen before; and all of them were prepared for a massive demonstration on Saturday. They said that all their friends and acquaintances felt the same way.

The mass meeting adjourned and people began to leave. I went inside the church for the strategy meeting, and it was obvious immediately that it was the most heavily attended session that we had had for many days. The key matter came to the fore. It was clear right away that everyone on the strategy committee had accepted the idea of a massive demonstration on Saturday, including the NAACP staff officials, who gave the impression that there had never been any question about it. To this a youth leader said quietly, "You knew there would be a demonstration, whether you all agreed to it or not." The old element of bitterness began to enter the situation.

We learned that "something," as it was put, had been worked out with the Jackson officials in such a way that a mass march would be allowed—could take place without arrests. We were told that there could be a mass march following the funeral, all the way from the Masonic Temple to the funeral parlor on Farish Street to which Medgar's body would be returned before being carried to Arlington National Cemetery. Police protection would even be provided for the marchers— by the officials of Jackson.

Someone said, "The city has done us no favor. Thompson knew we'd march, one way or the other."

Several of the ministers had already secured formal permission from the city officials for the march.

A controversy broke out. The issue of the several ministers' as well as the NAACP staffs' making unilateral decisions without consulting other members of the strategy committee came up immediately, but since it had already been done, the discussion moved to other matters.

A number, pointing out that mass arrests clearly disturbed the Jackson officials—since police time was tied up, the city was brought into national focus, and everyone arrested had to be fed something—now proposed that some of the marchers be arrested. We said that there should be at least several hundred arrests. The route had been laid so that it intersected with Pascagoula Street, which led right up to the City Hall, as well as with Capitol Street itself, which entered the heart of the downtown area.

We felt that part of the march could, in an orderly and nonviolent fashion, break ranks from the main body and try to march up one of those two streets, either to City Hall or into the downtown area.

The NAACP staff condemned this with great vigor, as did several of the ministers. Other clergymen appeared to give the idea close consideration.

Then a minister arose with tears in his eyes. He had given his word to city officials that the march would follow a prescribed path, that nothing would take place that in any way would disturb the plan. Certainly there could be no civil disobedience, he said, and there could be no arrests.

His voice was emotional as he finished. "Do not ask me to break my word." There was silence; then the embittered controversy resumed. The minister who had given his word had swung most of the other clergymen with him. An informal vote was taken: our direct-action group voted for civil disobedience and arrests. But there were many more, mostly the ministers, who voted for the march that the clergymen and the Jackson authorities had agreed upon.

As the meeting adjourned, we were asked if we would abide by the decision. We said that we would. In its way, the fact that a mass march could "legally" be held was something of a victory in Jackson and in all of Mississippi; it marked a milestone. But all of us knew that it had been "allowed" only because of the sentiment that existed at the grassroots.

We talked with a number of the ministers. Although they had voted against us on this issue, they said that there was no question but that there would be more massive demonstrations in Jackson in the days ahead, and that these would involve arrests. We were assured that they were in full agreement.

That in itself was a victory.

We were up early Saturday morning, and weather forecasters predicted the hottest day yet. The news reported that a white youth had been shot in the shoulder while he and companions drove through a black neighborhood in the early-morning hours. Bill Kunstler and I, and Ed and Jeannette King, went to the Jackson airport to pick up Dr. Martin Luther King and the delegation from SCLC. A number of the NAACP staff were already there to meet others. The police were much in evidence in and around the terminal building, and a large number of newsmen were present.

I scanned the front pages of Saturday's *New York Times*. There was a long article on Jackson, datelined Friday and written by the veteran civil rights journalist, Claude Sitton, that dealt with the past two days, and it was clear that Sitton had determined the essentials.

His story pointed out that the NAACP had discouraged a mass march on Friday by telling people that "their almost certain arrest might prevent them from attending the funeral"; then it went on to indicate that there was "widespread sentiment for a proposed mass march after the funeral services," but that NAACP officials "feared that because of the repressive police tactics and the animosity among Negroes such a demonstration would lead to serious violence."

Claude Sitton had indeed figured things out:

> Besides the feeling among participants in a month-long desegregation drive here, and their sympathizers, the association officials also were under indirect pressure from other civil rights groups. Representatives of the latter were urging Negroes to press for direct action. . . . There were indications that adherents of the Rev. Dr. Martin Luther King were seeking to bring the Southern Christian Leadership Conference, of which he is president, into the struggle.

The article then had a brief discussion of Bill Kunstler and me, and mentioned our group as the "chief advocates of continued mass protest." But he neglected to mention the vigorous spirit at the grassroots.

With some understatement, Sitton went on. "Some association officials were said to be resentful of the efforts of the [M. L.] King faction to move into the Jackson picture."

By this time our plane was arriving. Followed by a large number of police, we stepped out of the terminal to the passenger gate. Several dozen white people joined the police in observing all of this. Newsmen pressed to the front. The plane landed and unloaded. Led by Dr. King, and with a whirring of television cameras, the SCLC officials arrived in Jackson. We greeted them, talked for a few moments, then went to the cars. Bill, I, Dr. King, and one of his aides got into my car, and the others rode with Ed and Jeannette King. The police, apparently fearing that an attempt might be made on Dr. King's life, formed to escort us to the Masonic Temple.

It had been understood, we felt, that our serious discussion of the internal problems of the Jackson movement would take place after the funeral and any demonstration. Now, with the police moving us along very rapidly over the short distance from the airport to Lynch Street, we talked only of the general situation: the intense heat of Mississippi, the spirit of the people, and Medgar Evers. Within minutes we were at the Masonic Temple. Cars were parked everywhere for many blocks around, and a wave of humanity was pouring into the doors of the building. It seemed clear that several thousand people had come to the funeral.

There was obviously no parking space. I let Bill, Dr. King, and the SCLC aide out, then drove down many blocks before I found a place to park. The sidewalks were full of people walking to the Masonic Temple. Police cars drove by, back and forth, but I could see none parked. I reached the door of the building at 11 A.M., the starting time for the services. Inside the corridor, where people were packed wall to wall, someone told me that even the standing room was gone inside the auditorium. The music was beginning.

I stood a long time in the packed corridor. Then the music stopped, and I could barely hear a prayer being given and after a time a speech. I attempted to move down the corridor toward the back, hoping to be able to hear what was going on, but I made little progress. After a time, the people around me began talking, and I joined in, asking them from where they came. They told me, naming many places besides Jackson: big towns, little towns, rural hamlets all over Mississippi. There were people from the Delta and from the hills in northeastern Mississippi, from the Gulf Coast area, and from the pine country down in the southwestern part of the state. The ripples of Medgar's death and the Jackson movement in general were reaching out a long, long way—stirring people and places into which no civil rights workers had yet set foot.

I saw several Tougaloo students and Youth Council leaders who were unable to get into the auditorium. It had occurred to me that many of the people on the outside might drift away from the funeral before it was over and miss the mass march. The youth leaders and I began to spread the word, asking people to stay around for the march. It became clear that everyone intended staying around; indeed most had heard that a march was to take place. I made my way slowly upstairs. The upper corridor had fewer people in it, and most were clustered around a Coke machine. I got a Coke. An insurance-office door opened and a man, a close friend of Medgar's, looked out. He saw me and motioned me inside. Several other men whom I knew well were also there. Through a small space in the wall, we could hear the speeches being given.

A great deal of the oratory tended, to the obvious disapproval of the men who were listening with me, somehow to blend Medgar, and Mississippi, and the NAACP all together in such a way that the NAACP came out on top. But there were some good words spoken, among them those of Roy Wilkins, who said of Medgar:

> For a little while he loaned us and his people the great strength of his body and the elixir of his spirit. If he could live in Mississippi and not hate, so shall we, though we shall ever stoutly contend for the kind of life his children and all others must enjoy in this rich land.

Roy Wilkins called Medgar "the symbol of our victory," and said that "the bullet that tore away his life four days ago tore away at the system and helped signal its end. They can fiddle and they can throw a few more victims to the lions of repression and persecution, but Rome is burning and a new day is just over yonder."

As the funeral drew to an end, the announcement of the mass march was made. I went downstairs and made my way outside. There seemed to be even more people in the area than before. Then the funeral was over. A tremendous flow of people began to pour from the building. Many were crying. Bill Kunstler came out and suggested that I find someone who could take my car down to Farish Street, where the affair would conclude. I found a Tougaloo student who agreed to forego the march. The coffin was carried out of the Masonic Temple and was placed into the hearse.

A minister was calling on people to go out into the street and to line up three abreast. We walked out into the street. Police were out there, also giving directions. Someone remarked that the temperature was 102 degrees and due to go higher.

The head of the mass march began to take shape. Several of the Jackson ministers were in the front ranks, then the NAACP officials and

Dr. King. I was in the sixth rank. Ed King and Bill Kunstler were a little behind me. Then, as soon as the first dozen or so ranks had formed, we were off, and the rest of the mass march began to organize behind us like a thin stream of water flowing from a great pool.

Newsmen were up in front beside us. Looking down Lynch Street, block after block, I could see the blue helmets of the Jackson police at every intersection. We marched on, and as we began to pass the groups of police, we could see the hatred in their faces. It seemed infinitely hotter than I had ever known it in my life, and my clothes were soaked with sweat. At one point, I turned for a moment and looked back, and saw the long, moving line behind us. Then we marched through an underpass. Standing above us was one of the Jackson police officers who specialized in "identification." He looked bewildered. From his post, he could view a much longer line than we could see from the ground.

We marched on. Now Lynch Street was swinging over and we were moving onto another street that cut over in the direction of the downtown area. The numbers of police seemed to have increased; they seemed as endless to me as we must have seemed to them. We passed into an area where white people lived. They stood in front of their houses and business places, women and children standing behind their men. There was shock and hatred and fear mixed together on all of their faces; but they were silent and so were we.

We were on Farish Street, still in the white section, and the numbers of white people were increasing. So had the silent shock, and the silent hatred, and the silent fear. The tall commercial buildings of downtown Jackson were rising around us as we moved toward the intersection of Farish Street and Capitol Street. At that junction solid walls of police, rank after rank, had formed a cordon through which we passed; and on the other side of each of the two police walls were hundreds of white people who had come to watch silently.

Then we were in the other portion of Farish Street, the beginning of the black business neighborhood. There, in front of businesses and on the sidewalks, people stood and watched, with solemnity, tears, and hope. Now there were not so many Jackson police. Block after block down Farish Street we went until finally we were in front of the Collins Funeral Home, to which Medgar Evers's body had been returned, there to await shipment by car to Meridian, and there to be loaded aboard a train and carried to Arlington cemetery for another funeral service some days hence. One of the ministers up front held up his hand, and told us all to spread out from the street.

I walked over to the lawn in front of the funeral parlor. The people were coming, rank after rank, and coming over to the sidewalks and the lawns. Rank after rank they came. A newsman from out of state walked up to me and said that he and others estimated that at least 5,000 people were in the march. Even now, there was a huge number of people gathered around the area of the funeral parlor.

And inside was the body of Medgar Evers.

The Tougaloo student who had driven my car came up and, giving me the keys, said that it was parked right around the corner. I thanked him, but I was not planning to go anywhere. Ed King said that as nearly as he could tell no white Mississippians—other than he and Jeannette and Wofford Smith, Episcopal chaplain at the University of Mississippi— had been at the funeral. He was disappointed. Aaron Henry walked over and we talked briefly. He was hoping for some direct action up in Clarksdale.

Rank after rank came the people. I could well believe that there were at least 5,000 people in the mass march, and that probably many more than that had been at the funeral. Away up and down Farish Street, I could see the blue helmets of the Jackson police glinting in the sun.

It was very hot.

The ranks had stopped arriving. All the space around the Collins Funeral Home, including the street itself, was packed tightly with people who, sweat-soaked and quiet, said very little. All were just standing there. I looked around. Almost all the newsmen had left. I could see the NAACP officials walking together down the street. The affair was considered over. But the people were still there.

And inside was Medgar Evers.

It came to me that here was Mississippi—all together. The people around me were from every part of Mississippi. Inside was the man to whom they had come to pay homage, and he too represented Mississippi, as did that which had been dealt him. Up and down Farish Street were the police, and they represented Mississippi. The intense Mississippi sun was coming over the tops of the buildings to the west, and its heat had enveloped all of us. A great many things, all symbolizing the forces of Mississippi, were gathered together. Suddenly I recognized the feeling that flowed out to me from all of the forces meeting here, and I realized that the day was not yet over.

I was snapped out of this reverie by Bill Kunstler, who walked up with news that came as a great shock. Dr. King, he said, and the other SCLC people wanted me to take them immediately to the airport to catch a plane. He indicated that several of the SCLC staff had already caught rides to the terminal.

I looked at him and asked, very slowly, "Aren't we going to talk? The SCLC involvement?"

Bill Kunstler shook his head sadly. "I don't know what's involved," he said. "But they definitely want to go to the airport, right away."

"What about Jackson?" I asked, still stunned.

"They've got to catch a plane," Bill repeated. "Maybe we can talk with them on the way to the airport."

I gave Bill the car keys and said that I wanted to stick around for a few more minutes at least, and asked if he could bring the car from around the corner.

I was still in a daze. No group that planned to involve itself in Jackson would be leaving now, not at this point. Ed King had seen Bill and me talking and made his way through the mass of people to ask what had occurred. I told him. He looked sick at heart.

People were still standing quietly. It was still hot. The police were still up and down the street. Medgar Evers still lay inside the funeral home. This was still Mississippi.

Bill Kunstler came up again. He had the car about two blocks away and Dr. King and an aide were in it. Steve Rutledge and Dave Dennis were going to ride to the airport, Bill said, and perhaps we could all talk with the SCLC people.

It was time to go, he continued, and he said it sadly.

Then the SCLC aide came through the crowd of people. He said that Dr. King could be shot, sitting in the car like that, and that they absolutely had to go immediately.

I told Bill to take the car, that I thought I would stay.

He hesitated for several moments. Then the SCLC man again pressed for immediate departure. Bill told me that he'd bring the car back and meet us at the funeral home. They left.

Something was beginning to happen out in the street—out where the people were really massed together. It looked as if a woman was weeping and pointing toward the funeral parlor. Ed King and I moved closer.

Everything was suddenly very still.

Then someone—probably someone who had heard the song sung at our many mass meetings in the past month—began to sing, "Oh, Freedom," and it came, softly and mournfully, over the people:

> *Oh, oh Freedom,*
> *Oh, oh Freedom,*
> *Oh, oh Freedom over me, over me.*
> *And before I'll be a slave,*
> *I'll be buried in my grave,*
> *And go home to my Lord and be free.*

Now we were all singing.

> *No more killing,*
> *No more killing,*

> *No more killing over me, over me.*
> *And before I'll be a slave*
> *I'll be buried in my grave*
> *And go home to my Lord and be free.*

There was a brief pause. Then, again suddenly, came another freedom song, a much more spirited one, "This Little Light of Mine":

> *This little light of mine, I'm going to let it shine.*
> *Oh, this little light of mine, I'm going to let it shine.*
> *This little light of mine, I'm going to let it shine,*
> *Let it shine, let it shine, let it shine!*

Everyone sang on—a mighty roar:

> *All over Capitol Street, I'm going to let it shine.*
> *Oh, all over Capitol Street, I'm going to let it shine.*
> *All over Capitol Street, I'm going to let it shine,*
> *Let it shine, let it shine, let it shine!*

Capitol Street! Capitol Street! And now, all of the forces of Mississippi, all of the forces that were gathered together, began to react. *Capitol Street!* Out in the front of the funeral parlor, even as they sang, the people, in a great spontaneous surge, turned toward Capitol Street—object of the boycott, scene of many arrests, far off and inaccessible goal of the mass marches. In a mighty wave the people moved down Farish Street toward the heart of Jackson. Hundreds and hundreds of people poured from the sidewalks and lawns and porches to join the throng. Quickly I followed them, and so did Ed King and Jeannette, and Eddie O'Neal. Behind us came another great wave of people, and another, and another. We were all swept up in the stream of surging Mississippi people, flowing down Farish Street—toward Capitol Street. There was sporadic singing, there were cries of "We want Medgar's killer! We want *freedom! Freedom! Freedom!*"

Ahead of us several blocks were a number of Jackson police, themselves running down toward Capitol Street—running from the huge, singing demonstration that had suddenly poured forth.

And far ahead of us, down at the intersection of Farish and Capitol streets, through which we had all walked only a short time before, we could see the massing of the battalions of blue and brown helmets.

There were people everywhere—in the street and on the sidewalks. Some were old and some were young; some were well dressed and some were not. But in all the faces and in all of the singing, and in all of the cries of "Freedom! Freedom!" there was no fear, no fear-based apathy, no servility, no more of the past of Jackson and Mississippi, not even a spirit of violence—only the toughness bred by hard lifetimes combining with the hopes and the aspirations of generations into a determined and powerful forward thrust.

As we jogged along, occasionally pausing for a moment to catch our breath, Ed and I and Eddie O'Neal talked. This was the tremendous awakening of Jackson, maybe even of Mississippi, and this was the time to get Martin Luther King, now gone to the airport. He would come if he knew this was happening. But how to get him? We looked at a watch. Scarcely ten minutes had passed since everything began, and the car had left only fifteen minutes before. We pressed on with the people. Now we were close to Capitol Street. Directly ahead of us, blocking the entrance to the downtown area, slowing the momentum of the demonstration to a brief stop, then causing it to commence an ever so slow retreat, was Deputy Chief J. L. Ray and what appeared to be a huge army of many hundreds of lawmen of all kinds blocking all of Farish Street. Some people were pressing forward to get a closer view of the countless ranks of police; other people were moving back. Half a dozen freedom songs were being sung at the same time.

How to get Martin Luther King, now gone to the airport, before he left Jackson forever? The car must be arriving at the terminal.

We looked up. We were standing under a set of second-story offices used by black professional people, doctors, dentists, our lawyers. Some office must be open, some telephone available. There was still time! Still time for a call to the airport!

Still time for Martin Luther King!

Quickly we mounted a flight of stairs—Ed, I, Jeannette, Eddie O'Neal. An office was open, its window overlooking Farish Street. We dashed in, looked for a telephone. There was none.

For a very moment, before getting ready to try other offices in the building, we looked down at Farish Street and saw the tremendous throngs of milling people, saw the ranks of blue- and brown-helmeted police, saw the sunlight, felt the heat—all of the forces of Mississippi in motion. Then even as we were turning to seek elsewhere for the precious telephone, the police, having seen us either entering the building or looking out the window, poured into the building into which we were. They were at the top of the stairs in seconds.

Within two minutes both Ed King and myself were arrested, taken downstairs, prodded with clubs, and thrown bodily into a paddy wagon.

It had occurred with amazing speed, and we lay there stunned as the door closed on us. But there was still hope! Eddie and Jeannette had apparently not been arrested. Now all we could do was pray that they could in the next few minutes find that telephone.

There was a small, barred circular window in the paddy wagon. I looked out. All I could see were vast numbers of city police and highway patrolmen and contingents of sheriff's deputies—men with rifles and bayonets and shotguns and revolvers and police dogs—marching on Farish Street. I could hear shouts and yells and freedom songs. The paddy-wagon door opened and a man was pushed in with us, his head bleeding where he had been struck with a club. He told us that the lawmen were not arresting many at all but were pushing the demonstration back and forcing the people from Farish Street. The door opened again. A woman, her dressed ripped, was shoved in with us. She was crying. Ed King took out his Bible and began to pray.

We told her that, soon perhaps, the U.S. troops would come. The door opened again. A boy, blood all over his face, was pushed into the wagon. He was crying. Ed resumed his prayer.

Outside, we suddenly heard a volley of shots being fired, then another. Then we heard screams.

The others had expressions of horror on their faces, as I must have had on mine. I could think only "Sharpville." I could see nothing from the little window.

Again the door opened and a man with a bloody head was thrown inside. He had been clubbed, and told us that the police were firing over the heads of the people, and that they were shooting out the windows above Farish Street. More time passed. There were more shots. More people were thrown into the paddy wagon. Ed read aloud from his Bible. I glanced out the little window. Suddenly I looked again.

Long lines of heavily armed lawmen were marching past into Farish Street. Police dogs were being led. Trucks were going past, loaded with police. But standing in the middle of all of this, leaning against a lamp post and looking as if he were observing passing traffic in New York City, was Bill Kunstler.

I yelled, "Bill! Hey, Bill!" Ed King came over and looked out the window.

Bill Kunstler was looking around. "Bill!" I called again. "It's me, John!"

"John!" he said. "Where are you?"

"In the paddy wagon!" I answered. He looked in our direction, and I pushed my fingers through the little window.

He saw them immediately and started over to us. A dozen men with rifles then stepped into view. They pointed their guns at Bill Kunstler.

"Who are you?" one asked.

"Gentlemen," he said, "I'm an attorney. I have clients in that wagon."

They moved toward him, rifles still pointing. He stepped back onto the sidewalk and moved down the street, out of view.

"Thank God he wasn't arrested," I said to Ed. "We need him." Then I realized something.

Eddie O'Neal and Jeannette King had not reached Martin Luther King. If they had, Bill Kunstler would have been with the SCLC leader, not by himself. I looked at Ed. His face showed the same realization. Neither of us spoke for a long time.

The paddy wagon was now almost full. The shouts and yells, even the shots, were much further away. Then the engine started and the wagon gave a terrific lurch. We tried to sit on the floor, but the vehicle was maneuvered in such a fashion that we slid from one side to the other. We were traveling up Farish Street in the direction of the funeral home. I looked out the little window.

What had happened was obvious. Windows had indeed been broken by the police; glass was all over the sidewalks. Lawmen were everywhere. We passed a parked fire engine. I saw police holding groups of people at gunpoint, and nightsticks were drawn across the throats of several. I could not see the main body of the demonstration, although shouts and still some freedom songs were now very clear. Then the paddy wagon turned off Farish Street, and for a moment I saw Bill Kunstler and Steve Rutledge standing on a sidewalk.

Then we traveled fast, the driver taking each turn with screeching tires, sending all of us skidding back and forth. The injured people moaned. One woman appeared to have fainted.

We were passing through an edge of the downtown area. I looked out at Jackson, its commercial buildings shimmering in the late-afternoon sun. I hated it, at that point, more deeply than I had ever hated anything. Then I suddenly realized that Jackson was not *quite* as it usually was—there were scarcely any cars or people anywhere. The whole heart of Jackson was virtually deserted.

We were at the fairgrounds stockade. The paddy wagon stopped; the gate was opened; the wagon entered. The door was opened. I helped the woman who was almost unconscious to her feet. She climbed out. I stepped to the ground. The officer in charge pushed me over to one side, looked at me with a twisted face, and said, "Inciting to riot!"

Another said, "We ought to kill you right now!"

I stood there, slowly realizing for the first time that they felt that I, and perhaps Ed too, had organized and led the huge demonstration. Then I realized fully, for the first time, that these men, and unquestionably most of the white people, not only were totally incapable of realizing the role of Mississippi in producing protests but were totally unable to realize that black people could, themselves, lead themselves.

I looked around. There were dozens of police officers gathering where we stood. In the hot sun, leaning with arms out against the side of a long building, were about two dozen other people who had been arrested. Obviously the policy against mass arrests had been foregone.

We were searched, taken to a table, and one by one were booked.

A number of lawmen, clubs in their hands, gathered around Ed King and me, cursing us continuously. It was clear that they hoped to provoke us into doing something, or even saying something, that would give them the "right" to club us into the ground. We stood there, saying nothing, looking at them. Ed and I were the last to be booked, and as I sat down in the chair by a table, I gave only my name, age, address, and occupation. The officer, who knew of course a great deal about me, went through, one after the other, all of the questions. As I refused to answer, he became increasingly angry. The muscles on his face jerked and he became very pale; finally, furiously, he pushed my arm from the table and cursed me as someone whom he would "dearly like to put a slug or two through." Ed went through the same routine.

When all had been booked, we were ordered to lean against the wall under the still-hot sun of late afternoon. Ed and I moved to join those who had been in our paddy wagon, but we were pushed by the police to a section of the wall by ourselves. As we leaned, arms out against the wall, the police walked back and forth behind us, still cursing, still threatening. I was drenched with sweat and I noticed that my coat was torn. A black mourning band that I had put on my arm for the funeral was hanging limply by a safety pin.

About an hour passed. From what we could hear, the police were holding various conferences behind us. Suddenly we were ordered to turn around. With several of those who had been in our wagon, along with a number from the other group, we were placed in a paddy wagon again and taken to the city jail. One of the men with us was a Mr. Withers, whom I had met once months before, a photographer from Memphis, Tennessee, who did considerable work for black publications. He told us that he and other newsmen had left the area after the mass march from the Masonic Temple, then, hearing of what was developing, had returned to the Farish Street area. But the police had blocked the newsmen from taking pictures, and had threatened them, forcing several away at gunpoint. A TV cable had been cut by a deputy sheriff. Because he was black, Withers had managed to slip into the crowd and had begun taking pictures, but the police had broken his camera and had arrested him.

There were no Women for Constitutional Government at the city jail as there had been two days before, and it seemed clear that a wave of real fear must have swept white Jackson. We were formally booked again, and before I was led off, I gave Withers some cigarettes. The police officers in charge had evidently told the white prisoners in the cell block who I was because, as we passed their cages, screams came, "Give him to us! Let us get him!" But I was placed in a cell by myself.

I was extremely tired but I could not sleep. What had occurred on this day in Jackson, especially the massive upheaval at Farish Street, had been the largest black protest in the history of Mississippi. It was inconceivable that it could not have a positive impact on the power structure, and the more I thought about it, especially the widespread police brutality, the more I felt that the Federal government *must* be sending troops into Mississippi's hate-filled capital.

I knew that the developments of the day were going to have an effect upon the Jackson movement itself. I could not see how, after everything that had occurred, the effect could be anything but constructive: larger and more intensive mass marches. All of us, especially the people at the grassroots, had now reached the point where we could never, never turn back.

I heard the police coming down the corridor. I was taken from my cell into the main office. Attorney Carsie Hall was talking with Ed. The lawyer told us that we were being bonded out. The charges, which were disturbing the peace and interfering with officers, were, as he put it, "minimal, at this point." He went on to say that there might be additional charges levied against us. I asked about Withers and the others. He said that many of them were already out and that everyone would be out by nightfall. Several were receiving medical care. He told us that he would drive us to Tougaloo.

We went outside. Police gathered to look at us as we walked down the sidewalk, but once in the attorney's car, we relaxed. Soon we were going past the state capitol building, and I looked down Capitol Street, into the downtown area. Although it was Saturday evening, there was virtually no activity.

I asked Carsie Hall what had happened—the demonstration, the Federal government, what had been going on?

He knew nothing except that the fact that the demonstration had gradually dissolved and everyone had left the area, although large numbers of police were traveling through the black neighborhoods. Most of the prominent national figures who had come for the funeral, he continued, had either left before or during the Farish Street demonstration, and others had left on the late-afternoon flights. He had been busy getting bail-bond money.

Then we were at Tougaloo and a large number of students and some faculty gathered to greet us. Jeannette King, Eddie O'Neal, Bill Kunstler, and Steve Rutledge had all made it through the Farish Street situation, were back on campus, and had a great deal to tell us. We went into the Kings' home to talk.

Immediately we wanted to know, although the answer seemed obvious, if Jeannette and Eddie had been able to get in touch with Martin Luther King. They told us that they had been unable to find any office open in the building. By then, hundreds and hundreds of lawmen were down on the street, and since they knew Dr. King's plane had left, they had logically enough stayed out of sight. Eventually, they had joined forces with Bill and Steve.

I asked Bill Kunstler if anything had developed with Martin Luther King and the SCLC during the drive to the airport. He shook his head sadly. The degree of inter-organizational conflict that would develop between the NAACP and SCLC if SCLC involved itself in Jackson would, it seemed, be of a serious and drastic nature.

They told us about the demonstration.

It had gone on, they said, for at least forty minutes after we had been arrested, and police brutality had mounted steadily as the army of officers sought to disperse the people by forcing them back, block by block, along Farish Street. It had been by far the most brutally repressive situation since the beginning of the Jackson movement.

After a time, they said, following the shooting out of the windows and several very bloody and conspicuous clubbings, some youths began to throw bricks and bottles at the long lines of advancing police.

Bill and Steve told us that the NAACP officials had been many blocks away when the action had begun, arriving back on the scene well after the demonstration was under way. The NAACP staff had attempted to persuade the people to go home but had been ignored, even after one staffer had borrowed a bullhorn from the police and had begun calling for everyone to leave the area.

When the bricks and bottles were thrown, Bill said, everything had become extremely tense. At that point the representatives from the U.S. Department of Justice, who had observed all of this, moved into the situation. John Doar, a key government man, had stepped out into the street and had pleaded with the people to go home. Finally, they did.

Governor Ross Barnett had gone on radio and television to call out the Mississippi National Guard to active duty on a standby basis, and at least five Guard units were at the Jackson armory.

But there were no Federal troops, not even Federal marshals.

Jeannette said that she had heard that Mayor Allen Thompson had gone on radio and television, telling all of the people of Jackson to stay away from the whole downtown area.

We were told that news media all over Mississippi were taking the position that Ed and I had instigated everything.

I began to tell them what the police had said to me at the fairgrounds stockade, but Bill Kunstler cut me short. "It isn't just the news media and the police that are taking that position," he said. Then he told Ed and me what had happened.

After the demonstration had been dispersed, Gloster Current and some other NAACP staff people had called an emergency meeting of the strategy committee and, with a number of the ministers, had gone to a church. Bill and Eddie had talked with several people on the street for a few moments. Then it had occurred to them that this was definitely one strategy committee meeting that they should not miss. They had gone to the church, arriving a few minutes after Gloster Current and the ministers had begun the meeting.

When he and Eddie walked in the door, Bill went on, Gloster Current was calling for the immediate expulsion of Ed and me from the strategy committee, charging that we had incited the "riot." Most of the ministers expressed shock and horror at the developments on Farish Street, especially at the Jackson black people themselves. But several of the clergy who had pressed Gloster Current and other NAACP staff people for tangible evidence of the involvement of Ed and me were told that the Jackson police had evidence to this effect. Indeed, it was even pointed out to the strategy committee that we had been arrested.

Bill said that he and Eddie had observed the course of the strategy committee meeting, interested in how it was being handled, and for a time kept silent. Several of the ministers were not certain that the Jackson police were the final authority on any of this, and a prominent NAACP attorney, from New York, had joined them in expressing these doubts. Someone had raised the point that perhaps Ed and I should be allowed to present our case to the strategy committee after we had been released from jail.

But Gloster Current had called again for our immediate expulsion from the strategy committee, and most of the ministers present appeared to support him.

At that point Bill Kunstler, who had defended me in segregationist courts in Mississippi, arose to defend me and Ed before the NAACP and the Jackson ministers. First, he pointed out that the Farish Street demonstration, a large part of which he had observed after returning from the airport, was not a "riot" in any sense of the word, and that whatever brick- and bottle-throwing had taken place, undesirable as that might be, had occurred only after incredible police brutality.

He had then presented to the strategy committee his star witness, Eddie O'Neal, a minister himself, from Meridian, president of the Tougaloo student body, who had of course been with Ed and me up to the moment we had been arrested. Eddie O'Neal quietly told the strategy committee that the demonstration itself had been the purest expression of the feelings of the people—that it had been as spontaneous as anything could be. He had talked at length, and when he sat down, the strategy committee took the position that neither Ed nor I would be expelled.

Bill and Eddie said that several hundred lawmen had cordoned off the black neighborhoods in Jackson.

I asked them about the strategy committee—what else had gone on?

They told me that the ministers, with sound trucks and under a police escort, were canvassing the black neighborhoods, pleading with the people to remain calm. No public mass meetings had been set for the next few days, but another strategy session had been scheduled for early Monday afternoon.

The whole account of the afternoon's strategy committee meeting made me angry. It seemed that in the final analysis, not only white Mississippians but the NAACP staff and, apparently, a number of the Jackson ministers as well, could not really believe that the people could lead themselves.

It sounded as though the Jackson movement internally was by no means healthy, that many more crises lay ahead.

"The people are moving," I said, "and the Jackson movement will keep going. We won't let it stop."

Then Bill Kunstler indicated that he was returning to New York City the next day, Sunday. I asked him again if he felt that there was any chance that SCLC would involve itself in Jackson—especially in view of the huge demonstration of the afternoon. And even Bill's normally high degree of optimism failed him. Again, he shook his head sadly.

I walked outside. One of the Tougaloo administrative officials came up and we talked at length. A tremendous number of threats were pouring into the college, he said, concerning violence against me, against Ed, against the school. As we talked, a group of about twenty students came through the twilight. Many were carrying guns. We asked them what they were doing, and they indicated that they had set up a guard detail to watch the college that night. We nodded and thanked them. It seemed under the circumstances a logical enough step.

Steve Rutledge came out of Ed's house and said that a radio report indicated that the Women for Constitutional Government had levied quite a verbal attack against me.

Next, two FBI agents arrived, again to discuss the Thursday beatings on Rose Street. There was now, they said, considerable doubt that the police who had struck me and who had struck the others could be conclusively identified. I pointed out that every major television network had carried film sequences of my beating, at least, if not the other incidents, and that the faces of the police involved were clearly seen. They shrugged and indicated that there would still be difficulty.

I went back into the King's house. Jeannette was cooking supper for all of us. The telephone began to ring, and it was an unidentified white man reading scripture to us. We hung up, and the phone rang again. We answered with "Joe's Bar." He hung up. It rang again.

"Madison County Dancehall," we said. He hung up. It rang again, and we took the telephone off the hook.

All were extremely tired and talked only briefly after dinner. Once again, there was no question but that the Jackson movement had to continue, with continuous mass demonstrations. Although we knew the position of the national NAACP, we were concerned about the attitude of the ministers and felt that they had reacted to the situation with panic. Obviously there was going to be no direct action on Sunday, but there would be a strategy session on Monday. And more important than anything else, the people were moving forward. One way or another, we decided, the Jackson movement would continue ahead—intensively.

By this time, the body of Medgar Evers was well on its way to Meridian, to the train that would carry him out of Mississippi forever.

11

IT WAS INTENSELY HOT the next day, but the weather forecasters felt that rain might be coming. I took Bill Kunstler to the airport. He was not at all optimistic about the Jackson situation; although he tried hard to regain his optimism, he never quite succeeded. People were going to church as we drove into the city, and as we passed the National Guard armory, we could see the Mississippi troops still on standby duty. Bill left for New York City, and I picked up a copy of the Jackson Sunday newspaper with its banner story charging that "agitation" had taken over the funeral march.

I returned to Tougaloo, ate a late breakfast, and Steve Rutledge and I drove into Jackson. There was no activity anywhere. The police, it appeared, had all been withdrawn from the black neighborhoods. Most of the people whom we knew were either sleeping late or attending church. Those with whom we did talk, however, including several of the youth leaders, were convinced that the Jackson movement had to go forward. After a time, the police began to follow us, and we then drove down Farish Street. It too was very quiet. The city officials had moved quickly to clean up most signs of physical disorder—although, of course, the windows were still broken. We stopped at a small Farish Street newsstand. All of the newspapers, many from out of state, were talking about the Jackson "riot," and most said little or nothing about the police brutality, emphasized that the demonstration was led by non-blacks, and said much about blacks functioning violently and throwing bricks and bottles at the police. We drove back to the college. The police followed us for a time, then swung off.

By now it was early afternoon. We learned that half a dozen students had left to see if they would be admitted to "white" Jackson church services. As yet, no one knew whether they had succeeded.

A reporter from the *New York Times,* Jack Langguth, arrived to see me. We had talked before and there was no question about his integrity. He wanted to know, off the record, precisely what I thought would be happening in Jackson. I told him that those of us who believed in massive direct action intended to press very zealously for that. He was silent for a long time.

Then he said that word was going around that the large-scale direct-action phase of the Jackson movement was over. I asked him how he knew that. He shrugged and said that it was just going around. I told him that the people clearly wanted meaningful action and that they intended to secure meaningful changes. He was silent again. Then it developed that he had heard rumors that, behind the scenes, the Federal government was becoming very much involved in the Jackson situation. I told him that unless there was a really drastic change for the better in Jackson, mass action would still be necessary and would undoubtedly take place. But it was clear that he had doubts about the possibility of such action occurring.

As if to underscore that, he said that most of the out-of-state newsmen were leaving Jackson. He himself was taking off; his main reason for coming to see me, it seemed, was to get some biographical material in case, as he put it, "something happens."

I joked, "Sounds to me like you're trying to get my obituary, Jack."

He didn't smile and said that that might be possible. I gave him the information. He left, then, to get some biographical data from Ed King.

I was thinking all of this over when someone came in with the news that the students who had gone off to seek entrance into the white churches had all returned. Four, it developed, had been admitted to St. Andrew's Episcopal Church right across from Governor Barnett's mansion. The others had been turned away from other churches. The Tougaloo students were very eager for more mass direct action in Jackson.

A little later Dr. Allan Knight Chalmers arrived at Tougaloo. He had come to Jackson Saturday night and had been spending the day studying the situation. I had met him before, at the home of Dr. A. D. Beittel, of whom he was a close friend. Dr. Chalmers, I knew, not only was a professor of applied religion at Boston University but had endeavored for a lifetime to apply his religion to secular situations. Long involved on behalf of civil rights, a spearhead of the defense effort in the Scottsboro "boys" cases in Alabama a generation before, he was now president of the NAACP Legal Defense and Educational Fund. He had been one of the men to whom I had, well over a month before, sent a carbon copy of my letter to Laplois Ashford asking national-office support behind direct action in Jackson.

Several of us, including Ed King, who knew Dr. Chalmers, talked with him at great length, indicating that we felt, as did the people at the grassroots, that the Jackson movement absolutely had to go forward in a massive and intensive fashion: to crack Jackson and to start cracking Mississippi. He was extremely sympathetic, and when several of us, much later that evening, accompanied him to the airport for his return flight north, he indicated that he would definitely do his best to help.

When I returned home late that night, I was gripped by a feeling of deep gloom. It was the first time that I had really felt that way since the first stirrings of the Jackson movement away back on that cold day in

December when the six of us had been arrested in front of the Woolworth store. The visit with Allan Knight Chalmers had given me a temporary boost, but over it all lay the feeling that the Jackson movement was enmeshed in its most serious crisis. Bill Kunstler's pessimism, much as he had tried to transcend it, had shown through before he had left for New York. Jack Langguth felt that matters were essentially over. Certainly, in the light of everything that had happened for the past several weeks, if not before that, it required no extrasensory powers to see that the Jackson movement was facing some serious problems.

The feeling of gloom increased. I reached for the dozens of letters that I had been receiving over the past several weeks. Most of them were from well-wishers located all over the United States: people like Harry Stamler of Scottsdale, Arizona, whom I knew; others from people of whom I had never heard. Students and faculty at the Department of Anthropology at the University of California at Berkeley had sent a long letter. Another, signed by sailors of half a dozen nationalities, had come several days before, postmarked, of all places, Capetown, South Africa. Wofford Smith, Episcopal chaplain at the University of Mississippi, had sent a kind communication. I looked through all of them, wondering what these people would say if they knew some of the terrific internal conflicts occurring within the Jackson movement.

Some of the letters were not from well-wishers but were hate communications, generally unsigned. One was nineteen hand-written pages long, and its mildest term was "cobra snake." Another, quite short, was addressed simply to "Professor John Salter, Agitator of Negroes, Jackson, Mississippi"—and on it the Jackson post office had written, "Tougaloo College, Tougaloo, Miss." Its message had informed me that "it don't take courage to intrude upon a man's property, and let people pour catsup on you. It only takes a fool who thinks he's educated. Why don't you go to Africa and you can smell all the Negro stink you want. In fact, you can even be a nigger." It was postmarked Flagstaff, Arizona—my home town.

I went out to a telephone and attempted to call Eldri but could not reach her. On the way back to the house I saw several Tougaloo students who told me that, because several cars full of white youths had been seen on the road near the college, and because some more threats had come in over the college telephones, they were going to stand guard again that night. I told them to awaken me if anything occurred.

For the first time in weeks, it was raining a little. The feeling of gloom was even stronger just before I dropped off to sleep. Finally exhaustion took over and I slept, but it was a restless night, filled with strange dreams that I could not recall when I awakened early in the morning.

It was Monday. The sky was cloudy; a little rain was falling; and it was cooler. Later in the morning, several of us drove into Jackson to attend the strategy committee meeting due to start right after lunch.

The first shock came when we saw that there were no police cars anywhere around the Masonic Temple. As we stood on the sidewalk, we saw a police car going by, but the men who looked out at us were wearing soft hats, not blue helmets. Then from across the street some SNCC workers hailed us. They were people we knew who normally worked up on the Delta but who had come down to Jackson from time to time and had been in the city since Medgar's funeral. The SNCC workers were furious. Not only did they recognize the severe internal problems that gripped the Jackson movement, but thinking that they might stay on in the city and work for a time, they had earlier that morning asked if they, or at least one of their representatives, could be placed on the strategy committee. But the minister with whom they had spoken had been, they felt, extremely evasive and had finally said that the question of their being seated on the committee would have to be discussed at length. We told them that we would fight for their place on the strategy committee, and that we would let them know what happened.

We went up to the NAACP offices, where we received another surprise. Inside were several people we didn't know, people from out of state, and they were working with maps and card files of names. They told us that they were setting up a city-wide voter-registration campaign.

I felt sick at the implications of this.

We asked if Gloster Current was in, but he was not around. Ruby Hurley, we were told, would be in shortly. A copy of the *Jackson Daily News* was on a desk and I read through it briefly. There was a news item to the effect that Medgar's brother, Charles Evers, a Chicago businessman and teacher, who had been in Jackson for the funeral, had been appointed new NAACP field secretary for Mississippi. I asked if Charles Evers was around, but no one appeared to know much about that either. Another item in the newspaper quoted Roy Wilkins, who in a speech the day before at Alexandria, Virginia, had attacked SNCC, CORE, and SCLC as seeking "publicity, while the NAACP furnishes the manpower and pays the bill." Roy Wilkins had said that the NAACP is the "only organization which can handle a long, sustained fight," and had told his audience that they shouldn't give money to other organizations "when it should be given to us."

Ed King took the newspaper from me and read the article. Shaking his head, he threw the paper back on the desk.

In groups of twos and threes, the other members of the strategy committee were now arriving. We saw Ruby Hurley, who nodded rather curtly in our direction. A number of ministers came up to us and shook hands, and it was obvious that they felt apologetic about the nature of the Saturday-afternoon session of the committee. We too were quite friendly. Several of the youth leaders arrived and we talked briefly. Some more NAACP staff people came. Outside, the rain was coming down in a drizzle.

As soon as the strategy committee meeting began, it was clear that it was going to be anything but amicable. More significantly, it was apparent from the outset that the key decisions had already been made.

Several of the NAACP staff people made it clear that the situation in Jackson was of such a nature that any mass demonstrations would be ill advised and that the Jackson movement was now into its "new phase"— voter registration and work on the boycott. A number of the ministers agreed vigorously with all of this.

At that point I raised, as I had been doing for weeks, the necessity of immediate, massive direct action, saying that the alternative was simply a dead Jackson movement. A minister arose, crying, and talked at length about the "riot" of Saturday, saying, "We don't want that any more, no more of that."

Many others agreed.

Rather heatedly, I pointed out that the Farish Street situation of Saturday had not been, by any stretch of the imagination, a "riot." We had had many mass demonstrations that were much more "organized" than Saturday's had been. Those who had always supported the mass direct-action position, such as the youth leaders and Ed King, agreed, adding strong statements of their own. The argument went on and on.

As I looked around the room, it became clear that the discussion was as hypothetical as anything could be: the position of the NAACP staff was obvious, as it had been for at least two weeks. With few exceptions, and none of them vocal, the position of the Jackson ministers was more conservative than ever. It was indeed clear that for all practical purposes the decision to end mass direct action had been made before this meeting had convened. Then I remembered the absence of police outside and the soft hats worn by those driving by. With quiet bitterness within me, I began to wonder if the decision had already been conveyed to the city officials.

At this point, a new element entered the discussion, what Jack Langguth, the reporter, had hinted about the day before: Federal involvement. Now we were told that some prominent Federal officials were working behind the scenes, right at this time, on the Jackson situation, and that one of the Jackson ministers was himself in Washington, D.C. Very little was being said about the matter of the Federal government since, we were told, no one really knew what was happening. But we were all assured that top Federal officials were definitely involved.

Federal involvement! If any possibility, however thin and remote, had existed concerning strategy committee approval of massive direct action, this injection of "Federal involvement" into the discussion completely destroyed it. *Federal involvement!* It did sound good—except, when you thought about it, what kind of involvement?

We raised this question immediately. Again, no one appeared to know much about the role of the Federal officials—only that some prominent government men were definitely working on the Jackson situation. We of course indicated that, unless a settlement of the Jackson conflict was *really* constructive—and at least all of the demands of the Jackson movement should be met—then massive direct action was very definitely going to be needed. Indeed, we pointed out, it should be currently going on, in order to emphatically ensure a genuinely substantial victory.

But it was quite apparent that there was to be no massive direct action in Jackson.

We wrangled on and on. I talked about the people at the grassroots and their great awakening, and their forward thrust through the paralyzing climate of fear, in search of a good and meaningful life. But it was only too clear that it had been the grassroots people who, on Saturday at least, had frightened most of the strategy committee.

We asked if there were going to be *any* demonstrations in Jackson. Rather vaguely, we were told that there would probably be some smaller ones from time to time. One of the younger NAACP staff, who was not opposed to our position as were the others, thought that perhaps there could sometime be a mass march of people to the voter registrar's office. Arrests, this staff member felt, would be difficult to make because voter rights were, in theory at least, protected by certain aspects of clearly defined Federal law. It was a good word on behalf of the militant position, but it became quite obvious that there would not even be that sort of mass demonstration.

By this time the discussion concerning large-scale direct action was essentially over. Several of the NAACP staff people now left the room, and the elderly minister who was acting chairman moved the gathering on to more mundane matters, such as mass meetings. We then moved to bring up SNCC representation on the strategy committee. We pointed out that since this was a major civil rights group that was much involved in Mississippi affairs, and since it might well be assisting continuously in the Jackson effort, it should definitely have a voice in matters.

It became very obvious that here, too, a decision had been reached. The elderly chairman hedged. Others indicated, for reasons that were not stated, oblique objections to SNCC representation. Several NAACP staff people returned to the room and took a negative position. Indeed, at one point in the discussion, I saw the chairman looking several times over the heads of all of us, and I quickly turned around. An NAACP staff member, standing in the back of the room was shaking her head with great vigor.

The argument concerning SNCC representation on the strategy

committee of the Jackson movement dragged steadily onward. Finally it was left on the basis that if a SNCC representative were to sit in on the discussions, *maybe* it would be all right.

Eventually the meeting adjourned. Several of us, including a number of the youth leaders, walked out of the Masonic Temple and as the rain filtered down on Lynch Street we talked. We were angry and bitter. Several of the SNCC people joined us. They were disgusted. We talked some more and decided to get together in a day or so. Perhaps we could develop some worthwhile direct action in Jackson. This had been the first real mass movement in the most intractably segregated state in the Union, a movement that had the full support of the grassroots people and that had plowed through mass arrests, widespread police brutality, and murder. To all of us, the fact that this could now be ended, just as if a water faucet was being turned off, and ended with no real prospect of any bona fide settlement, seemed not only incredible—it seemed like a nightmare.

None of us said much as we drove back to Tougaloo in the still drizzling rain. At the college, several students asked us what had been happening. We told them. Although not really surprised, still they were stunned.

I went home and had just put on some coffee when a car pulled up outside. Steve Rutledge, who had left in the middle of the strategy session to keep an appointment with the FBI concerning some police brutality incidents he had witnessed, came inside. With him were two FBI agents who had given him a ride to Tougaloo. One of them was from Arizona; a few days before, we had talked about our home state. They had some coffee and prepared to leave. Then the Arizona man told me, very carefully and very quietly, "Take care. Be very careful." I nodded and they left.

Steve told me that nearly all of the police were gone from the downtown area.

A number of us ate supper at Ed King's home that night and talked briefly. An aura of deep gloom seemed to cover everything. It was still raining when we left. No carloads of white youths had been seen and the telephoned threats had diminished somewhat; and other than the regular night watchmen, no guards were posted that night. As I drifted off to sleep, I was still thinking of ways in which we could reactivate the Jackson movement.

Then it was Tuesday, June 18. It was still cloudy but the rain had stopped. I was up early and met my summer-session classes, which by mutual consent had been ignored for the past several days. The students were eager to hear what was occurring, and bluntly I told them. Their reaction was somber and angry.

About 10 A.M. Ed King came to see me. A telephone call had just come for us, he said. It had been from Jack Young, the lawyer, who had indicated that it was imperative that Ed and I go into Jackson immediately to confer at length with him. Aware of the prevalent wiretapping, the attorney had not wished to go into details over the telephone, but he had made it clear that some extremely serious legal problems were arising for the two of us. We had a cup of coffee, got into my car, and drove into Jackson. The city looked calm and serene, almost as if it knew that, temporarily at least, the active phase of the Jackson movement had ended.

We parked a block from Farish Street and walked to Jack Young's office. Everything was quiet and placid, except for a police car parked across from the building in which the lawyer's office was located. I told Ed King that it looked to me as if we just might be arrested once again. We looked at the police and they stared back at us. Then we went up to see the attorney.

He greeted us pleasantly and we sat down. Then he came to the point: he had just learned, he told us, that the city officials, taking the position that they now had "new evidence" concerning the mass demonstrations on Saturday afternoon, were planning to indict us both for "inciting to riot." That came as no particular surprise to us, and I told him so. He did not take this turn of events at all lightly, however, and said that the whole situation could become extremely complicated. Suddenly, it was clear to me that even Jack Young himself was uncertain about the role of Ed and me in the Farish Street upsurge. There was nothing to tell him other than the fact that the massive demonstration was the purest expression of feeling on the part of the people—that it was completely spontaneous. If the city indicted us for "inciting to riot," I told him, then it indicted us. We would have to fight that through court along with all of our other cases. He told us that he would keep us informed. We then left.

Outside, the police car still watched.

We went into a newsstand, bought some newspapers and magazines, and came out.

The police car still watched.

We crossed Farish Street, walked up to my car, and got inside. Another police car passed slowly by us, its occupants staring.

Strange, I thought, all of this attention. Yesterday, there had hardly been a police officer in view, not even around the Masonic Temple.

We drove down a block and turned into Farish Street, heading back to Tougaloo. I could see a police car away back, two or three blocks behind us. Then we turned up past the Blair Street AME church and through a black neighborhood, then through a white residential area. Now we were out onto a main road, the route which we almost invariably followed which headed north through Jackson, out into the country and to Tougaloo. Neither Ed nor I said much and both of us were thinking, I suppose, of the Jackson movement and our expected "inciting" indictments. From time to time I looked in my rear-view mirror, but could no longer see anything resembling a police car. We had been followed constantly, for weeks, but somehow all of the attention given us by the police on Farish Street shortly before, and the fact that they followed us as we left the Farish Street area to head back to the college, disturbed me very much. I drove well under the speed limit, traveling only about thirty miles an hour.

It was about 11:30 A.M. There was rather heavy traffic in our lane. In the opposite lane, coming toward us, traffic was almost as congested, and cars were coming at closely spaced intervals.

We drove on. Now we were about a mile from the outskirts of Jackson, going through a white suburban area. Traffic was about as it had been, heavy in both lanes.

Suddenly, in one split second, I saw what was happening:

Some yards ahead of us, lunging out of a sidestreet to our left and past a stop sign, came a car driven by a white youth in such a fashion that another car coming down toward us in the other lane was forced, by the white youth's car, into our lane, approaching us head on while the white youth quickly manipulated his car over to the side. I was throwing on my brakes and so, probably, was the other car—but it was too late. We hit head on.

I was semi-conscious, moving as if I were in some sort of dream. Blood was all over my face and I tried to wipe it away. Very slowly, I looked in the mirror, then slumped back, realizing that only one eye seemed to be working. That eye saw a great hole in the windshield, over on Ed's side, and then I saw Ed slumped against the door, and covered with blood. I called to him, but he didn't answer. I looked out of my window. Cars were parking everywhere and a great many people were talking and pointing—white Jackson people. They saw me looking at them and one of them waved and smiled. Then several others smiled.

Hazily I wished that I had a gun.

None of the people was coming over. Then I saw the police, talking with the people and looking toward us. Somewhere, finally, I heard an ambulance scream.

Police officers came to the sides of the car with ambulance attendants, pulled me out, and I stood there. Someone else was holding Ed, who was moving slightly. They maneuvered us around to the back of the ambulance. Still the white faces stared at us, some smiling; and again I wished that I had a gun. Then the attendant was asking me a question: to what hospital did I wish to go? I tried to think. Then I told him, St. Dominic's, the Catholic hospital. Now we were in the back of the ambulance, on cots. Ed was moving around a little, very slowly regaining consciousness.

"Wreck," he muttered, "their car forced another into our lane, forced it . . ."

"We're on our way to a hospital," I told him, "the Catholic hospital. We'll be there in a few minutes."

He said nothing, but he was alive. I looked at the ambulance attendant, a white man, who was in the back with us. He looked at me, expressionless. Then the ambulance stopped. The door opened and we were carried out. Dimly, I could see that we were not at St. Dominic's; we were at the Baptist hospital.

We were carried inside. The police now seemed to be everywhere, wearing their soft hats, not the blue helmets.

I was in a receiving room, stretched out on a kind of table. They put Ed in another room, off to the side. Someone was looking at my eye, telling me that the eyelid was hanging off, but that the eye would again be functional. Then I drifted off into a strange semi-sleep, fading back into consciousness and then into a deep haze, weird dreams wafting through my mind.

Someone was speaking to me. I opened my eye and slowly looked up. It was Jeannette King. She asked how I was. I told her I was still alive. She said that she had been in to see Ed and there was no question but that he'd live. Dr. Beittel had come, she went on, and although there had apparently been some difficulties concerning our being admitted to the hospital, all of those problems had been satisfactorily resolved and we would go into surgery later in the evening. We were lucky to be alive, Jeannette said, and she told me that my car had been completely wrecked. Men were standing at the door, looking at me—some in business suits, some in police uniforms. Something was moving around in my mind, something to be asked. Then I knew what it was.

"Who was driving the car that forced the other one into our lane, forced it to hit us?" I asked. "Who was it?"

She told me a name and said that he was in his late 'teens. Very hazily, I thought the name over. And then I remembered. "His father," I said.

Jeannette nodded. The youth's father, a former public official, was one of Jackson's most prominent Citizens Council members.

She thought that there would be some sort of investigation.

"The driver of the other car," I asked, "the one that was forced into hitting us, was he hurt?" Jeannette shook her head and told me that, although the other car had been substantially damaged, the driver, a black woman, had received only minor injuries.

Then I slipped away into some kind of dream again, thinking of my brothers in Arizona and the rifles in the closets and on the gun racks. I wanted to see my brothers, wanted to see our guns.

I was awakened again by someone talking to me. It was Dr. Beittel. They were contacting Eldri, he said, and expected her to leave immediately for Mississippi. He said he would talk again to the hospital officials and would try to get us into a private room. He left to talk to the hospital administrators.

Then, into the room where I lay, came the police, slowly, in a single-file. Among them was one of the detectives who had followed me so often in past days and who, just a week before, and only hours before Medgar's murder, had been riding with the man who kicked their car door open, almost knocking me off my feet.

As if I were on a bier, they walked by, slowly, some staring at me grimly and some smiling. There were almost two dozen of them, and as they walked by, I remembered the police on Farish Street, an hour and a half or so before, who had seen us going into Jack Young's office, who had seen us leaving the office, who had seen us get into my car, and who had followed us for a while—and who had seen us heading toward Tougaloo, along our usual route.

Now, through my one eye, I looked back at them with the purest kind of raw hatred. Then some of them turned their heads away. Again and again, as they passed, I wanted my brothers, wanted our rifles from Arizona.

A long time later, it seemed, I was wheeled down a corridor and left outside a room in which there were doctors. People passed by, looking down at me, and many of them whispered to one another. A doctor came out of the room, stared down at me, then grimaced. I looked back at him. Then he went inside the room and came out again with a bandage which, very delicately, he placed over my injured eye.

Then I was taken for X rays and, finally, wheeled into an elevator and taken up to another corridor, then into a room, and into bed. Ed lay in another bed and appeared to be sleeping. A nurse came in, cheerful and friendly. She began to check us over and said that we would go into surgery in a few hours. Then she gave me something and I slept.

When I awoke, feeling drugged, it was late in the afternoon. Rain was drizzling down outside and there seemed to be mist arising from the hot ground of Jackson. Jeannette King was in the room now, sitting by Ed, who still seemed to be sleeping. She saw me move about, trying to sit up, and she came over.

They had got in touch with Eldri, she told me, who would be arriving in Jackson the next day. She asked how I felt. I told her that I seemed all right. Then Jeannette reached over to a table and showed me the front page of the *Jackson Daily News*.

Squinting my one eye slightly, I could make out the headlines.

There was a picture of the police standing by my wrecked car and, under it, a caption saying "Integration Leaders Hurt Here," and a big headline, "Salter and King Hurt in Wreck." The story had just barely made it under the day's news deadline.

Then there was a banner headline, "President Calls Jackson Mayor."

And a smaller one, "Negro Groups Quarrel Over Policy Here."

Still feeling drugged, I asked her what was happening. Managing a lopsided smile, I told her that we knew about the wreck, but what about the other developments? She read parts of the other stories, sometimes verbatim, and sometimes she just summarized.

There was not much at all concerning the "Negro Groups Quarrel"— a statement from Willie Ludden of the NAACP, indicating that the SNCC workers were "operating independently" and that the NAACP was not in any way involved with SNCC. Down at the end of the article was a little more: "The NAACP, here, now headed by Southeastern area official Ruby Hurley of Atlanta and Evers' brother, Charles, of Chicago, were reported advocating vote registration and court suits as the key to integration of Jackson facilities."

I swore very quietly at that and asked Jeannette if Charles Evers was in town, but she did not know. She went on, then, to the other story, the one about the President.

Although it had not apparently been publicly disclosed until just a few hours before, it developed that both the President and his brother, the Attorney General, had been busy Monday on their telephones. Robert Kennedy, the news story said, had talked at length Monday with a number of the Jackson business leaders. The President had called Allen Thompson Monday afternoon, while the mayor was at the Jackson airport waiting to receive Alabama governor George Wallace, and Thompson had talked with the President on an airport telephone.

"Monday," I thought. "Just as we were having the strategy committee meeting."

The news story mentioned, again the first that we had heard of it, that in past days Attorney General Kennedy had talked a number of times with the mayor and the businessmen. There was mention also of the fact that the Attorney General had talked to the mayor at length on this day, Tuesday.

The story gave no real indication of what had been said in any of these discussions, although Allen Thompson was quoted frequently in a context of recalcitrance and had apparently told the President "just exactly what we have been doing, what we intend to continue doing, and what we expect to do in the racial activities here." He had informed the President that all racial tension in Jackson would cease if the President would give "just a word because the people would listen to you."

There was a picture that showed Allen Thompson holding a telephone. The caption read, "Peace Will Return." Under it was a sentence, "Mayor Allen Thompson says Jackson will again be peaceful for both races when the outside agitators are defeated and leave town."

Then, very slowly indeed, Jeannette King read something else: "A meeting requested by a group of Negro ministers will be held at City Hall at 3:30 P.M., with Mayor Thompson and city commissioners."

"*Today?*" I asked. "Today?"

Jeannette King nodded slowly. I looked outside again. It seemed very late in the afternoon. "It's going on right now," I said. "And maybe it's even over."

She nodded again. I remembered the absence of the police from around the Masonic Temple on Monday—remembered how the decision to end demonstrations had been so obviously made even before the strategy committee had convened.

"What do the students think?" I asked. "The ones that you've talked with?"

She began to tell me that they were all very much worked up about Ed and me, that girls had cried. But I interrupted and asked again, "What do they think about this?" I pointed to the newspaper.

"You know what they think," she replied. "They know what's happening."

Then a nurse came in and Jeannette turned to go. But before she left, she told me that other than she and Eldri when she came, no one was being allowed to see Ed and me. There were those, it seemed, and Jeannette gave a wan smile, who felt that attempts might be made on our lives.

The nurse told me to rest and said that I had broken ribs and broken facial bones. I lay back. "Meeting on Tuesday afternoon," I thought. "And what will the city fathers offer the Jackson movement now?"

Again, as I moved off into sleep, I thought of the police who in the late morning had seen us go into our lawyer's office, who had seen us come out, and who had seen us head back to Tougaloo.

When I awakened, it was time to go into surgery. I was to be first, then Ed. I was wheeled down the corridor into a room. Several doctors and nurses were there, all of them wearing white—and all of them were white. They pumped anesthesia into my arm and slowly my mind began to detach itself from my body. Then, very distantly, I heard my voice saying to a doctor who, wearing a mask, was bending over me, "You'd like to kill me, wouldn't you?"

He shook his head.

Then, I awoke, back in my room. It was morning, Wednesday morning, and it was raining outside. Much of my face seemed to be bandaged. Nurses were moving back and forth and greeted me. I was fine, they told me, and so was Ed. But one of them went on to say that Ed would have to have many more operations. A large portion of his face had been sheared off when he went through the windshield.

A doctor came, apparently the man who had done most of the work on us. He was cordial, repeating what the nurses had said.

I slept again. When I awakened, it was later in the morning. Ed seemed to be moving around and talking very slowly to Jeannette. I greeted them both. I felt very drugged and I could hardly move. For the first time I saw that Ed's face was almost entirely covered by bandages.

Jeannette came over. She told me that Eldri was arriving in Jackson within the hour, but that it had been felt best to leave Maria with her grandparents in Minnesota. I asked Jeannette if she had a newspaper. She hesitated, then brought over the morning paper, the *Clarion-Ledger*.

She showed me a picture on the front page. Several of the ministers were talking with Allen Thompson, and the caption read, "Reach Agreement." We looked at one another. Then Jeannette read what was under the picture:

Jackson Mayor Allen Thompson chats with group of Negroes following meeting Tuesday afternoon at which he and the City Council announced the hiring of Negro policemen, placing of Negro guards at Negro school crossings and upgrading certain Negro city jobs. Thompson also reported on his Monday talk with President Kennedy.

Jeannette put the newspaper down. Everything was silent, and outside the rain continued to drizzle. "What else?" I finally asked. "There must be more."

Again she hesitated, then read parts of a news story under a large headline "Council's Talks Moving Toward Racial Solution":

Jackson chalked up some progress in racial solutions Tuesday as leaders of the Negro community talked with the City Council in the afternoon. . . . Hiring of Negro police and school crossing guards and upgrading of Negro employees in the city's sanitation department were the particular points of discussion at both the small afternoon meeting and the larger meeting at night, when spokesmen who talked with Mayor Thompson and the commissioners made their report.

The story went on to say that one of the ministers, as spokesman for the "committee of five which met with the Council, recommended acceptance of the proposals agreed upon at City Hall. The resulting vote was estimated at about ten to one in favor of acceptance."

I cut Jeannette off. "Ten to one?" I asked. "Ten to one, where?"

Very slowly, she replied. "At a mass meeting, last night." She paused, then went on. "But I'll tell you about that in a moment."

I felt more heavily drugged than any medicines could make me as she continued reading: "Mass demonstrations would be checked under the agreement. Attention diverted from mass demonstrations would be concentrated on increasing voter registration, it was said."

"There's another story," she told me. "Right under this one. Do you want me to read that?" I nodded slowly, drearily.

Mayor Allen Thompson presented four proposals to Negro leaders here Tuesday in an effort to ease racial tensions in Jackson. The proposals are: Hiring of Negro policemen for Negro areas; Hiring of Negro school crossguards for Negro schools; Upgrading of Negro employees salaries; A continuation of meetings with the Negro leaders to hear grievances, complaints, and recommendations.

"We understand as a result of this there will be no further unlawful mass marches, demonstrations or violence," the mayor said. Thompson stressed that there had been "no pressure and nobody has yielded."

Other earlier Negro demands which were not considered in Tuesday's proposals were: Removal of segregation signs in public buildings; Formation of a bi-racial committee; Desegregation of eating places and public facilities; Eventual desegregation of public schools on a voluntary basis.

My head was hurting. "But he's given nothing," I said. "Nothing at all that he hasn't put out time and again—nothing!

"The people," I went on, "the people at the mass meeting—they didn't approve this! They couldn't!"

Then she told me what she had heard, from Tougaloo students and several Youth Council members who had gone to the meeting the night before. No one had known what was developing, the students had told her, other than the ministers and the NAACP staff people. The "concessions" of the mayor had been presented to the people at the mass meeting as a great beginning and a victory, and the name of the President had been invoked many times. The students had reported to her that the ministers and the NAACP staff had all recommended acceptance. There had apparently been great confusion, and the young people and others had begun stirring. One minister, and the students had named a man who was among the most conservative, had ended an appeal for acceptance by saying that if matters did not work out, they would march, march, and march again. Then those in charge of the meeting had called for immediate approval of all of this. Many of the people who had heard the "march" pledge had thought that they were approving mass demonstrations. Some, still confused, had said nothing. Some had indicated disapproval. Jeannette said the students told her that it had been over in moments, and that the meeting had then been shifted to other matters—voter registration.

"But they'll never march," I said. "They never will."

She nodded sadly. "But the people don't know that," she said. "They think that, any day now, it will all begin again and go onward."

"The students," I said. "They know what happened."

Again she nodded. "They know."

Then, as I stared out at the rain, she told me other news: an arrest was expected soon in Medgar's slaying. And on this day Medgar's funeral was being held at the Arlington cemetery. Then we were silent.

After a while, she went over to see Ed. And I looked out at the rain falling on Jackson.

REFLECTIONS ON AN ODYSSEY

FOR ME—AS FOR SO MANY OTHERS—there was not, of course, any turning back to more conventional modes of life. Whatever the significant junctures through which a person may pass, there is always a point where the soft slopes and easy resting places of the stream one travels shift sharply and irreversibly into the high walls and rushing water of the River of No Return. That came for me during the blood-dimmed days and nights in the forests and deserts of Jackson. Both Eldri and I—and Ed and Jeannette King—could only go forward.

I left Tougaloo quite amicably and for the better part of the next four years worked in various parts of the South with economically poor people, mostly non-white, on the development of grassroots community organizations. It was a spread of time that saw the belated passage and partial implementation of the 1964 Civil Rights Act and the 1965 Voting Rights Act, northern urban disorders, the oft-problematic superimposition of the Economic Opportunity Act, the increasingly explicit opposition of stratospheric corporate liberalism and its more localized appendages, Viet Nam—and the achievement of some gains at the grassroots and the promise of more in those sections where strong, local leadership and genuine people participation had been carefully developed.

I spent the two years immediately after the Jackson campaign working as a full-time human-rights field representative for the trusty Southern Conference Educational Fund—that admirably uninhibited collection of mavericks that had been so supportive of our work in Mississippi and of human rights across the land: the Rev. Fred Shuttlesworth, the Rev. Howard Melish, Dr. Jim Dombrowski, Carl and Anne Braden, and an old friend indeed, the social action poet John Beecher. SCEF had recently been joined by long-time mover and shaker Miss Ella J. Baker, who years before had been with the NAACP national office and more recently executive director of SCLC, and founder and key adviser of SNCC.

Amid well-grounded rumors of death threats and with a .38 Smith and Wesson Special revolver tucked away in my attaché case, I worked across the South—from the lower Black Belt away up to the mountains of West Virginia. Increasingly, I came to concentrate my SCEF efforts in certain economically exploitative, thoroughly Klan-ridden northeastern

240

North Carolina Black Belt counties. There, joined by such sparky examples of committed activism as SNCC workers J. V. Henry (white) and Douglas W. Harris, Jr. (black), and carried along by the enthusiasm of such local leaders as Reed and Willa Johnson, the Rev. A. I. Dunlap, and Jet Purnell, and with the tangible encouragement of Floyd McKissick of Durham, we developed a strong grassroots movement in Halifax County and used boycotts, nonviolent demonstrations, and successful Federal lawsuits to break the hard lines of resistance to social change, open up the voting process to non-whites, breach most aspects of the segregation system, and curb the terror of the Ku Klux Klan. Then we turned the movement successfully into adjoining Northampton and Bertie counties, where such figures as the indefatigable Rev. W. M. Steele put me through an itinerary of meetings and movement that circumvented any weight gain from the excellent sustenance provided me by these impoverished but generous Black Belt families. Then we spread the movement into adjoining areas.

At the end of the summer of 1965, strong grassroots movements existed in the northeastern Black Belt of North Carolina. A good organizer should not leave *too* soon but, in the interests of bona fide self-determination, should not camp too long. Things were settling and I no longer carried my revolver.

By now, Eldri and I had another child, John III, born at Raleigh. We junketed up to northern Vermont, where I spent a pleasant academic year at Goddard College, returning to North Carolina at various times to provide technical assistance to the Black Belt movements.

Times were changing across the nation. The social-class dichotomies of the civil rights movement, now joined by the integrationist/separatist debates—all of this in the context of some important victories, much tokenism, and continuing massive economic poverty—were combining to fragment whatever solidarity had initially characterized the movement in its springtime.

I fought one more campaign in the South. The recently developed North Carolina Fund was a state-wide "anti-poverty" agency initially funded by the Ford Foundation and increasingly tied to the U.S. Office of Economic Opportunity. The Fund, echoing the rhetoric of OEO, was talking about maximum feasible participation of the poor in decision-making and ostensibly planning the elimination of poverty in the state. Friends in the lower echelons of the Fund, some of them Black Belt movement veterans, asked us to return to North Carolina to help out in the organization's stated mission. With some misgivings, I accepted the post as Director of Training, working with young Indian, black, and white people around the techniques of mobilizing the poor. At the same time, I began to work with my old colleagues and friends in the Black Belt to organize—in Bertie, Halifax, Hertford, and Northampton counties

—a grassroots anti-poverty program which we called the Peoples' Program on Poverty. All of this was far too heady for the leaders of the Fund, who promptly fired me. There were massive protests from my trainees and friends and from people and groups around the state, and these, coupled with legal action and the impending plans of Black Belt people to "come in numbers" to the central offices of the Fund at Durham, led to my reinstatement as a "consultant" with no strings attached. I continued to work with the Black Belt People's Program until we secured, from the Fund and collateral sources, large-scale funding for this poor people's movement.

By now, it was clear that OEO nationally and its appendages were primarily committed to the political enhancement of the national Democratic party, and that with the exception of situations like the People's Program on Poverty, where the grassroots poor were well organized and depended only on themselves, the funding was merely enough to pit local people against each other and never enough to do much against poverty.

We moved on, in the summer of 1967, to the Pacific Northwest, where I taught low-income Indians, blacks, and whites in the shadow of Mount Rainier in Washington and with an old friend, Professor Nat Gross, developed successful minority hiring and training programs in industry/labor. Martin Luther King, Jr., and Robert Kennedy were shot to death, and from our disparate geographical locations, old Mississippi movement colleagues—Ed King, Joan Trumpauer, I, and others—talked by telephone far into those funereal nights. I declined an offer to join corporate management in Seattle, and we spent a year teaching at Coe College in Cedar Rapids, Iowa, where my students and I organized a solid local union of the American Federation of State, County and Municipal Employees.

It was spring, 1969. The Chicago Commons Association was one of that city's largest and oldest private social-service agencies. It had been founded by Dr. Graham Taylor, a colleague of Jane Addams and William Salter, in the 1890s. Graham Taylor's daughter, Lea, in her late eighties, was still active in Commons affairs and was an old friend of my parents. She and a colleague, Dr. Arthur Hillman of Roosevelt University and director of training for the National Federation of Settlements and Neighborhood Centers, were instrumental in bringing me to Chicago to become the first Southside Director of the Commons. I developed a first-rate staff—among them Jim Richardson and Marshall Klein (white), Emily Garcia (Chicano), Jesse Howard and Geraldine Howard (black). I found my old Tougaloo student and Jackson-movement co-worker, Bette Anne Poole, who promptly left her job with the Illinois Central Railroad office to join us. Our geographic sweep was an immense piece of Near South Side area: about four miles long and three miles wide, including the old stockyards. Most of it was changing racially as vast numbers of white people moved out and large numbers of non-whites moved in. Our program focus was the grassroots community organization of those "persons of the fewest alternatives."

We were in Chicago for more than four years. In the course of it, we had our third child, Peter, and helped low-income people, primarily non-white, overcome the most profound interpersonal alienation, fear, and apathetic futility to organize more than 250 block clubs and form two large umbrella groups. All of this focused, with increasing success, on a wide variety of problems: civic services, education, employment, health, housing, police/community relations, race, and welfare. Racial tensions were extremely high; killings were not uncommon; we received constant threats from white racial groups and covert opposition from the regular Democratic party of Mayor Richard Daley. But strong grassroots leadership and participation, and the "oak wood" slow and steady commitment of our staff, carried things through. By 1972 and 1973, the community organizations were well established, alert and resistant to attacks, and inoculated against co-optation.

At the same time that all of this was progressing, I became much involved as a volunteer in the American Indian programs on the north side of the city. As always, I was impressed by the commitment of our Indian people—22,000 in Chicago—to family/clan/tribe/tribal-culture even in the often tragic circumstances found in the urban context. Native Americans have been forced into the cities by economic privation on the reservations and the ill-motivated, land-coveting urban-relocation policies of the Federal government. I began working extensively with such people as Susan Power (Sioux), Bill Redcloud (Chippewa), Steven Fast Wolf (Sioux), Willard LaMere (Winnebago), Elmira McLure (Potawatami), Mona Kitchell (Chippewa), and Martin Eder (Assiniboin).

The commitments in that world deepened quickly: program planning for the American Indian Center, working as an officer of a native American newspaper which we founded, serving as a committee member of the technical-assistance-oriented Great Lakes Resource Development Project of Americans for Indian Opportunity. I helped develop and then served for several years as chairman of the Native American Community Organizational Training Center, which trained Indian people in such critically needed areas as adoption/foster homes, health services, youth/cultural preservation, welfare, and resource development—all of this from an activist perspective.

The work was demanding but quite productive and enormously satisfying. It was also thoroughly interesting from a number of standpoints, including the fact that, vis-a-vis my Southside Commons work, where most of the people were non-Indian and seeking deeper roots in the general context of U.S. culture, the Indian focus, of course, was to remain outside of that and firmly within the framework of the traditional way. My sense of healthy, bi-cultural schizophrenia became sharpened. But to sound modestly ethnocentric, I have always tried to inculcate the time-honored and tested native social principle of "tribal responsibility"— the individual has an obligation to the community, the community has an obligation to the individual—into everything that I have helped organize.

We left Chicago in the summer of 1973 for the University of Iowa, Iowa City, where I accepted a position in the Graduate Program in Urban and Regional Planning, teaching, among other things, community organization. We were only four hours away from Chicago and I continued my involvements in the native American programs there, including my chairmanship of the Training Center, and also worked with such vigorous Iowa people as Alice Hatfield Liljegren (Micmac) and Elliot Ricehill (Winnebago), Isabelle Deom (Mohawk), Gene Rave (Winnebago), Darlene Wind (Chippewa) and many Mesquakies: John Buffalo, Donis Mitchell, Andrew Roberts, Iva Roy, Don Wanatee, and Robin Youngbear. We developed Indian programs at the university and secured technical resources for native groups in the area, and helped develop a very successful American Indian Cultural Center at Iowa State Penitentiary.

At the same time, working with non-Indians—Professors Jim Harris and Dave Ranney and Urban Planning students such as Patricia Anderson, Mike Crist, Clemens Erdahl, Scott Johnson, Edith Sontag—I continued my involvement in other types of community organizations: fight against urban renewal, fight for flood control, tenant rights, day-care political action. Time passed productively with my Iowa and Illinois involvements. In my classes and student consultations, I found myself regarded as something of an elder statesman, a repository of veteran wisdom. But although the Indians' position remained as committed as ever to the native values, and the aforementioned non-Indian stalwarts at Iowa continued their involvements, and my classes were certainly full, times were changing on the Iowa campus. The dimension of creativity and social commitment was ebbing in the new but somewhat nineteen-fiftyish atmosphere: career orientation in the most primary sense, the avoidance of controversy, and, in many professional circles, the hiring out to and otherwise supporting the power structures.

In the late summer of 1976, I answered an advertisement in the liberal *National Catholic Reporter* that indicated an opening for the position of Director of the Office of Human Development, the social-justice arm of the twelve-county Roman Catholic Diocese of Rochester, New York. The people there were interested, among other things, in someone with a broad background in community organization. On my way to Rochester for an interview, the train in which I was riding derailed at 60 m.p.h. in a massive wreck, but I was unhurt and continued by air.

At Rochester I was met by Tim McGowan, an OHD staffer—young,

Irish, sharp, committed, and responsibly wild. I liked him immediately, as I did another staffer, Carol Schwartz—young, ethnic, unassuming but with a firm and forthright candor that has toppled more than a few adversaries. Both Tim and Carol, and another thoroughly congenial soul, Kevin Cullen—articulate and analytical and something of an Irish nationalist—were interested in doing bona fide community organizing. Their spouses—Theresa McGowan, John Schwartz, and Teresa Cullen—have always been solidly committed. Some others in the OHD circle were, it seemed to me, much less interested in the action approach, and no community organizing had ever been done by OHD. I was eventually hired for the director's position, with the backing of Tim, Carol, Kevin, and others, but against the strong wishes of another group of staffers. The man whom I replaced, Father Charles Mulligan, was moving into the new position of Diocesan Director of Social Ministry, to which I would be responsible.

We moved to Rochester in early December, 1976, as soon as I could complete the fall term at Iowa. Immediately we began to develop new dimensions of grassroots community organization and advocacy at OHD on behalf of those "persons of the fewest alternatives" whatever their religious, racial, or cultural backgrounds. At the same time, I continued support of the older programs, which were essentially charitable food and clothing giveaways.

With enthusiastic support from Tim, Carol, Kevin, John Erb (who later left OHD for an honest and effective political career and who remained very supportive), and Mike Krupiarz, intense and philosophizing (who came to OHD later on), we got into many good things—and they rolled on and on.

Tim, Carol, and I—later joined by Mike—launched a multi-issue, multi-racial block club project at St. Francis Xavier parish, where we had the firm backing of hardworking Father Ed Golden. Kevin developed new training approaches for church volunteers which stressed community action and grassroots involvement, and he organized many elderly persons into action groups. Carol became a major figure in the fight to secure public ownership of municipal power in Rochester.

For almost thirty-five years, Algonquin Indian mink skinners had been brought down every fall from Quebec to work on the fur farms of Ontario County, just outside Rochester. The wages were extremely low and the health and housing conditions were abysmal. The plight of these people had been ignored by the church and by state and Federal agencies. Tim and I, joined by Elliot Ricehill, an old Winnebago friend from Iowa, went into the fur-farm situation and helped the Algonquins organize and carry out a successful strike that substantially raised wages and made all of this retroactive to the beginning of that fur season. We forced state and Federal officials into the situation, developed broad ecumenical church backing and support for native American groups—with the result that the living conditions of the Algonquins improved considerably.

With Tim as political coordinator and prime mover, we pressed international human rights issues with vigor in the governmental context: Chile, southern Africa, Panama, and much else. We also began putting the New York State Catholic Committee behind native American rights, with special reference to Iroquois land claims.

We pushed many more issues. In the process, we reached out to form strong relationships between Roman Catholic social action and a broad variety of grassroots organizations, including organized labor, racial groups, civil rights and liberties bodies.

In all of this, we received many accolades from the grassroots poor and from local clergy and parish staffs. Open opposition mounted from several other OHD staff who, bound up in the food/clothing approach, expressed great fear and doubt about community organization and advocacy. There was a visibly growing strain and coolness from diocesan officials, including Father Mulligan, my predecessor and Director of Social Ministry, who at various points seemed opposed to this direction.

In June, 1978, Father Charles Mulligan, with no advance warning, fired me abruptly or, to use his terminology, "terminated" me. The reason given involved "a breakdown in communication." His action was backed up by Bishop Joseph Hogan and by some other diocesan officials. A cautious priest, opposed to community organization and advocacy, was quickly appointed in my stead and an effort was made to lock me out of my office.

Immediately, a widespread protest developed in which the most unusual coalition I've ever known sprang into being—and did so with astonishing spontaneity: my community organizational colleagues and friends at OHD: Tim, Carol, Kevin, Mike, and some others; the Rochester Catholic Worker movement; native American groups; the eighty-nine unions making up the Rochester-area AFL-CIO Central Labor Council; the Teamsters Union; various community organizations; a number of Catholic clergy and nuns; and Catholic and Anglican laypeople. John Erb, formerly of OHD and now an active Democratic county legislator, served as coordinator. My reinstatement was vigorously requested by this extraordinary alliance, which also protested the lack of due process and the obviously precarious commitment to social justice exhibited by the institutional church and its bureaucratic functionaries.

Despite weeks of public protests and a flood of letters and petitions, the hard-driving coalition was not successful in securing my reinstatement. The bishop would neither meet nor talk with the coalition leaders, most of whom were deeply committed Catholics. But the entire matter, and all of the attendant issues were aired: including the plight of lay and minority and social-action persons in the church and the whole future of social justice. The coalition has remained intact as the Rochester Catholic Social Action Group to ensure that there are no more instances of what happened to me and that the social-action activities at OHD are continued without interference and, hopefully, someday with diocesan support.

We left Rochester in the late summer of 1978: myself, Eldri, Maria, John, Peter, a dog, three cats, and five kittens—pulling a huge U-Haul trailer. We came to the Southwest. But I was back at Rochester in October to give the address at the first convention of the Northeast Block Club Alliance—the multi-issue, multi-racial grassroots association of poor people that Tim, Carol, and I had begun to develop away back when I first came to Rochester. There were Tim McGowan and Carol Schwartz —the very best of friends that a campaigner like me could ever have— working as vigorously and creatively as ever. There was Father Ed Golden, the kind of priest, and Sister Betty, the kind of nun, who—along with such others as Monsignor George Cocuzzi, Fathers George Hill and Dan O'Shea and Larry Tracy, and Professor Joe Torma of St. Bernard's Seminary—set the kind of example that can't help but keep one, despite bitter disappointments with the institution, in the church. There were the grassroots people—some American Indian, some black, some white, some Puerto Rican—all representing their now actively organized sections of this inner city area. It was their meeting, that of the grassroots—the people who had forced the City of Rochester into providing effective services to the area and whose community-development plan had just been accepted and funded by the city. The people could have been the dispossessed stirring at any point all the way back through my years and beyond—and Tim and Carol the refreshingly eager, working organizers of any of the scenes through time.

Fifteen years have passed since the blood and the betrayals and the high courage in Jackson. From where I sit now, I can see, just to the north, the very beautiful and serene Lukachukai (Chuska) Mountains, away up here in the isolated Navajo country. Those, like other special mountains—Katahdin of Maine—give strength. One is reminded of the Cheyenne leader Black Kettle's death song in 1864 at Sand Creek, Colorado, as the U.S. Army closed in to kill the unarmed Indians huddled for protection under a U.S. flag: "Nothing lives long/Only the Earth and the Mountains."

The Earth and the Mountains, living for such a long time, have seen a great deal. From his perspective, the Creator certainly has. No one of us, given our brief sojourn here, can grasp the Totality and it seems presumptuous to try. But I am an itinerant half-breed, and not too reticent with some advice and opinion. I have a certain tenure along the trail, with all of its shadowy places and all of its turbulence. I have, I think, a respectable set of scars and a reasonable amount of earned paranoia in my psyche. In our human quest for full measures of liberty, material well-being, and spiritual rapport, I think we can be basically optimistic. Maybe it's the kind of thing one senses intuitively rather than tabulates empirically.

In the way that I have always seen humanity dichotomized—the people who serve their communities and whose words make things grow and, on the other hand, those people who serve only themselves—I believe that we have more and more of the former than we do the other. The river that we travel can indeed be rough, but we can only go on, into waters ever deeper. For all of us, then, it is a River of No Return and the pulse of history in the Creation is beating. But the sun comes down upon the water, gives us courage and strength, and much, much more than just a fighting chance.

Tsaile
The Navajo Nation
Fall, 1978